ME:

UNDERSTANDING MYSELF AND OTHERS

Audrey Palm Riker, R.N., Ed.D.
Psychologist, Wabash Center, Lafayette, Indiana;
co-author with Holly Brisbane: MARRIED LIFE;
co-author with Charles Riker: UNDERSTANDING
MARRIAGE and UNDERSTANDING PARENTHOOD;
author of professional and popular articles on child
development; consultant to author Holly Brisbane:
THE DEVELOPING CHILD.

Charles Riker, Ed.D.
Associate Professor of Child Development and
Family Studies, Purdue University.

ME:
UNDERSTANDING MYSELF AND OTHERS

By
Audrey Palm Riker

Charles Riker
Contributing Editor

Ｂ

CHAS. A. BENNETT CO., INC.

Peoria, Illinois 61614

Dedication

To Paul Van Winkle

Acknowledgments

Textbooks always result from the generous efforts of many persons. My special thanks go to the following:

• To my husband, Charles Riker, whose wise advice, patient support, and careful editing made ME possible.

• To Susan Riker, who generously contributed her letters and diaries, thoughts, and experiences.

• To Greg Riker, Kevin Smith, Mark Hale, Julie Pearlman, and the hundreds of other adolescents who shared their case histories, agreed to be interviewed, completed questionnaires, and helped select the title, ME.

• To my mother, Evelyn Palm, who did the medical research for ME.

• To Jerry Santangelo and all the Bennett sales force, whose surveys and useful suggestions helped define the topics for ME; and to Mildred Nauer, who typed the manuscript during its revision and completion stages.

• To consulting teachers Jan Horner, Donna Liska, Katie Houghton, Dwilla Bloom, Sharon Kolbourn, and Beverly Miller, whose insights and experiences gave direction to ME; to family historian William J. Goodman, who provided background on family life-styles.

• To photographer Natalie Leimkuhler and her family of superb models, and to photographers David Snodgress and Kathy Tuite, and to illustrator Diane Pollock.

• To readers Steve Riggs, Wendell Riggs, M.D., Linda Froberg, M.D., and Kim Froberg, M.D. for helpful criticism.

• To Steve Davis, who kept the Riker typewriters in top repair.

Preface

"How can I tell you how I feel if I don't know myself?" asked a teen.

Perhaps you have thought the same thing at times.

Early adolescence—the age you are now—is a time of change. How you look changes. Your moods and needs change. Everything may seem to be shifting and uncertain. You want to know yourself better as a person. You also want to understand why others act as they do. You want to develop ideas, opinions, and goals for life that are yours alone.

ME is a psychology (sy-KOL-uh-jee) book about the first few years of adolescence. It will help you know yourself better. Psychology is the study of people and why they act as they do.

The basic theme of this book is *relationships* (ri-LAY-shun-ships). Relationships comes from the word *relate*. It means how you get along with yourself and those close to you—parents, brothers, sisters, other relatives, teachers, neighbors, and friends.

Years ago you learned to read and write words, and to work with numbers. Reading, writing, and solving problems force you to think. *Thinking* helps you figure out what's going on around you. Thinking helps you to reason, and to make decisions. Your ability to think is a super gift. It sets you apart from the lower animals like horses, dogs, and birds.

However, thinking isn't your only talent. You also have an *emotional* (ih-MO-shin-'l) life. Another word for emotions is feelings.

Your emotions, or feelings, switch back and forth across a wide range. At one moment they can keep you *calm* and *comfortable*. Another time your emotions may make you giggle with *joy* or be impatient with *anger*. Sometimes they can cause you to feel *sad* and *lonely*.

Human behavior means what people do. A good way to learn *why* you do what you do is to understand how your thinking and feelings work together. While reading ME you'll learn more about your emotions and how they influence what you think and how you act.

It's exciting to be an adolescent today. No one older than you has ever lived in a world so complicated and at the same time so full of new opportunities. The secrets of life are being discovered every year. Scientists press their search to help people live longer by replacing diseased body organs and by wiping out killing afflictions.

However, your world isn't perfect. The daily news also includes reports of energy shortages, divorces, broken families, drug abuse, juvenile crime, and mental illness.

This book does not attempt to offer simple answers to these demanding social issues. Instead you will be encouraged to discover that there may be a number of ways for you to react to any one of them. In other words, when you encounter a problem, there may be several approaches available for you to solve it. You will be encouraged to discover why one method may be best for you.

ME does not offer any "right way" to study the subject of adolescence. The text includes research findings from leading experts in the fields of psychology, medicine, and education. A *researcher* is a person who carefully collects information about a certain subject. Research projects are called *studies.* The results or conclusions that researchers come to are referred to as *findings.* The findings of research studies in psychology, medicine, and education will help you to understand why persons act as they do in certain situations. ME includes the results of research studies about adolescents.

WRITERS

The author and consulting editor of ME are wife and husband, and parents of a son and daughter. Audrey Riker is a psychologist at Wabash Center in Lafayette, Indiana, a community agency for children and adults with physical and mental problems. Charles Riker is Associate Professor, Department of Child Development and Family Studies, in the School of Consumer and Family Sciences at Purdue University.

RESEARCH

Research for ME included the author's experience as a mother and psychologist, plus more than ten years of professional work in testing, teaching, and counseling. The book also benefits from the thousands of personal histories the editor has read and listened to during his more than twenty years as a teacher and counselor of adolescents.

Just a few years ago, the Connecticut State Board of Education published a book titled *Teach Us What We Want To Know.* The authors—Ruth Byler, Gertrude Lewis, and Ruth Totman—surveyed thousands of schoolchildren in every grade to find out the students' real concerns about their physical and mental health. The results—what those boys and girls wanted to know—served as another guide for the selection of the main topics covered in ME.

While writing ME, the author also asked questions like the following of her teenaged son and daughter, and their friends.

"How does life seem at your age?"

"What do you enjoy most?"

"What do you like least?"

"What do you want out of life?"

"What are your biggest problems?"

"How do you try to solve them?"

"What do you want to know about understanding yourself better?"

"What do you need to know to understand others better?"

"What kind of advice from parents, teachers, and counselors helps you most?"

THE PLAN FOR ME

The spirit of this book encourages learning in several ways. Learning can be both exciting and fun, especially when you are discovering new information about yourself. Four proven learning methods follow.

1. *Success improves learning.* In reading ME, you will be reminded that *you are valuable* as a person and that *you can learn* as a student. Both these points are true no matter how well you have done in the past. When you do a good job with your studies today, tomorrow's learning becomes easier.

2. *Listening improves learning.* In ME you will be encouraged to listen closely to both yourself and others, and to learn to sense the emotions that may cause certain behavior in you and them. Such an attitude requires two forms of listening. The first type pays close attention to the *words* used by you and others. The second kind listens "between the lines"

for *possible causes* of statements and actions. Both types of listening improve chances for learning.

3. *Discussion improves learning.* Students also improve chances for learning when they are willing to share experiences during class discussion without trying to prove that one person is right and the other wrong.

4. *Laughter improves learning.* No one likes to be laughed at. However, the kind of laughter that admits, "I've made that mistake, too," often relaxes everyone in the group. This type of good humor can soften anger, melt hard feelings, and even fix a broken friendship. In ME you are encouraged to learn to laugh *at* yourself. You are also invited to laugh *with* others, not *at* them.

SPECIAL FEATURES

To make the study of yourself and others both interesting and valuable, the book includes the following subdivisions.

CASE EXAMPLES

Each case is a short story about someone like you. Case examples are set apart by the format used here. Boys and girls contributed the facts about their own lives. Their real names have been changed. The familiar thoughts and words in the cases will make it easier for you to understand the particular topic you are studying at the time.

Some cases run just a few lines. Others are longer to include important details. There is no single case that solves any particular problem. Many cases remain unfinished so you can practice thinking what decisions or actions might be best for the persons involved. By reading and think-ing about the case studies, you can begin to figure out why others act as they do. You can also start to discover the reasons for the things that you do and say in certain situations.

Activities. Activity titles indicate how you might spend more time on particular questions. Throughout the book you will find activities that match the topic you are studying at the time. These short exercises will always be set in the kind of type face you are reading now.

Activities allow for *individual differences in learning. Some require more* time and work than others. So, depending on how much you want to learn about a subject, you can pick an activity that will let you do your own research at your own speed.

Some *research* activities challenge you to discover information in reference books like dictionaries and encyclopedias.

You may be asked to *interview* someone with special knowledge or experience.

In some activities you will be required to make a *decision* as if you were the person who needed to solve the problem.

You be the counselor is an activity that invites you to give advice to a person your age who is troubled and unhappy.

In other activities you will take *Time out* to think about certain issues from a different point of view.

The question *What about me?* shows up often. This activity reminds you to stop and think about the ideas you just read and how they might apply to you and your life.

Guidelines for living. Lists of suggestions are spotted throughout the book so you can check your present way of doing things against the list. You may discover that you can get more done with less energy by making certain changes in your life.

Private and personal. Not all study questions and activities are intended for class discussion. Always consider other students when personal topics are mentioned that might hurt or embarrass anyone else in class. *Private and personal* usually appears with issues and ideas best kept to yourself. If your parents are divorced, for example, you can consider how the breakup affects you and others in your family. Your group can talk generally about the subject of divorce without discussing the details of your home life. At other times you may want to volunteer information that could help the class members understand something that you know well.

• *Unfamiliar words*. Unfamiliar words are broken down to help you say them correctly. They always appear like this in parentheses (puh-REN-thuh-sees). To pronounce words you have not seen before, put stress only on the sounds in the BIG letters. Then repeat the entire word a time or two for practice.

• *Recap*. At the end of each chapter, highlights are repeated briefly. Recap comes from the word recapitulation (REE-kuh-PICH-oo-LAY-shin). This word means a short summary.

• *Terms*. Key words and phrases are listed after the recap in all but the last chapter.

• *Photographs*. Most of the pictures in this book show adolescents when they are alone or with brothers, sisters, parents, or friends. However, persons of all ages show up in the photographs to remind you that human development continues for each person from childhood through adolescence and adulthood to old age. While you are growing and developing, people of all ages touch your life.

POSSIBLE USES FOR ME

Many teachers have asked for a book like this one to help prepare students for the Marriage and Family Living course in senior high school. ME has been written to meet that need.

Me can also be used as a basic text for the study of adolescence from a special point of view—the teenager's.

Following the trend for shorter courses, any unit, chapter, or combination of both can be used to construct a learning module or mini-course.

OUTLINE FOR THE BOOK

ME includes six units and twenty chapters. Each chapter covers a particular subject, or part of an important topic. Each chapter also features text, activities, and recap. Each unit serves as a building block from the one that came before it to the unit that follows. However, any portion of the book can be studied by itself.

CONTENTS

Unit I includes information about why people behave as they do, about the physical and psychological changes of adolescence, and about what it means to grow up in today's world.

Unit II talks about parents and how to get along with them as you gradually gain your own independence.

Unit III explains the strong influence of brothers and sisters (or lack of them) on your life.

Unit IV draws attention to social life outside the home. You'll discover how friendships get started and break up. You'll also read about popularity, acceptance, rejection, and loneliness.

Unit V describes reasons for your interest in members of the other sex, and for their interest in you.

Unit VI presents some special problems that can make growing up more difficult. You'll find out how young persons can learn to keep growing stronger even in families that suffer from serious problems.

THE AUTHOR'S POINT OF VIEW

Throughout this book the author *stresses realism.* Realism means the way things really are, not the way we might like them to be. There is no attempt in ME to make things seem better or worse, or to suggest that real life is not the way it is.

The author also *stresses honesty, decency,* and *responsibility.* You will read about opportunities in your life to make important choices. You will be encouraged to continue the process of becoming a good, fair, honest, and kind person, taking time to think of others and their needs.

For certain activities you will be asked to decide what you would do in a particular situation. Obviously you are free to live the type of life you favor. However, in this book you will always be encouraged to make choices that build your character and incline you to be considerate of others as well as a good citizen.

Our society always needs responsible men and women. Our society needs you at your very best. By studying this book you will learn how valuable you are and how much you have to contribute to your family, your friends, and your community.

Table of Contents

UNIT I
Me

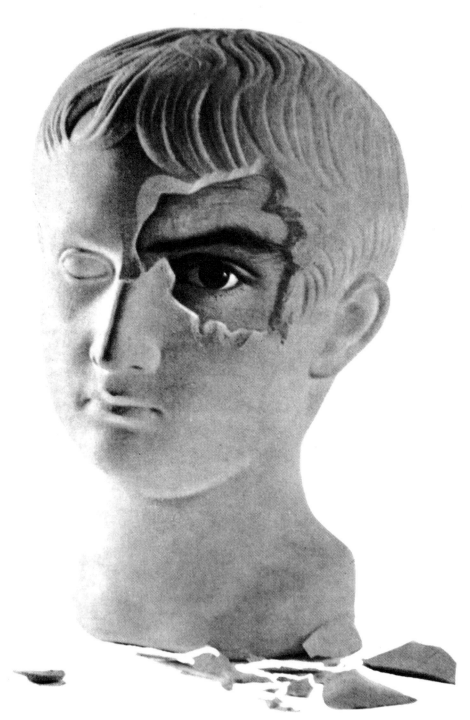

I wonder what I'll be.

CHAPTER I

Goodbye, Childhood

"Sometimes I want to be grown up, and on my own, and all that. I feel like going out—downtown or something. But at other times I get sick of everything. I'd like to be nine again and go play ball," sighed Caren, age fourteen.

You probably know what Caren means. One day you may want to grow up faster. The next day you may need to hold tight to some of the simple fun of childhood. If so, that makes you like practically everyone else your age.

Perhaps you have been told the same thing that Caren heard when she acted like a nine-year-old:

"You're too old to behave that way anymore."

Sound familiar?

To be an adolescent means many things. Adolescence is an in-between age. You may be *too young* to get a driver's license, to live alone, or to work full time. On the other hand you are supposed to be *too old* for temper tantrums, for crying on your mother's lap, or for getting away with telling a lie.

During early adolescence—between the ages of twelve and sixteen—you leave childhood behind you forever.

You change *physically*. (You don't look the same.)

You change *mentally*. (You don't think the same.)

You change *emotionally*. (You don't feel the same.)

Despite all these changes you are not yet an adult. As an adolescent, parents expect more of you. Teachers demand more of you. However, to your advantage, you are free of serious burdens during these few in-between years. For example, you probably don't have to earn a living or support a family. Adolescence is a time to learn, a time to move ahead, and a time for fun.

The teen years can be wonderful and exciting. If you were to ask Caren, she'd

Adolescents develop physically, mentally, and emotionally.

Kathy Tuite

17

RELATIONSHIPS THROUGHOUT THE LIFE SPAN

Time of Life	Age Range	Number of Relationships
Infancy	From Birth to Age 2	Family members and baby-sitters only
Early childhood	2 to 6 years	Family, close neighbors, day-care centers, nursery schools.
Middle childhood	6 to 10 years	Contacts increase at school, church, playgrounds and other recreational centers.
Late childhood	10 to 12 years	
Early adolescence	12 to 15 years	Acquaintances increase rapidly; total will never be greater.
Middle and late adolescence	15 to 20 years	Interest in other sex begins; acquaintances decrease slowly.
Young adulthood	20 to 40 years	Marriage and parenthood; contact with friends decreases.
Middle age	40 to 60 years	Children leave home; acquaintances continue to decrease.
Old age	60 years and older	Contacts limited to close friends and relatives.

From infancy, your relationships with others gradually increase in number. They reach a peak in your adolescent years, then gradually decrease.

admit that she really enjoys her chances to make decisions for herself. She also likes her increasing independence. She welcomes more attention from boys. However, she also worries about popularity. At times she dislikes the way she looks. She often quarrels with her parents and fights with her brothers.

Caren is on the last lap of a long journey that started when she was just a baby. It will end in adulthood. Like you, she must say goodbye to childhood and hello to the uncertain years of adolescence.

RELATIONSHIPS

Adolescence is worth understanding. There are many ways to study yourself and other teens. However, the main theme of this book is *relationships*, or getting along with yourself and others. Relationships comes from the word *relate*, which means to *connect with* as in family *rela*tives. When you think about it, nothing is more important to understand than your own self and how you get along with those close to you.

INGREDIENTS

A chocolate fudge cake is made of many different things—eggs, flour, sugar, shortening, and chocolate. Still, these separate ingredients by themselves don't make a cake. The portions must be measured, blended, and baked. Only then does everything combine to become a cake.

Complete and mature persons are also mixtures of many different ingredients. For example, all persons have the following.

• *Genetic inheritance* means all the mental and physical equipment passed on to you from your parents before you

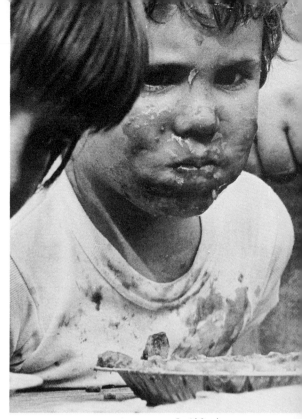

David Snodgrass,
Herald-Telephone, *Bloomington, Indiana*
Kenny's family claims that he inherited his love for apple pie from his father. However, Kenny won this pie-eating contest all by himself.

were born. Genetic (juh-NET-ik) inheritance includes all of your physical self plus your basic intelligence (your ability to think) and disposition (the type of person you are).

• *Life experiences* mean all the important things that happened to you from before birth until now. You may have lived most of your life in a large city, in a suburb, in a small town, or in the country. Many of your major life experiences will depend on where you have spent most of your time and the type of family in which you were raised.

• *Personal values* refer to what you believe to be important and what you

19

are willing to work for. Your personal values help decide the kind of life you live and especially the way you treat other persons.

Something to think about. The subject of personal values receives a lot of attention in this book.

Can you think of one belief that you have today that will never change as long as you live?

When your personal values are clear to you, life becomes a lot easier, especially when it is time to make an important decision.

In this unit you'll read mostly about getting along with yourself and some of the things that make you a special, one-of-a-kind person.

PHYSICAL GROWTH AND DEVELOPMENT

Moving on. If you were planning a long trip, you'd need extra clothes and something to carry them in. You might pack a favorite book or picture. The rest of this chapter describes what you will need for your journey to adulthood and maturity.

In talking about the teen years, a few words are used a lot. In fact, these terms may seem to overlap because they are all tied to the process of getting older. However, these simple definitions will help.

- *Adolescence* refers to all the changes during the teen years. Physical changes are the most obvious. You also change in many other ways. For example, you become more capable and stronger. You also improve your ability to understand unfamiliar ideas.
- *Growth* means a gradual increase in body size.
- *Development* means growth in progress, and a gradual improvement in abilities.

- *Mature* means to complete or finish growth and development.
- *Rate* means how fast you complete growth and development. Some boys and girls grow rapidly and complete their physical growth in two years. Others with a slower rate may require four or more years of body changes to reach their physical maturity.
- *Timing* refers to the age when you begin and finish your adolescent growth spurt.
- *Puberty* means all the body changes that make a boy or girl capable of starting another human life. This means the person can become a mother or father. Puberty may start any time from an early age of eight to a late age of thirteen. These body changes for girls usually begin at least six months ahead of those for boys. However any one boy may be larger and heavier. He may develop faster than a girl of the same age.

In human growth and development the physical and mental equipment inherited from parents, and all the nutrition, health, and other life conditions decide how fast you will complete your adolescent years.

Growth and development rules. Good rules not only say what is expected, but also allow for some exceptions. Suppose, for example, your parents set a rule to be home by 10 P.M. after a varsity game. One evening you are late because the bus broke down. Should you be punished? Lose privileges? Or should you get a chance to explain why you were forced to break the rule?

Rules of growth and development tell you what's expected, but they also have exceptions. This short list includes only those rules and exceptions that seem most important for your study of adolescence.

- *Normal growth and development follows an inherited plan.* Inherit means to transfer something of value from one person to another, usually property or money. In this case, *inherit* refers to the transfer of physical traits such as facial features and body build from your parents to you. Your physical inheritance was set permanently when your life began nine and one-half months before birth. Your own basic genetic plan remains the same throughout life, even as your body changes and develops.

- *Normal growth and development stays on course.* Even though your basic plan may halt temporarily because of illness or accident, "detoured" development always tries to catch up and return to the genetic blueprint set before birth.

- *Normal growth and development is continuous.* One stage blends into another. No time is separated from all others. Although physical growth will stop, body changes will continue as long as you live.

- *Normal growth and development goes through important stages that can't be repeated.* Put another way, for some things there are no second chances. For example, severe shortage of the right foods for a mother during pregnancy could hold back mental development in her baby. Even the best nutrition later in life could not make up for the early brain damage.

- *Normal growth and development is predictable, but unique for each person.* Although you go through the same stages as everyone else, you are an original. No one else is exactly like you. If you are a so-called identical twin, your fingerprints, your voice pattern, even your natural body odor are one-of-a-kind. Given a sniff of clothing, a bloodhound can easily tell one twin from another.

Natalie Leimkuhler

Preteen Jean ready to cut her tenth birthday cake.

- *Normal growth and development cannot be separated from personality development.* Physical changes common to all teens are always accompanied by many other changes in interests, in attitudes, and in relationships with parents, teachers, and friends. Put another way, as your body matures, your opinions about life and the people around you also change. Mind and body mature together, but at different rates. As you grow physically, you change mentally, emotionally, and socially.

Growth spurts. Growth and development are the master keys to understanding adolescence. Both words suggest that *changes* are happening. Of course, change is not new to you. All your life you've been changing, sometimes very fast, sometimes more slowly. For example, you've already lived through two of your three growth spurts.

The *first* was before birth when you grew at super-speed. By the twelfth week of life your unborn self was in-

Natalie Leimkuhler

Near the end of her physical growth spurt Jean welcomes her fourteenth birthday with a smile.

Everyone agrees that baby Sean inherited his mother's happy disposition.

Ted Hug

creasing in size and weight at a rate of six times per month. When you were born you were almost one-third of your total adult height. So you can see that the rate of growth is much slower after birth than before.

Your *second* growth spurt occurred about age two.

Now, during adolescence, you are in the process of your final one. Without this *third* and last spurt, you would be forever a prisoner of childhood. A few more pounds and a couple of inches transform you permanently and unmistakably into an adult—a man or a woman.

Growth patterns. Adolescence begins before puberty and continues until after puberty is completed. However, neither the start nor the end of adolescence is clearly marked. Physical and mental changes usually begin slowly and quietly. They taper off the same way. No stage of growth is completely separate from any other stage. In every time of life, what happens early always influences what happens later.

Body parts and systems have different functions, or jobs. However, they all work together. Each depends upon the other. For example, the *digestive* (dih-JES-tiv) *system* breaks down and digests food for the body to use in growth and for energy. The *circulatory* (SUR-kyoo-luh-TOR-ee) *system* carries nutrients (food) dissolved in blood to the cells of the body.

All body systems mature during adolescence, but they do so at different times and rates. Sometimes one system leaps ahead while others lag behind. For example, your brain grew rapidly when you were very young. From birth to your first birthday it doubled in weight—from about 0.33 kg [12 ounces] to about 0.91 kg [32 ounces]. By age six your brain was practically as big and heavy as it will ever be. During adolescence, the long bones of your arms and legs grow fast. You also reach your full adult height.

PERSONALITY

When people say, "He has a great personality!" what do they mean? You can't weigh or measure personality. You can't examine personality under a microscope. Yet personality is as much a part of you as your weight or height.

Personality includes everything about you, including your basic disposition, your emotions, your behavior, and everything you learn that becomes part of you. Following you'll read about some of the parts of personality that are especially important in your study of relationships.

Basic disposition. Each child is born with the beginnings of a particular personality. Some babies are very active at birth, others less so. Some cry softly, others yowl. Some establish regular times for eating and sleeping. Others become night owls.

Brand-new personalities can be measured. Modern electronic equipment is used to tell the difference between bouncy, active newborns and more quiet, passive babies while they are still in the hospital nursery.

When such children are studied as they grow older, tests seem to back up what parents suspected all along.

• Babies are quite complicated at birth.

• Babies tend to keep certain personality traits (such as being very active or noticeably quiet).

Babies undergo great changes in the way they act as they grow older.

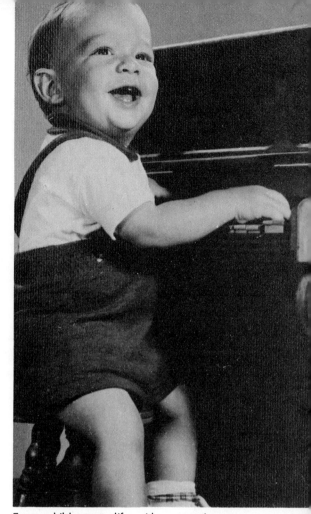

Every child starts life with a certain type of personality. As a baby, Greg was active, outgoing, and curious. His love for keyboards and music began early.

Traits are parts of personality that don't change. Traits are ways of behaving that a person repeats so often that others learn to expect certain phrases and actions. In time, most persons are described by their personality traits. You've probably heard comments like these: "Deann is selfish and lazy, but Lois is generous and hard-working."

Of course, everyone is a combination of many different traits. In fact, someone once counted all the words in the

23

As a young adult, Greg is more mature, but still developing his talents. He remains active, outgoing, and curious. And he still loves music. Greg now works as a sound engineer for a rock band.

English language that describe the behavior traits of humans. The list came to almost 1,800 words!

Following is a list of common personality traits. Some are considered desirable. Some are not.

Desirable Traits	Undesirable Traits
Calm	Aggressive
Cautious	Critical
Cheerful	Demanding
Cooperative	Fickle
Friendly	Lazy
Funny	Mean
Generous	Meek
Gentle	Quitter
Good-natured	Shy
Loyal	Suspicious
Mature	Tough
Outgoing	Unhappy

When doing any of the following activities, DO NOT WRITE IN THIS BOOK.

Look up the words. Use a dictionary. Write out definitions of words you do not know.

Make a list. Checking both columns, list five personality traits that describe you best.

What about me? Set down the traits you would like to have. Then, in a short paragraph, describe what you would need to learn or how you would have to change to develop the traits you would want to be yours. (Hint: You may have to learn something unfamiliar to you. Also, you may have to change a favorite way of doing things in certain situations.)

Behavior is part of personality, too. Behavior means what you do and say. Behavior is learned, not inherited. Behavior develops as a result of give-and-take with parents, brothers, sisters, other relatives, teachers, and friends.

Suppose a new boy shows up at school. You might want to get to know him better. How would you go about it?

Chances are you'd study his behavior and watch how he acts in different situations—in class, at lunch, after school. You'd probably ask your friends about him. You might keep an eye on how he gets along with others.

Finally, with a chance to meet him, you might ask him about himself. What does he like? Dislike? How does he feel about school, rock music, girls? Gradually you'd fit the pieces together and get an impression of his personality. Based on his behavior, what he says about himself, and what you learn from others, you'd decide if you want to know him better or not.

Emotions are also part of personality. Emotions are the strong feelings that develop when you become aware of an unexpected sound, movement, or a new bit of information. Emotions can be happy and pleasant, as when you are surprised with a gift you've long wanted. Emotions can be unpleasant and sad, as when someone you love dies or goes away.

Some emotions can help you to organize your life and escape from danger. Others make you feel disorganized or unable to make a decision, even when it's very important that you take action.

Emotions affect the body because the brain and the body always work together. Strong emotions like anger or joy can make your heart beat faster, make your mouth feel dry, cause you to sweat, or make your stomach feel tight.

Interview.
Ask three adults the following questions:
1. Are emotions good or bad? Good ___ Bad ___
2. Would you root for a player who cries after losing the big game? Yes ___ No ___
3. Would you vote for a politician

Natalie Leimkuhler

Emotions are strong feelings that can be positive or negative. What emotion do you think David is feeling?

who shows emotion by getting "choked up" during a campaign speech? Yes ___ No ___

List the results of your poll on a chart for the class bulletin board.

DO NOT WRITE IN THIS BOOK.

To learn more. What emotions did you feel while taking the poll?

After you heard the answers?

Any idea why you reacted that way?

Compare your reactions with those of classmates who did this activity.

Everyone is born with emotions. Positive or pleasant emotions are those that make you feel good. Negative or unpleasant emotions make you feel bad. Out of a baby's tiny cry will develop emotions like anger, fear, jealousy, disgust, and sadness. From infant sounds of contentment will come joy, love, generosity, and kindness.

By adolescence you are capable of feeling many different emotions, and each with different degrees of intensity.

25

For example, if someone makes fun of you, you may feel a *little* embarrassed, *very* embarrassed, or *extremely* embarrassed.

As you get older you will become more aware of emotions and the need to understand them, to enjoy them, and to keep them in check.

NEGATIVE EMOTION

No one has much problem with positive and pleasant feelings like success, joy, or happiness. However, learning to handle negative and unpleasant feelings like jealousy, shame, or worry is a lot harder.

Frustration, fear, and *anxiety* are a few of the negative emotions you'll learn about in ME. Frustration is a feeling that comes when you are blocked from getting what you want. Frustration often leads to anger.

Fear and *anxiety* are really part of the same emotion. Fear usually develops because of some outside threat that you can see or feel—like a snarling dog, or an approaching tornado.

Anxiety is part of fear. Anxious persons worry and fret that something bad will happen. But they are not always sure what makes them so upset and nervous. At times a little anxiety is helpful, as when it sharpens you for a test or keeps you alert in a dangerous situation.

However, no one can live all the time in frustration, fear, or anxiety (or any other strong emotion) without becoming mentally and physically upset. That's why healthy people try to get rid of the strong emotions that bother them.

Next, you'll read about some of the ways that persons use to cope with negative emotions and frustrating problems.

What about me? Everyone has basic emotional needs. Some of the more common emotional needs that contribute to a person's mental health are:

- *Belonging* (the need to be part of a family, group, or team).
- *Approval* (the need for praise when you have earned it).
- *Achievement* (the need to succeed).
- *New experiences* (the need for variety in your life).
- *Security* (the need to be free from fear).
- *Love* (the need for someone to accept you as you are).

On a separate sheet of paper write one example of how you try to meet *each* basic need.

DO NOT WRITE IN THIS BOOK.

COPING WITH STRESS

Everyone meets *problems* in learning how to live comfortably with self and others. Everyone meets *conflict*. Everyone experiences some disagreement with others. Everyone uses *defenses* or ways to protect self from unpleasant feelings. Everyone must make important *decisions* about how to act in certain situations. Everyone must grow more mature or remain childish. Much of this change takes place during adolescence.

Nikki's story helps explain what happens when someone meets a conflict that causes feelings of stress. Her case may sound like some of your struggles. As you read, try to put yourself in her place and think what you would do.

CASE EXAMPLE

For several days Nikki's mother asked her to pick up the clothes and papers in her bedroom. Now it is Saturday and Nikki wants to go out with her friends. Mother insists that

the work be done before she leaves. Nikki feels caught between something she wants to do and something she doesn't want to do. She also feels frustrated, angry, and a little guilty for avoiding the work.

Nikki is face-to-face with a real conflict.

Time out. Before reading on, stop for a moment to imagine what emotions you would have if you were in Nikki's place. Would your emotions most likely be positive or negative? Would your emotions cause you to feel better or worse? *Time in.*

Nikki feels uncomfortable, a little anxious, and frustrated. She has three ways to cope with her strong emotions.

• *Approach.* She can deal directly with her problem. That way she will either solve it or make it worse. For example, she might take direct action by tearing into the mess, working fast, getting the job done, and still meeting her friends. Or she could make even a greater effort and do more than mother

asked—dust the furniture and clean the windows. Or she could try to argue her mother out of the assignment. She could make a deal to do the work later. She might blame her roommate sister for the mess. Or she might scream, kick the furniture, and fling even more clothes on the floor. In each case she *does something* to get rid of her strong feelings. She takes action, but not necessarily the kind of action that will solve her problem.

• *Avoid.* Nikki can try indirect action. She can escape by moving away from the conflict. Sometimes retreat of this type makes sense, as when a bully threatens you with bodily harm, or when you need extra time to think about a choice you must make. Other times, avoiding the problem simply prolongs the trouble or makes it worse. For example, Nikki could lie on her bed and

What about me? How do I solve problems?

Think of some recent trouble that you had to face. Which of the three problem-solving methods did you use?

Approach?

Avoidance?

Do nothing?

Is that your usual method for solving problems?

Is it possible that another method might do you more good?

DEFENSES

To survive and fight again, a boxer must dodge deadly body blows. In much the same way, everyone tries to protect self against personal attacks. No one can stand unharmed against repeated blows to personality or character. Cruel criticism, cutting insults, and unkind remarks are the kind of painful jabs everyone can do without.

To guard against the upsetting feelings caused by such attacks, everyone uses *psychological defenses.* Simply, these defenses are learned reactions to emotional upset. Defenses help drain tension, hold off anxiety, and keep the person in emotional balance.

Some defenses are useful. Defenses that help you to get along well with others, to avoid violent behavior, to learn ways to cope with problems, and to stay mentally healthy are called good adjustments.

Learn. For example, if Nikki decided to deal with her conflict directly and sensibly, she might clean her room. In doing so, she'd please her mother, feel better about herself, and get rid of feelings of tensions and guilt. She might also learn that *direct action* is often a good way to solve a problem. All this would add up to a good adjustment.

Now, let's say Nikki tried another approach to her problem. The conflict with

daydream about the time in the future when no one can tell her what to do anymore. Or she could plot to slip away unseen. Or she might develop a real headache from the upset caused by her own angry, churning feelings, plus the pressure of her mother's nagging.

• *Do nothing.* Nikki can decide to do nothing. Some people take no action when under pressure. They can't tackle the problem and they can't run away from it. They feel caught in a trap. They seem unable to cope with even the smallest frustration. Nikki might do absolutely nothing except feel tense, upset, and anxious. In such a state she probably will be unable to think clearly or to regain inner calm.

mother upsets her. Her muscles tighten, her heart beats faster, her head pounds. (Remember, strong emotions cause body changes.) Nikki complains that she feels sick.

And suppose mother is sympathetic and forgiving and willing to forget about the messy bedroom. Nikki may learn that becoming sick is a good way to escape from things she doesn't want to do. When persons claim to be sick in order to avoid anything unpleasant, they usually have trouble dealing with the ordinary problems of life.

We tend to learn and use defenses that make us feel better, even if the improvement lasts only a short time. Many persons use defenses to protect themselves and don't even realize it. In time, these tactics to avoid threat can become part of personality traits. Nikki, for example, might never realize when or how she learned to moan, "I've got a headache," to avoid everything from homework to chores around the house. Such "avoiding" habits are learned and can become part of her personality.

Defenses come in many other forms. You might know people who become sarcastic under pressure. Others may offer excuses for not keeping their word, or make up reasons to explain why they cheat, lie, or steal.

Some defenses cripple the personality. These methods to avoid what is difficult may relieve strong negative emotions, but the price is high. For example, telling a lie is a defense against getting hurt, but it also works against the user. If you lie every time you are under pressure, you might reduce anxious feelings for the time or even avoid a conflict. However, you'd also become known as a liar. Then you'd have even bigger problems.

Natalie Leimkuhler

As an adolescent you'll make many important decisions.

Something to think about. You have probably been in situations where you were sure that another person was telling a lie, cheating, or stealing.

Pause a while. Try to think of some reasons *why* they needed to act so?

Do you believe that dishonest people *prefer* to act that way?

Try to think of one good reason for your answer.

DECISIONS

While on your journey through life, you'll make many important decisions that will affect the kind of person you will become as an adult. When you were younger, parents made the big decisions for you. You were directed from the outside. As a teen, you are on your own more and more. Also, others hold you increasingly responsible for what you say and do. Now, you become more "inner-directed."

Suppose a toddler wanders into a neighbor's back yard and yanks the tulip tops from the stems. After seeing the ruined flowers, the neighbor may get angry and ask the parents to keep the child home. However, if you did the same thing, you would probably be called a delinquent.

As you read this book you will get a better idea how your own development as a person moves from the past to the present, and what can happen in the future. Keep this past-present-future sequence in mind as you read more about decision-making.

Inherited. Part of the way you make decisions today was inherited from your parents. You read earlier that basic temperament is present at birth. Tests show that some babies react faster than others to sights and sounds. Children tend to keep such basic reactions as they grow older. Some are fast, some are slow. For example:

• *Fast.* Fast reactors "fly off the handle" or "shoot from the hip." They act quickly and often without careful thought.

• *Fast and right.* Some persons are both quick and accurate. You know classmates who not only finish exams first, but also get the best grades.

• *Slow.* Some people are slow in making decisions, but they are seldom wrong. Called "cautious" or "deliberate," they may annoy others by taking so long to make up their minds. However, rarely do these slow but steady persons make a really bad decision.

• *Slow and wrong.* Taking a lot of time to think doesn't guarantee good decisions. Although some people take a long while to make up their minds, their decisions are still not the best.

• *No decision.* Some people seem unable to make any final choices. They

may feel anxious. Or they may be so sure that they'd be wrong anyway, that they avoid making a decision even when the delay causes them to lose out.

What about me? Regardless of your basic temperament and decision-making style, thoughtless and quick-without-thinking behavior often seems to be part of adolescence. A great increase in energies, new restlessness, and a need for action and excitement can lead to poor and hasty decisions. For example, most persons blurt out an insult once in a while. Later they wish they hadn't said it. Some teens risk serious injury with a dangerous show-off trick. And who hasn't spent money foolishly, or thought about running away from home?

Excited, tense, or angry people of every age and temperament sometimes act too quickly and later regret it. However, during teen years, even impulsive and unthinking acts may serve an important purpose. You can learn to develop limits and controls for your life. You test what's real and what isn't. In your search for who you are and what you can do, you measure yourself against others.

CASE EXAMPLE

Imagine that you attend a meeting to plan an upcoming dance. Volunteers are needed to help decorate the gym. You jump to your feet. Before you can think twice, you agree to head the committee. You spend hours trying to assign workers, purchase supplies, make decisions. You soon regret your quick action at the first meeting. The gym walls won't hold the tangled crepe paper, so down goes the colorful arrangement you planned. You may also learn that you are not yet the world's greatest organizer, or that you are a better follower than leader. Or you may discover that you are a natural leader and a truly talented decorator.

Guidelines for living. This is a good time for you to learn a little about your natural temperament. Use the following checklist to learn which type of decision maker you tend to be.

DO NOT WRITE IN THIS BOOK.

What Kind of Decision Maker Am I?

• Do I start many projects eagerly but finish very few?

• Do I often blurt out wrong answers instead of planning what I want to say?

• Do I often get low grades on tests because I don't read the questions carefully or don't re-check my work before turning it in?

• Do I usually take the first offer in a trade instead of bargaining for something a little better?

• Do I often use teasing or sarcasm that hurts others, and then regret my words?

• Would I accept $2 today rather than wait for $5 next week?

• Would I choose one day at Disneyland now rather than wait for a guaranteed week-long trip next year?

If you answered yes five or more times, chances are you tend to be quick and impulsive and wrong more often than you'd like to be. If you answered no five or more times, you're probably a more cautious and thoughtful decision maker.

If you are not satisfied with the way you are making decisions, you will have many chances to discover why you act as you do when you study the chapters in ME—which are all about you.

To learn more about me. To give you an idea of the many choices you face daily, keep a log of all the decisions you must make in a normal school day. Include selections of food and other items, and opportunities for work, play, and recreation.

Keep your record on a separate sheet of paper.

DO NOT WRITE IN THIS BOOK.

MATURITY

Physical maturity means to complete your growth and development. Persons who act their age are called emotionally mature. No matter how old they are, mature persons know how to make best use of their talents and energies.

It's important to remember that no one is perfect. At times everyone makes mistakes and uses immature or even harmful defenses.

A personal checklist. The best test of a strong personality and growing maturity is in the *total* picture of you. Ask yourself these questions.

• How well do I manage life overall?

• How do I get along with friends and family?

• What things do I value most?

• What kinds of decisions do I usually make?

Throughout this book you will read about ways to deal with negative emotions. You will learn to substitute useful defenses for harmful ones. You will learn to build better and more enjoyable relationships with others. You will learn to consider your values. You will learn ways to gain inner control and increased understanding of self.

Everyone can change old and useless ways of doing things. Everyone can get help with problems, even when they seem too big to manage. An exciting and satisfying life lies ahead of you if you are willing to work for it.

What about me? On a separate sheet of paper write one way that your life has been influenced by:

• Your environment.

• A particular experience that happened to you.

David Snodgress, Journal and
Courier, Lafayette, Indiana
"Adolescence, here I come!"

• The heredity received from your parents.
• Your personal values.
DO NOT WRITE IN THIS BOOK.
You have just done some important research about your own life. Read what you have written. Does this new information tell you about the possible causes for the way you live your life today?

To learn more. Select one idea or topic from this chapter that applies to you and the way you live your life.

On a separate sheet of paper describe your selection in one sentence.

In no more than three sentences explain why you chose it.
DO NOT WRITE IN THIS BOOK.

RECAP

Adolescence is the part of your life journey after you are a child and before you become an adult. The teen years are an "in-between" time. You are no longer a child. However, you are not yet an adult either.

From the time you were a baby, many things helped decide the kind of person you are today. Your genetic inheritance came from both parents. Both where you live and what happens at home help to build your personality. The values you hold also shape your growing self.

Relationships make up the basic theme of this book. Relationships mean what happens between you and the most important people in your life. Relationships also help mold your personality.

Adolescence includes all your growth and development—physical, social, intellectual, and emotional. *Growth* and *development* refer to increases in body size and abilities. *Puberty* means all the many changes in the body that make a boy or girl capable of starting a new life or becoming a parent. *Mature* means to complete growth and development. *Rate* refers to how fast a person grows. *Timing* means the ages when you start and complete a growth spurt.

Adolescence includes your last important physical development. Adolescence usually begins slowly, picks up speed, then tapers off gradually. Although all body parts mature during the teen years, some systems grow faster than others. Just as no person could live alone completely isolated from other humans, no body system could function alone. Each depends upon the others.

Good rules tell you what to expect, they offer general guidelines, and they allow for exceptions. Normal growth and development:

• Follows an inherited, or genetic, plan.

  • Stays on course.

  • Is continuous.

• Goes through important stages that can't be repeated.

  • Depends on timing.

• Is unique, or not exactly like the growth and development of anyone else.

• Cannot be separated from personality development.

Personality means everything about you, including the way you look, the way your body works, your mental abilities, and your emotions, or strong feelings. The way you learn to understand and manage your emotions also influences your personality development.

Behavior, or how you act with others, is also part of personality. *Traits* are the behaviors that become permanent parts of personality.

Conflict and other upsetting problems seem to be part of everyone's life experiences. There are three ways to deal with upsetting problems:

• *Approach* the difficulty, and try to solve it.

• *Avoid* or try to escape from the problem.

• *Do nothing* at all.

Defenses are the behaviors that people use to avoid or fight off upsetting events—especially those that make the persons feel bad. Some defenses are useful. Others help get rid of anxious feelings for the time but may, in the long run, harm the person using them.

Adolescence is a time when young persons learn to make important decisions. A decision-making "style" may be partly inherited, partly learned from parents, and partly the result of personal experiences and learning.

Mature persons of any age keep trying to manage their lives well. They think about their problems, and try to work out different ways to handle strong emotions. They try to live in ways that hurt neither themselves nor others.

As an adolescent, you've lived long enough to pick up an amazing collection of facts, ideas, skills, attitudes, and behaviors. However, there is still a lot of work to be done before you will be ready to live as an independent, mature adult. Learning to manage relationships with others is one way to achieve independence and maturity.

TERMS

Adolescent	Personal values	Growth spurt	Traits
Physical	Adolescence	Personality	Conflict
Mental	Growth	Emotion	Approach
Emotional	Development	Frustration	Avoid
Relationships	Mature	Fear	Defenses
Genetic	Rate of growth	Anxiety	Decision
Inheritance	Timing of growth	Anger	Maturity
Life experience	Puberty	Behavior	

CHAPTER 2

A Framework for Brainwork

Your brain is the most important part of your body. Your brain stores millions of bits of information and performs hundreds of important duties. It is so necessary for life that when a person's brain stops working the owner is considered dead.

The brief story of the brain that follows is included to help you understand yourself and others better. With this new knowledge you will be ready to learn more about why your body and mind work as they do.

OVERVIEW

Your brain plays a part in everything you do. Your brain controls your personality, your thoughts, your emotions, your character, all of your skills and abilities. Your brain regulates your growth and development. Ride a bike. Throw a ball. Write a poem. Your brain makes everything work.

Your brain also decides your relationships with other persons. It tells you when to get involved, or when to stay apart. For example, suppose you see an injured person who needs help. Your brain sorts out the pros and cons of the situation. "If I stop and help I may be late for school . . . But if I don't help, the other person may not get to a doctor on time." Your brain is the part of you that makes the final decision to offer help or to pass by.

Kathy Tuite
Your brain coordinates everything you do.

BASIC EQUIPMENT

Your brain serves as the control tower of your body. A jellylike mass weighing 1.7 kilograms, or a little less than 4 pounds, the brain's color is greyish pink.

From its location under a thick, bony plate in your head, the brain speeds electrical and chemical messages along circuits of nerves to mix and blend everything you do, including thinking, talking, and walking. When you feel like shouting, for example, the brain signals the muscles of your tongue and face to move in just the right way to produce either a cry of joy or a howl of pain.

Your brain keeps you in touch with the world around you through your senses of sight, hearing, taste, touch, and smell. Your brain also switches your emotions from strong to weak, from positive to negative. It even repairs itself after some injuries.

UNSOLVED MYSTERIES

Some scientists call the brain the "last frontier" because it still contains so many unsolved mysteries about why people act as they do. Locked inside are the answers to these questions:

- How do people learn?
- How do they remember?
- How do they understand language?
- Why do some become mentally ill?
- How can they be made healthy again?

David Snodgress, Journal and Courier, Lafayette, Indiana

Billy just got the autograph of a famous athlete. Guess what sport Billy plans to play when he goes to college?

The brain is so complicated in the way it works and so stubborn in yielding its secrets that many scientists spend a lifetime studying nothing but one small part of the brain. Perhaps some day you will solve one of the mysteries of the brain.

BRAINWORK

In one of its most important tasks your brain helps you to *think*. Thinking is what pulls your life together. Your brain even has the amazing ability to talk with itself. Simply, you can think about what you have been thinking. Try it.

Your brain thinks in two basic ways. *Conscious* thinking means being aware, or knowing what thoughts are in your mind. *Unconscious* thinking happens when your brain works but you don't know about it.

When you sleep, you are unconscious. Dreams are a form of thinking with pictures. Even when you're awake, a lot of unconscious thinking goes on. Below the surface, unconscious thinking takes place as if hidden in another person inside you. Here are some examples:

• All of a sudden you get the answer to a problem that's puzzled you for days.

• You wake up in the morning with a plan for the day already worked out.

• In a flash you recall a name that you've been trying to remember.

In each of these cases your unconscious thinking has been at work.

Like a super-librarian, the brain collects, processes, and stores your experiences. During dreams, it flashes instant replays of the day's events in strange forms.

Some memories get filed away for future reference, without effort. Others are forgotten forever. It depends on how important each event is to you. You may forget buying a candy bar. However, you'll surely remember an insult.

Your body sleeps, but your brain never rests. Like an automatic door control with an electronic eye, your brain stays silently in charge of every body function while you sleep. It controls body temperature and monitors breathing and food digestion. It is always ready to wake you when strange noises occur. And it lets you sleep through most familiar sounds.

MATURITY

As your brain matures it gets better at what it does, just like the rest of your body. Imagine a curious baby named Bobby exploring his world. Given a fuzzy, red sweater he will touch it, study it, smell it. He may even taste it.

At first, babies check everything around them through their senses—by touching or tasting. As they grow older, infants depend more on thinking and memory. As the baby shifts from testing everything with fingers and mouth to conscious thinking, the brain develops. Bobby, for example, soon learns that sweaters are not to eat because they leave fuzz in his mouth. He stops tasting them, although he may keep sucking on a corner of his security blanket.

Between the ages of two and seven, a great amount of learning takes place. Bobby learns that a sweater has a name and a purpose. He learns its color—red.

Between the ages of seven and eleven, Bobby can do more and more. He discovers that a sweater like his costs several dollars. He also learns that it is only one of many kinds of sweaters. He can tell when it should be worn—for dress up or play, for a mild day or for a cold one. He may even know whether it is made of cotton, wool, or other fibers.

All normal children go through similar, orderly stages of mental development. You did the same thing when you learned to give names to certain people, streets, autos, and musical groups. You began to organize your thinking and to remember your experiences. You learned to use words to express your thoughts and emotions with increasing success.

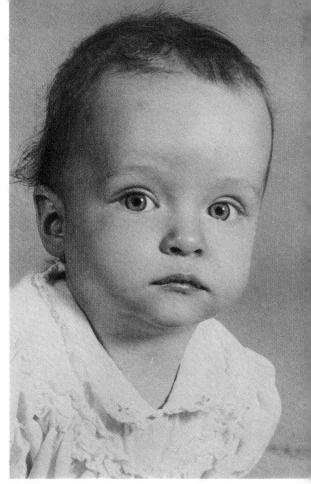

Like you, infant Susan learned what she needed to know through her senses.

For each person the order of mental growth is planned by nature in advance. You may already know this by living or working with young children. First, babies make funny sounds. Then they say single words. Later they speak in sentences.

Even though language development is much the same for everyone, each person moves at a personal pace. Some babies say simple words at one year. Others take longer. All are normal in their way.

Some children understand new ideas very quickly. Most go at average speed.

Like you, teenage Susan still learns through her senses. At this age she is responsible for her good health, for her developing intelligence, and for how well she uses her talents and time.

Even so, sooner or later all bright and average persons go through all the regular stages of mental development. These abilities to think unfold as the child grows older.

Write one paragraph. Early memories are very important in understanding your own development.

On a separate sheet of paper write a paragraph describing the first thing you can remember from your childhood.

Explain why that particular memory remains so clear to you.

How old were you at the time?

DO NOT WRITE IN THIS BOOK.

INTELLIGENCE

When you call someone a "brain" you probably mean that the person is intelligent. Intelligence ties together many different workings of the brain.

• Intelligence means your ability to use language to explain your thoughts to other persons.

• Intelligence helps you to make sense out of the events of the day.

• Intelligence helps you to work with numbers, to learn new facts, and to recall old ones.

• Intelligence also refers to your powers of reasoning and judgment. When you reason, you figure out how things work. When you use good judgment, you make good choices.

What about me? It is not unusual for a person your age to wonder, "Just how smart am I?" There is a simple answer. If you are reading this book and understanding most of it, you have enough intelligence to live a full life. You will be able to study, earn a living, and get along with relatives, friends and co-workers.

EXPERIENCE

It is still not known exactly how much heredity (what you get from your parents) contributes to a person's intelligence. It has been proved, however, that learning and experience also decide how intelligent a person becomes. Discoveries of recent years show that a person's intelligence can be improved. The upper level of how smart you can get in a lifetime may be limited. Experience helps you to reach that upper level. The more you try things, the better you get. Put another way, the more you use your brain the sharper it becomes.

No one is born with a fixed amount of intelligence that can't be changed. The

Kathy Matter, Journal and Courier, *Lafayette, Indiana*

As he listens to his favorite story, Chico imagines himself as a brave fireman. Pretending and daydreaming are important stages in every child's mental development.

David Snodgress, Journal and Courier, *Lafayette, Indiana*

This teacher helps his young pupils develop their intelligence.

intelligence you inherit from your parents is more like a rubber band. It stretches when you help it along with good experiences like food, rest, attempts to solve problems and puzzles, and regular study sessions.

ENVIRONMENT

Environment (in-VY-run-ment) means everything in your immediate life—people, places, and things. Environment makes a difference in the development of human intelligence. Take a

The more you use your brain, the better it works. To develop typing skill you must practice a lot.

Kathy Tuite

Rohn Engh

Stacey grew up in an environment that is clean, healthy, and uncrowded.

A poor environment can destroy the desire to learn and achieve.

William Johnson

package of radish seeds. Plant half of them in good soil. Then give them water, sunlight, and fertilizer. If you keep the weeds and rabbits out, your radishes will probably grow big, red, firm, and tasty.

Plant the rest of the seeds in the wrong place and forget about them. Your crop will be small and scrawny. In each case the seed was good, but the environment or surroundings decided the results. The first group of seeds had a good environment that helped them to grow. The second group had a poor environment that held back the growth of the radishes.

Look up the word. Environment is a word that you will read and hear many times.

To remember it better, look up *environment* in a school dictionary. Write out all the different meanings on a separate sheet of paper.

DO NOT WRITE IN THIS BOOK.

In a way, your life will be like the radish seeds. No matter what, you will grow. However, the better your environment at home, at school, and in your neighborhood, the better are your chances to accomplish all that you are capable of. Simply, your intelligence is likely to develop best in good surroundings. The saddest thing about a poor environment is that many fine people with talents for learning and working never get a chance to develop them.

FAST GROWTH

Your intelligence increases rapidly during adolescence and continues to develop long after your teen years. In fact, many thinking skills reach a peak later in life. Even much older persons who stay active and healthy both physically and mentally keep alert and quick as long as they live. They can think, study, and work out tricky problems far longer than others their age who sit and rock, or watch TV most of the time.

Adolescence is a time for fast growth and much learning. Nature takes care of the growth. Your body will get taller and heavier whether you want it to or not. However, you decide how much you will learn during your lifetime. You probably know students who use their intelligence regularly for study, homework, sports, hobbies, and social activities. Life is usually much easier for them.

Did you know? There have been recent studies at Harvard University on how children learn and why they succeed in school. The findings of the studies suggest that *home background* has more influence than anything else.

The results also show that success in school depends on:
- The quality of subjects taught.
- The amount of time a student spends in class.
- The amount of time a student spends on homework.
- The quality of the teachers.

You decide. Which one of the above best explains how you learn?

Write your answer to the question on a separate sheet of paper. Give at least one reason for your answer.

DO NOT WRITE IN THIS BOOK.

ATTITUDES

Your brain remembers past learning. Each time you want to read a book or tune the TV set, you don't have to learn how all over again. Memory stores such information and releases it on call.

Learning includes many things besides school subjects or skills. For example, you learn *attitudes*. An attitude is a way of thinking about something. Everyone carries many attitudes filed away in the brain. Attitudes lie ready for instant use when the right topic shows up. At split-second notice you can pro-

Most teens enjoy snack time.

duce an attitude complete with emotions. The feelings might be strong or weak, positive or negative.

For example, you may dislike a certain food. You may even be able to trace the start of your negative attitude back some months to a late night snack that made you feel sick. In such simple ways you learn pro (for) or con (against) attitudes about certain foods.

In human relationships, attitudes are not so simply explained. You learn attitudes about yourself and others so early in childhood, and from so many different experiences, that it's almost impossible to remember exactly when some of your opinions ever got started.

To learn more about me. Attitudes can change. In fact, what happens from day to day can make one of your attitudes either weaker or stronger.

In some cases a new experience might cause you to change an old attitude. When you change your mind about something, you are changing your attitude.

Think of a recent example of how you gave up an old opinion for a new one.

On a separate sheet of paper, describe in no more than three sentences

A great reader, Frannie uses her intelligence to learn and to remember.

what it was that made you give up your old opinion.

DO NOT WRITE IN THIS BOOK.

MOTIVATION

Motivation means how much you want to learn and how soon you want to learn it. Athletic coaches constantly search for ways to motivate or inspire their teams. How much you want to do things well helps you to decide whether you will use your intelligence to complete your schoolwork, or to avoid it. Strong motivation gets the job done. Weak motivation often leaves it unfinished.

Emotions and attitudes also play a part in intelligence and motivation. When you are upset or worried, you don't learn as much or as well. A negative attitude to school can interfere with your ability to think and learn.

To learn more about me. To get a better idea of what motivates you, complete the following sentences.

There are not any right or wrong answers, just yours. This is a game of self-discovery to help you find out what you value most.

DO NOT WRITE IN THIS BOOK.

On a separate sheet of paper jot down the first answer you think of in order to complete the sentence.

- If I had five dollars, I would . . .
- The best reward anyone can give me is . . .
- What I like to do most right after school is . . .
- When I do good schoolwork I'd like my teacher to say . . .
- Someday I'd really like to . . .
- I feel wonderful when I . . .
- I will do most anything to get . . .
- When I earn money I like to . . .
- If I had just one wish it would be . . .
- The first thing I'd buy on a shopping spree would be . . .

When you complete your work, review your answers. Try to think *why* you answered as you did.

SPECIAL BRAINWORK: VALUES AND MORALS

Of all of the many thinking duties of the brain some are especially important in your study of ME. In the remainder of this chapter, you'll read about the development of values and morals in your life.

Moral development. You are familiar with your rapid physical growth and your increased intellectual development. At this age you may also experience a spurt in moral development. *Morals* mean what you believe to be right and wrong. Morals also mean the values you live by. With moral development you don't add to your physical size or your amount of brainpower. However, you do begin to decide which human actions are OK and which are not. Consider these cases.

CASE EXAMPLE

Recently, in Portland, Oregon, a brave thirteen-year-old eighth-grader chased and captured a thief. Then the boy took the lawbreaker's gun.

"The money belonged to someone else and the robber shouldn't have it," explained the young hero. Then he added, "I hate crime." Obviously the thief-catcher has a strong moral sense. The difference between right and wrong is very clear to him.

In another city a fourteen-year-old boy won the National Soap Box Derby. Soon after, he was stripped of his title. Officials discovered that the winning race car had a secret battery and electromagnet for faster starts. The winner's uncle, the boy's sponsor, explained that since most contestants used cheating devices of some kind, he decided to help his nephew do the same.

What about me? How would you react in situations like these? Would you chase a robber who had a loaded gun? That is, would you risk your life to fight crime?

Or suppose you could be almost certain that no one would know if you broke the rules of a contest. Would you cheat in order to have a better chance for first prize?

These questions may be difficult. No matter how you answer them, the decisions that you reach are *moral* choices. They say something about your personal values. They indicate your present attitude about what is right and what is wrong.

You make similar moral choices every day. Under pressure, you decide to lie or to tell the truth. At certain times you may choose to avoid responsibility or to accept it. Or you may ignore what is fair and right just to avoid taking a risk. Only you can be sure what you would do in situations that demand a moral choice.

Moral beliefs don't develop as fast as your ability to understand math or science. Moral development is a longer and slower process that is tied to your age and general level of mental growth.

Did you know? Jean Piaget is an expert on children's mental development. He lives in Switzerland. Piaget was one of the first psychologists to study how a child's ideas of right and wrong develop. He discovered that moral beliefs build a little bit at a time. Piaget also found that ideas of right and wrong, once formed, tend to stay much the same as the person grows older.

When children are very young, right and wrong means not to make their parents angry. Later on, a little at a time, most children learn the rules of fair play on the playground, or in school. They want others to like them. They learn to avoid criticism or rejection by going along with the crowd.

A higher level of moral development begins about age eleven. That's when most boys and girls start to accept responsibility for what they do and say.

Children learn the rules of fair play in school, on the playground, and in the neighborhood.

Conscience. An inner voice, conscience reminds you to do right. Conscience is also a sense of responsibility that causes you to feel guilt or shame when you do something wrong. Your conscience develops gradually, and becomes stronger during adolescence. At your age, making a promise or giving your word puts more pressure on you than it did when you were a child.

Conscience can be helpful when it encourages you to live a good life, to stay out of trouble, and to act in an honest and responsible way. The feelings of guilt caused by your conscience can build so much discomfort and inner tension that the natural urge is to get rid of guilt fast. Here are some common ways that persons get rid of guilt:

- Apologize to the person offended.
- Make up for the offense by doing something good.
- Rationalize or make up a reason for the behavior.
- Deny the bad behavior and hide the guilt.
- Use humor. Laugh it off.

Guilt. Guilt lets you know the way things really are and sometimes gives you the energy needed to change your behavior. However, just as you judge others unfairly at times, you can also be too hard on yourself. Too much guilt causes fears, anxieties, depression, and overwhelming feelings of worthlessness.

In Chapter 1 you read about *defenses,* those thick, invisible walls of excuses and reasons that people build to protect

Concern about what's right and what's wrong begins during childhood. By age eleven most children start to accept responsibility for what they say and do.

44

themselves from the truth. However, defenses don't always work.

Sometimes persons feel so guilty that unconsciously they try to punish themselves by driving their cars too fast, by injuring themselves repeatedly, or by committing suicide.

No conscience. Not everyone has a strong and helpful conscience. Criminologists, (KRIM-uh-NOL-uh-jists) are experts concerned with youth who commit crimes that are brutal and senseless. The criminologists notice that such boys and girls do not know the difference between right and wrong. Also, these young offenders feel no sense of personal responsibility or shame for their violent acts.

Although there's no simple reason to explain why an adolescent would brutally attack or kill another person, these reasons are offered:

- Breakdown of the family.
- Changes in the ways that parents and children live together.
- TV and film violence. Watching violence can trigger imitation in young viewers. Studies suggest that children who watch TV will see thousands of murders and other violent acts by the time they reach fourteen.
- Racial attitudes of "get even" that wipe away feelings of guilt.

In later chapters, you'll read more about each of these forces and how they might touch your life.

Religion. Religion is a way to study and worship God. Members of the same church or temple usually agree about what is right or wrong. Most religions teach a moral code or belief called the Golden Rule. It reminds us to treat others the way we would like them to treat us. If you attend church services or religion classes you will be familiar with

Natalie Leimkuhler

Leslie's conscience hurts. She felt guilty about not finishing her lawn mowing assignment long before mother showed up to check.

the reasons for treating all persons equally and fairly.

Adult influence. Just hearing about what is right and wrong doesn't seem to influence the way boys and girls act very much. Living, studying, and working with adults who live according to the Golden Rule seem to have most influence on young children. For this reason boys and girls seem to learn most about right and wrong by imitating adults around them. So if the youngsters live, study, and work with fair and honest adults, they will probably become fair and honest adults themselves.

The opposite is also true. Children raised by, and attracted to, adults who are unfair and dishonest may learn to break the rules of right and wrong without feeling bad about it.

HARD CHOICES

Sooner or later most everyone gets caught between two sets of rules that don't agree. At such a time you will be forced to make a choice. You are really on your own. You will have to decide.

For example, at home you and your relatives may always tell the truth and try

Children learn about right and wrong by imitating adults close to them. Parents are the most important models.

to live according to the rules of your religious faith. Some of your classmates, however, may question your family's moral code or even laugh at it. The squeezed feeling that develops in such situations is called *conflict of values.*

It is possible that you have already been in situations where you knew what was best but had trouble doing what you believed to be right. Suppose, for example, that your friends decide to shoplift just for fun. You know that shoplifting is wrong. However, you decide to say nothing. Perhaps you are afraid to lose your friends or get teased for what you

believe. That's just one example of how the pressure to go along with the crowd plays a big part in moral decisions during adolescence.

Another confusing part of moral development is that hardly any actions are all right or all wrong. You probably realize that *intention,* or what the person has in mind at the time, helps to decide how good or bad an act is. Breaking a friend's bike by mistake is quite different from kicking the spokes on purpose.

Situation also has a lot to do with the way a person acts. It is difficult to predict from one time to the next who will

46

cheat and who won't. A boy who would never steal a penny might think it OK to sneak into class a few answers for a tough exam. Or a man who wouldn't drop a gum wrapper on the street might give the order to send polluted waste into the river behind the factory he owns on the edge of town.

So you can see that human behavior is very complicated. It's not easy to sort out the countless reasons that determine what a person will do in a certain situation.

Between the ages of ten and seventeen, boys and girls build their moral character that will last for life. You have already made some choices that will decide the kind of adult you will be. A set way of living your life begins to emerge. You tend to act that same way from one time to the next. In fact, your friends may be able to guess in advance what you would do in a certain spot. You can probably guess the same about them.

For private review. Think of three values you consider important.

Where did you learn them?

Who taught them to you?

How do parents help decide your values?

How do teachers, friends, sports heroes, and TV stars influence what you consider to be valuable?

CHARACTER

Your character decides the kind of moral choices you make. You may inherit good looks, a strong body, or a talent for music. However, no one is born with good character. Instead, good character must be earned from day to day the same way a truck driver must earn a safety record.

Adolescence is the time to build your character. You are old enough to make

David Snodgress,
Journal and Courier, Lafayette, Indiana

Queen Vicki earned her crown as a teen volunteer in the candy striper program. She gives many hours of cheerful and helpful service to patients in her local hospital. One of the best ways to develop your character is by showing concern for others.

sensible and honest choices, and to live by them. You are able to control impulses that might cause harm to others. You can learn to take responsibility for your actions. You can learn to be a decent person and a loyal friend.

As you feel more concern for others, you will also begin to be more responsible for persons outside your own family. When you realize that some words and acts can hurt others deeply, it will be easier for you to develop attitudes of friendliness, self-control, and consideration. Mature and responsible men and women try to live according to a moral code that puts them in charge of their thoughts and actions.

In fact, the more self-control a person has, the less need for controls from parent, teachers, or the police. In a real sense, self-control gives you personal freedom. And that's what growing up to maturity is all about.

Something to think about. Choose one event from your childhood that really shaped your life today.

Try to give reasons for your selection.

What is one inherited trait that you believe has influence on you now?

What are your reasons for your choice?

You decide. What kind of person do you want to be three years from now? Five years? Ten years?

On a separate sheet of paper write the qualities or traits you would like to develop as you grow older.

DO NOT WRITE IN THIS BOOK.

Following are some words to get you started.

If they would help you become the kind of person you want to be as an adult, add them to your list.

Rich
Kind
Creative
Powerful
Helpful
Generous

To learn more. Select one idea or topic from this chapter that applies to you and the way you live your life.

On a separate sheet of paper describe your selection in one sentence.

In no more than three sentences explain why you chose it.

DO NOT WRITE IN THIS BOOK.

RECAP

In building relationships with others, your brain directs everything that happens. In fact, the brain controls all that you think and say. It also monitors everything you do and everything that happens to you. The brain coordinates all movement. The brain also regulates the digestion of food and other body processes.

Your brain helps you to think in two ways. Conscious thinking happens while you are awake and aware. When you plan something on purpose, that's conscious thinking.

Unconscious thinking goes on while you are awake or asleep. It happens even though you are not fully aware of it. Unconscious thinking often produces thoughts and ideas to be used at some later time.

As you grew from infancy through childhood to adolescence, your brain got better at its thinking job. Today you have millions of bits of information stored away. You can recall past events and make sense of them. You can make decisions. You can do jobs today that require close attention and skills you did not have when you were younger.

The brains of all normal people go through the same stages of growth and development. However, each brain matures at its own pace. Also, some persons seem to use their brains better than others.

Intelligence is not limited to one single talent. It is more like a shopping bag stuffed with many different skills and abilities, each in assorted sizes. Some people carry a larger shopping bag with king-sized talents. Even so, every normal person gets at least a sample size of all human abilities.

Experience can help any person use intelligence better. Environment means all the things that happen around you. Motivation, or how much you want to learn, also helps to decide how much you will learn. An attitude means a way of thinking about something. Emotions can interfere with learning and motivation and attitudes.

Moral development, or ideas of right and wrong, also follows a set plan. Conscience is like an inner policeman warning you about right and wrong. Sometimes your conscience scolds you silently for what you said or did.

Moral development moves ahead best when children grow up imitating people who are fair and honest.

Religion means a way of studying and worshipping God and living your life.

By now you are able to make your own choices and decisions about good and bad. Depending on your experiences and environment so far, you may already have a strong or weak religious faith and moral conscience.

Almost everyone gets caught in moral squeezes. A desire to go along with the crowd might urge you to do something you know is wrong.

Few choices are all right or all wrong. Sometimes it is difficult to decide. Your intention (whether or not you mean to do something harmful) also plays a part. Try to remember that you won't make the right choice every time.

Character means your personal set of moral rules. You put the finishing touches on your character during the adolescent years. Most people build character through small, day-to-day actions rather than any one big decision.

Each time you use self-control, or choose not to lie, cheat, or steal, you build your character a little more. You also build your character when you learn to care for the feelings and wishes of others, and when you take responsibility for your words and deeds. It is possible to keep developing your moral character for the rest of your life.

Persons with good and strong characters enjoy their journeys through life. They also earn good reputations in the process. You can decide now to do the same.

As you study the rest of this book, try to keep a double goal for your self: to build a healthy personality and an honest character. While pursuing both goals your personal journey through life will be easier and more fun.

TERMS

Brain	Inheritance	Moral development	Conflict of values
Genetic	Intelligence	Values	Character
Thinking	Attitude	Conscience	
Conscious	Morals	Religion	
Unconscious	Traits	Adult influence	

CHAPTER 3

How My Looks Make Me Feel

Rusty is a high school freshman. Uncertain about his looks, he also feels clumsy. It seems he can't walk through a room without bumping or breaking something. He says:

"I'm a big guy, but I'm heavy. I'd like to be a lot thinner. I don't like my build because I'm too flabby. I grew a lot last year. In my stocking feet I'm five feet nine. I want to be taller.

"I weigh 175 pounds. I don't really look that heavy, because I fooled the weight guesser at the fair last fall.

"My face isn't the best, but it's OK, I guess. One thing really bothers me though. Last year I broke my nose playing football. Now there's a bump there that ruins my looks. Sometimes I look in the mirror and say, 'Boy, you are good-looking!' Other times I say, 'Ugly, what you need is a good nose job!'"

So far you've read about some of the physical and mental changes that bring you from childhood to adolescence. In this chapter you'll read about some of the typical behavior that goes along with bodies that mature early or late. You'll read about bodies that add padding or stay slender, and about some that grow tall or stay short. You'll also read about how the rapid growth and body changes of early adolescence can affect your

feelings about yourself and your relationships with others.

NEW INTERESTS

Adolescence is a time of great interest in body size and shape, in facial features, in clothing and grooming. Boys and girls study themselves in every light, from every angle. Girls experiment with makeup and hairstyles. They question, "Am I pretty enough? Am I as attractive to boys as other girls?"

Boys compare themselves with other boys to discover, "Am I as strong? As capable? As good-looking?"

Comparing yourself to others and wondering about your looks are normal events at your age. There will be times when it may seem that everyone else is watching you with the same critical eye with which you search yourself.

By age twenty-one, almost everyone has stopped growing. However, living through the final growth spurt can be a demanding experience. For one thing, you can't be sure of the end result. How tall will I grow? What kind of body will I end up with? Will others like what they see?

Body image. Body image means how you look to yourself and think you look to others. Body image is part of your total self-concept.

Self-concept. Self-concept means how you rate yourself. However, it means more than whether you like your body or not. Self-concept includes how satisfied you are with the way you think,

Normal people come in many shapes and sizes.

Natalie Leimkuhler
"I wonder how they'll like me in these."

perhaps you came to believe that you live in a mean and ugly prison.

Unhappy with looks? Sometimes, feelings about a person's body can get distorted. Distorted means a picture that isn't true, like the wobbly image you see of yourself when you look into clear, rippling water.

Suppose, for example, a clumsy boy is born into a family of super athletes. If the awkward latecomer is valued for himself, fine. However, he may receive continual criticism or rejection because of his average abilities. If that happens, his regard for his body is sure to suffer. In short, he won't like himself. Situations like these produce a self-concept that is weak.

Opinions about the body are so closely tied to feelings about the entire self that those who *feel* incapable often end up believing that they can't do something, whether they can or not.

Of course, no one slips through the adolescent years without some uneasiness and uncertainty. Sometimes a single critical remark can shake you thoroughly—especially if it highlights a weakness that you already suspected to exist.

A grown woman named Elly, now the mother of teenagers herself, still winces at the memory of a comment overhead in childhood.

First woman: "Isn't it too bad that Elly is so plain? Her sisters got all the good looks in that family."

Second woman: (Laughing) "Yes, she'll have a hard time finding a boyfriend."

Actually, Elly developed into an attractive young woman with many boyfriends. However, for a long time she feared that the thoughtless busybodies were right.

the way you feel, and the way you get along with others. Persons with a strong self-concept respect what they are and what they can do.

Learning attitudes. No one inherits attitudes about the body or the self. You *learn* to feel good or bad about the way you look. You also build your self-concept from the words and actions of important persons in your life—parents, relatives, teachers, and friends.

From the time you were a baby you began to discover that you live in a body. You discovered that your body has particular parts like arms and legs. You also learned that you could do some things and not others. For example, you probably learned to ride a bicycle, but discovered that flying from housetops is not possible.

Gradually, as a result of much trial and error, you may have decided that your body is not a bad place to live. Or

With or without unkind criticism from others, adolescence itself can cause temporary worries. Common physical differences like birthmarks, a chipped tooth, or big ears seem to be just horrible to the owner. Of course, these minor flaws won't prevent a normal life. However, they may cause the teen who has them plenty of misery for a while.

At a time when you are getting used to a changing body you may feel so unsure of yourself that you believe the most casual comments to be true. What you'll shrug off later in life as a catty remark can wound you deeply today. Such psychological injuries heal in time, but the memories may linger on.

Try to remember that body image and self-concept depend on the *majority* of experiences that happen to you, not just one. Also, what you really *are as a person* is much more important in life than how you seem to be (how you look).

Did you know? Feelings of self-concept are learned from others. These ideas of personal value begin when a child is very young.

Research studies show that by age three or four children can tell whether other people think of them as handsome or ugly.

In many cases the good-looking child receives praise and affection. The less attractive child may become the object of ridicule and neglect.

You be the counselor. How would you advise parents to help each of their children to build a strong self-concept, regardless of physical appearance?

What should the parents say?

What should they do?

Something to think about. Oliver Cromwell was a famous English statesman.

When Cromwell was having his picture painted, he told the artist, "Paint me as I am, warts and all."

What does that tell you about Cromwell's self-concept and body image?

Bernard Crumpton

A pleasant attitude and an easy smile both add to a person's self-concept.

What directions would you give to an artist who was about to paint your portrait?

Any idea *why* you would say that?

HOW FAST YOU MATURE

Boys. Faster-growing, bigger boys may get a lot of flattering attention in junior high school. During these years most girls are taller than most boys. Boys who mature first often gain some personal or social advantages that last into adulthood. Bonuses like these that go along with early maturing aren't earned by any special talent, but the lucky boys happily collect the prizes anyway.

For example, a boy with a large, strong build usually receives attention and compliments. Extra size seems to suggest that he really is more mature.

53

Boys who mature early usually have sturdy and muscular bodies. These adolescents often turn out for football.

As a result he not only acts more grown-up, but others also treat him more like a man.

Slower-growing boys must prove that they too are maturing, even though they continue to look child-like. It's not surprising that smaller boys sometimes learn to feel like nobodies when compared with their larger classmates. Sometimes these negative feelings about self hang on even after the late bloomer catches up.

Most boys measure themselves against the ideal and favorite male body type: tall, well developed, with broad shoulders and narrow hips. Openly or secretly, most boys compare themselves with other boys to measure their progress.

Body changes during puberty always alter the looks of the adolescent. Boys and girls may be concerned that they are developing wrong. Even though it is quite normal to worry at this age, the gradual progress into adulthood is smooth for practically everyone.

Sometimes a person of one sex seems to take on the appearance of a person of the other sex for a short while. This happens because plenty of male and female hormones are present in members of both sexes. For example, the female hormones in a boy may cause him to have slightly swollen breasts during early adolescence. Such swelling usually disappears in a few months. In the long run, nature makes very few mistakes.

At a junior high school dance, girls are often taller than boys. The boys catch up later.

Girls. Early maturing girls do not automatically collect the same advantages of faster-growing boys. The rate of growth and development and the arrival of puberty are closely tied together. So the girl who adds height fast may also be the first in her class to menstruate. Very early maturing girls may get some teasing or rejection from classmates who still look like "little girls."

Parents sometimes worry that their rapidly maturing daughters will attract older and more-experienced boys. However, early maturing girls are more likely to be quiet and not care as much about an active social life as do girls who mature when they are older.

If you are a girl, early maturation (MATCH-oo-RAY-shun) can seem unbearable at a time in life when looking different is that last thing you want to happen. However, later in adolescence, when physical differences even out and slower-growing girls and boys catch up, early maturing girls usually relax and enjoy themselves. They don't feel so different any more. Regardless of individual growth patterns, girls usually prefer to be slender, with delicate features, and not too tall or too well developed.

Male or female, two basic reasons account for the big differences in growth patterns between individual persons.

• Genetic inheritance from parents.
• Hormones released from glands in the body.

Both rate and timing of physical maturation help decide how the person will look when the physical changes have

55

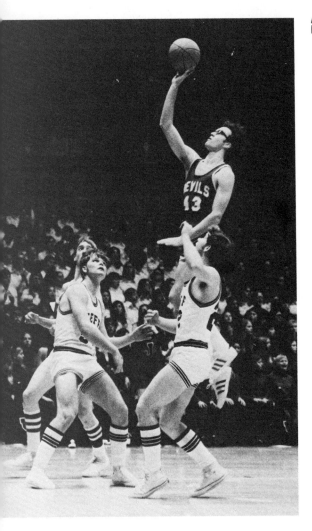

Being a few inches taller can be a big advantage in a game like basketball.

heavier than girls. However, at about age eight or nine most girls start to grow faster. From about ages ten to thirteen, girls are taller than boys of the same age. In late adolescence, boys catch up again, pull ahead, and stay ahead. Boys grow for a longer time than girls. Girls stop growing by age eighteen. The average boy keeps growing until age twenty-two or twenty-three. In both sexes, however, increases in height usually start in early adolescence, rush ahead for about a year, and then continue at a slower rate until late adolescence.

While the long bones in the arms and legs and the large muscles of the body are growing fast, some temporary effects result. You may suddenly feel very tired and want to sleep more than usual. All of a sudden, your feet seem farther away than they did a week or a month ago. You may feel like an awkward tangle of arms and legs.

Eventually, growth in all body systems catches up and evens out. You become a physical adult, better coordinated, more comfortable with your body and your self-image. Obviously, the more satisfied you are with yourself, the better will be your self-concept.

Don't like your height? Because height differences are so noticeable and seem so important during the early teen years, they deserve your attention.

CASE EXAMPLE

Even boys of average height may be disappointed because they don't grow taller. Others decide to make

stopped. Boys and girls who mature early usually develop bodies that are larger, heavier, and more muscular. However, early maturers are not necessarily taller than average. Late maturers, on the other hand, tend toward body builds that are slighter and thinner.

THE TALL AND THE SHORT

Boys start life slightly larger and

the best of what they have. Skip recalls that he was a "funny looking, skinny kid" in junior high school. He always wanted to be a basketball star. He never made it.

Now in high school, Skip explains, "At five feet seven, I'm no basketball material. But I sure can run. At track you can be a shrimp and still make it. Since I weigh only 130 pounds, I can't be a shot-putter either. So I taught myself to enjoy track, even though it wasn't my first choice. Like a fool, I run the half-mile, the mile, and the two-mile. The coach says I might get into a good college on a track scholarship. Skinny and funny looking or not, track has paid off for me."

Something to think about. What do you think of Skip's attitude? Did he give up too quickly on his goal to make the basketball team? Is he just pretending to enjoy track because he couldn't get what he really wanted? Has there been a time when you settled for "second best," only to find a new interest or talent?

Feelings about height. Did you ever notice that short girls may be called "cute" or "petite"? However, lack of height can earn a boy nicknames like "Shrimp" or "Peanut." Such labels can stick for years.

Junior high school is a time of short boys and tall girls. These years may be really difficult for the short boys. First, they lag behind their male friends. Then, in a society that seems to say that boys should be taller, it can be downright humiliating if girls are inches taller, too.

A word of encouragement: remember that boys continue to add height for a longer time than girls. After a while most boys grow tall enough to attract girls in their own age group.

CASE EXAMPLE

Tad's case shows that tall boys don't get all the benefits. When smaller, shorter boys decide to stretch their minds rather than their bodies, they can score some impressive results.

Tad is one of the shortest boys in his class. Chances are that he'll always be shorter than average. He doesn't enjoy being small. Often he starts conversations with "I'm short, but . . . .."

However, like most teens, Tad can do several things well. He's decided to put his efforts into work he does best. He has a special talent for writing and debating. In terms of words, no classmate produces more.

Recently Tad wrote a letter to the local paper urging citizens to ride the bus to save fuel and keep the air clean. He is a skillful debater who has already won a medal for his persuasive, insistent arguments.

Tad has earned the genuine respect and affection of his classmates. They recognize a human dynamo when they see one.

Tall girl. Some tall girls suffer as deeply as short boys. By age nine or ten a girl usually has a good idea whether she's going to be tall. One clue is when both parents are taller than average. Another clue can be found in X-rays of her growing bones.

Girls who grow fast and also inherit genes for tallness tower over boys their age during junior high school. Since girls develop faster than boys, a girl who matures before her classmates is certain to stand out in the crowd. During a time in life when interest in boys increases, the tall girl may feel shut out of girl-boy activities.

CASE EXAMPLE

A fourteen-year-old girl who signed herself Beanpole Belinda wrote the following to a doctor whose answer appeared in a newspaper column.

"Already I'm five feet seven inches tall. My mother is five feet eight. My father is over six feet. I'm scared I'll grow taller. I can't face being taller than all my friends.

"My mother says, 'I went through that too. It's better to be tall than short. You look nicer in clothes. Most models are tall.'

"But I'm not pretty enough to be a model. Kids tease me about my height. I feel rotten. Can you tell me how to stop growing?"

You be the counselor. Chances are that Belinda will probably end her growth taller than average. How would you help this unhappy girl? How could she help herself? How do you think the doctor answered her in the newspaper column?

THE FAT AND THE THIN

Now consider some other serious concerns of early adolescence—too much or too little body weight. A physician is the best judge of the best body weight for fast-growing adolescents. However, in those who have completed their growth, *overweight* usually means about 4.54 kg [10 pounds] too many for height and build. *Obesity* usually means that a person is 9.07 kg [20 pounds] or more over the ideal weight.

CASE EXAMPLE

Bozo is a professional eater. He is also obese. He makes his living by eating more food faster than anyone else. He weighs close to 136.08 kg [300 pounds] and holds a number of world records. In eating contests Bozo regularly defeats professional athletes and other big appetites foolish enough to challenge him. As a child he gulped down forty hot dogs during a nine-inning baseball game just to entertain his friends. Once he wolfed every fancy desert in a French restaurant. Another time he gobbled twenty-seven chickens at one sitting.

He trains for his major matches by forcing down food and liquids to keep his stomach stretched. He gains more than twenty-five pounds preparing for a really important contest. He says that speed, fast reflexes, and good coordination are the secrets of his success. Bozo's advice to those who want to learn his trade: "Get it down fast."

Bozo's story is amusing. However, there's nothing funny about too much body fat. True overweight is the most common body disorder of adolescence. It's given special attention here because about 15 percent of U. S. girls and 10 percent of boys suffer from too much fat. Even a greater number of adults are overweight. If an equal number of young persons had cancer, the nation would be horrified. However, obesity (the medical term for excess pounds) shortens life to a startling degree.

It would be hard to add up the emotional penalities in unhappiness and bad feelings about body and self caused by extra fat. More than that, overweight is like an illness. The *longer* one stays fat, the heavier the person gets and the greater are the chances for health problems.

The exact connection between disease and too much bulk is hard to pin down. In general, though, fat adults are more likely to die of heart ailments including diabetes, hardening of the arteries, and high blood pressure. Obese adults also get backaches and suffer diseases of the weight-bearing joints like the spine, hips, and knees.

The *cost of living* is higher for heavyweights. They pay more for insurance, spend more for food. They need more effort to walk, breathe, and even sleep. Overweight men and women even suffer job discrimination.

Why fat? Like Bozo, some people are fat because they eat too much. However, extra pounds are not always due to overeating. To get fat and stay fat, you must inherit at least a moderate amount of "heavyweight" genes.

Fat runs in families. For example, adopted children take after their natural parents in body build. One study showed that among children of normal-weight parents, only 8 or 9 percent were found to be very heavy. However, add one fat parent and 40 percent of the children became overweight too. In families where both parents were fat, the proportion of overweight children rose to 80 percent.

Overweight teens of either sex usually inherit larger bones and muscles, broader hands and feet, and shorter, wider body builds. Not only are their overall body dimensions greater, but they tend to mature earlier and grow larger than more slender friends.

Of course, heredity and environment always work together. Children *learn* attitudes about food. For example, if you grew up thinking that no meal was complete without a rich dessert like pie or cake, that's a learned attitude. Also, fat parents often place great value on food. Without knowing it, they may overfeed

Kathy Tuite

Both heredity and environment influence body size and shape.

their babies. Infants and very young children who eat more than they need can develop extra fat cells which may remain throughout life.

Other causes of fat. No one knows just how much heredity influences your desire to be active, or your tendency to gain weight if you are not. Nor is it known exactly how positive emotions like happiness or negative ones like despair affect weight gain and loss.

DAILY FOOD GUIDE

	Child	Preteen and Teen	Adult	Aging Adult
Milk or milk products (in cups)	2–3	3–4 or more	2 or more	2 or more
Meat, fish, poultry, eggs (in servings)	1–2	3 or more	2 or more	2 or more
Green & yellow vegetables (servings)	1–2	2	2	1
Citrus fruits & tomatoes (servings)	1	1–2	1	1–2
Potatoes, other fruits & vegetables (servings)	1	1	1	0–1
Bread, flour & cereal (servings)	3–4	4 or more	3–4	2–3
Butter or margarine (tablespoons)	2	2–4	2–3	1–2
Highly recommended: 3 to 5 cups of fluids per day				

The American Medical Association recommends that you eat these foods daily. This is not a program to lose weight. The guide includes selected foods for persons who want to combine good nutrition and normal weight control.

However, it is known that being overweight often results from a moderate food intake combined with a very low rate of activity. Your activity level may be inherited along with your body type. Right from birth, thinner babies move around more and actually eat more than children of normal or heavier weight. Fat babies move less and eat less. Both types of children seem to keep their low and high activity levels as they grow older.

Solutions. Although overweight children often become overweight adults, a person with an inherited large frame and heavy muscles won't automatically become fat. Nor will an adult with extra fat cells necessarily be overweight.

If you inherit a tendency to gain weight easily, you need not accept defeat and grow fatter. Wise choice of food, increased activity, and regular daily exercise can control body weight.

Think of the larger persons you know. Many of them are well proportioned, solid, and healthy. No matter what your body constitution is, to become obese you must keep eating more food than you need for growth and energy.

Feelings about fat. Although serious overweight should be avoided, it's easy to get overconcerned about normal body curves.

Chubby girls win beauty contests in some Middle Eastern countries, but not in the northern hemisphere. The cultures of the United States and Canada admire and reward extreme thinness. Pick up a newspaper. Glance at the clothing ads. Except in those ads of shops that sell extralarge clothing or in a TV commercial, have you ever seen a fat model display the latest styles?

A problem develops for some because not everyone is naturally slender. Thinness may get so much attention that some teens may feel upset about their own normal curves. Because everyone is seen as fat or thin, even a few extra pounds are viewed with dislike or fear.

CASE EXAMPLE

Michele is slightly below average in height and toward the upper limits of normal weight for her age and build. She's certainly not thin, but neither is she fat. Yet she feels distressed about her appearance.

"My build is terrible. I am big-boned, short and fat. My body causes me to be self-conscious. I get tongue-tied around boys. I can't think of anything to say because I keep wondering if they think I am fat."

Too thin? There are many skinny adolescents—especially girls—who are the envy of their better-padded friends. However, any boy or girl who inherits a slender frame with long, narrow hands and feet probably will not gain weight easily no matter how much is eaten. He or she simply lacks the "storage vaults" for fat. If you inherited lighter bones and stringy muscles at birth, and then mature later than most of your friends, chances are that you will stay slender for the rest of your life.

As you know, some teens just grow at a slower rate than others. As they move into middle and later adolescence, many former stringbeans add heft as well as height.

However, if you are really worried about too little (or too much) body weight, a physician is the best judge of what level is best for you. Also, a doctor can discover and treat hidden causes of too few or too many pounds.

For example, sometimes a condition called nutritional anemia causes poor

David Snodgress, Herald-Telephone, Bloomington, Indiana
Active adolescents are rarely overweight.

appetite and underweight. Blood tests may show a shortage in body iron, especially in girls who lose iron during the monthly menstrual flow. In such cases, doctors usually prescribe iron-rich foods such as liver, egg yolk, and dark-green vegetables. Extra iron can also be taken in pills or liquid medicine.

No matter what your build or weight is, if you want to stay healthy and look your best, a well-balanced diet is the first and most important step.

Living with self. Adolescence can be a time of dissatisfaction with many things, including body shape and size. In one study of boys and girls, two-thirds of the teens wished they could change their looks. In another, most of the girls wished to be smaller and weigh less. However, most of the boys wanted to be larger and weigh more! So, if you feel

Most teens love snack foods. You can help meet your daily food requirements from the tasty delights in this picture.

dissatisfied with nature's work on your looks you are probably a lot like others your age.

However, some things you can change and some you can't. What's important is to know the difference. For example, what can you do about some permanent, inherited physical trait that you dislike, such as body build or height? Sulk? Cry? Blame your parents for bad genes?

Such reactions may sound silly. However, if you think about it, you probably know some people who do let some normal part of their appearance strongly influence their lives. For example, a short boy may feel that he must compete with larger males to prove his worth as a person.

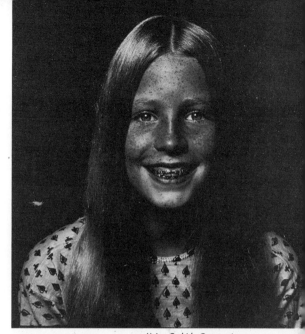
Union Carbide Corporation
Braces don't keep Dawn from smiling.

WHEN SOMETHING IS REALLY WRONG

There's a big difference between not liking a normal healthy body and coping with a real physical problem. Adolescence is usually a time of great health and fresh good looks. Yet sometimes things do go wrong.

When a serious problem develops in growth and development, it is best to seek expert medical attention. Caught early enough, crooked spines can be straightened by body braces. Medical tests and follow-up treatments may help very slow-developing boys or girls mature at a more normal rate.

Plastic surgery. Many birth errors can be totally corrected or greatly improved early in life before concern about body image ever gets started. Delicate operations of the mouth mend a cleft, or split, lip and close open palates. Surgeons can even fashion new body parts, like a missing ear. They also pin back cup-handle ears, trim unwant-

ed nose bumps, modify protruding jaws, and build up receding chins. Plastic surgery can improve ugly scars, remove unattractive moles and disfiguring birthmarks.

Plastic surgeons and other qualified doctors are called "artists of anatomy," because they make over face and body features that might otherwise prevent people from living a normal life. Some of their work is·cosmetic, done to make a person look and feel more attractive.

Dentists are artists, too. They improve appearance by capping chipped or discolored teeth. Dentists also straighten crooked teeth and repair damaged and decayed ones.

Psychological benefits. Many people do look more attractive and feel more confident after plastic surgery. However, boys and girls who blame lack of popularity or school failure on floppy ears or a crooked nose will be disappointed in cosmetic surgery. The best

63

Natalie Leimkuhler

Clothes make the person.

feel good about themselves and their special talents.

GROOMING COUNTS, TOO

Skin, hair, nails, and teeth make up the "outside you." Like a billboard they advertise how well you take care of your body and what value you place on your own appearance.

Regardless of your body build, facial features, skin color, or hair texture, you can improve your body image. Simply, when you make an effort to look your best, when you carry your body well, you improve your body image. When you wear clothing that is clean and in style, you get an extra psychological lift that boosts self-confidence and makes you feel good about self. All these experiences add up to a strong self-concept.

Countless books and magazines about basic grooming and the selection and care of clothing are available for teens. In fact, so much is written that it's easy to get the idea that you must spend a lot of money on makeup or clothes to look good.

The fact is, you can get by with a simple daily routine, very little equipment and clothing, and still look clean and fresh, well groomed and attractive.

A GUIDE TO GOOD GROOMING

- *Skin.* Take a bath every day. Shower or wash using lots of soap and water. Follow with use of deodorant or antiperspirant. For skin problems such as serious acne, consult a dermatologist, or skin doctor.
- *Hair.* Brush and comb your hair daily. Regular shaping or trimming contribute to basic grooming. Shampoo every few days or when your hair separates, feels oily, or loses its clean look.

surgeon can change only a physical feature, not a total personality.

Also, remember that adolescent growth is uneven. A nose that seems out of proportion in the early teens may look just right a few years later when the person reaches full growth.

Even young persons with permanent physical defects and crippling diseases still can grow up to be comfortable and stable adults. Warm and solid family acceptance makes the difference. When families love and respect children who look or act a little different, the children are off to a good start. Parents and brothers and sisters help children develop a healthy body image and a strong self-concept by teaching them to

- *Nails.* Use nail file, emery board, and clippers to keep your nails clean, well shaped, and free of snags.
- *Teeth.* Brush at least twice a day. After meals is best. Use a toothbrush and dentifrice (powder or paste). Use dental tape or floss to clean between all teeth and remove trouble-causing plaque. Visits to the dentist twice a year help prevent and control dental decay and other problems.

A well-balanced diet, plenty of rest, and exercise also contribute to good grooming and good looks. A daily routine of attention to body, clothing, good food, and regular exercise can become a lifetime habit.

HOW IMPORTANT ARE LOOKS?

Perhaps you've thought, "If only I were better looking, my problems would vanish." The idea that handsome men and beautiful women always get everything in life is just not true. In fact, when a child is raised with an overemphasis on appearance, more important personality growth may be neglected.

Given a choice, almost anyone would pick a well-proportioned attractive body and a pleasing face. Such assets would probably make adolescence an easier time. However, sunny, carefree teen years don't always lead to good times later on. For success in adulthood, beautiful girls and handsome boys must also learn how to make a living and get along with others. Look around you. Successful, contented persons come in every size and shape.

One of the most popular fashion models of the 1970s has a big gap between her front teeth. Only a few persons are *perfectly* beautiful or handsome. Even fewer are total disasters. Everyone has some feature of face, or form, or person-

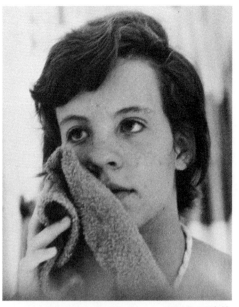

Natalie Leimkuhler
Good grooming begins with soap and water.

ality to build on, like nice hair, a bright smile, or a friendly attitude. Fortunately, important qualities of honesty, kindness, decency, and loyalty have nothing to do with how a person looks.

It is good to remember that when children are given attention, admiration, and praise too much and too soon, they may miss an important part of growing up. Some conflict, some doubt, even some bad experiences may actually help build a strong adult personality. Without a little struggle when you're growing up, the desire to succeed later in life may never develop. Of course, too much failure and too much criticism are also harmful to personality development.

IT ALL ADDS UP TO WHAT?

Adolescence can be a tough and competitive time. Rivals in the race for

Did it ever seem that you were "all hands" or "all feet"?

status and attention from the other sex sometimes scorn or ridicule each other's appearance. Even a joking comment from a friend or relative can arouse worries that something is terribly wrong. Comments like "You're too short, too tall, or not developing right" are no help at all.

When criticisms or jokes about looks are *meant* to hurt or repeated many times, the youth on the receiving end may develop a permanent dislike for a normal, healthy body. If someone gives you a bad time about your appearance, remember that those who pick on others are also most unsure of their own looks and worth.

Even if no one comments unfavorably on your changing body, you may still feel ugly, clumsy, or just like a hopeless case. Few teens feel comfortable about themselves in all situations. In fact, if you feel critical, embarrassed, self-conscious, or at times proud and pleased with your body image, you are totally normal.

As the uncertainties of adolescence fade, most persons feel more satisfied with themselves. Also, overconcern about appearance is something that means less if you continue to grow as a *person*. What you admire at age fourteen may seem silly at eighteen. Values change as you mature.

You probably know some self-centered older adults who still rate clothes and looks above everything else. Rarely are they the kind of people to be admired or imitated. Often they are vain and insecure, still trying to use their fading looks to get by.

Did you know? Body image and self-concept are learned attitudes. Image means how you see yourself. Self-concept means how you feel about yourself. Both body image and self-concept can change for the better. For example, you may notice now that when things go well you are more satisfied with your appearance. Friends comment, "Hey, you look great!" Of course, you looks don't change. However, your expression, your smile, and your posture do change. You seem more attractive. In the same way, when persons feel ugly, they often act ugly, wear a sour expression and turn away those who might be friends. Others are surprisingly willing to accept our own estimates of self-worth and treat us in terms of the way we rate ourselves.

Something to think about. Appearance is important during adolescence. Teens (and older persons, too) often judge each other in terms of looks.

However, the true value of a person often has little to do with physical appearance. In fact, there are many ways to build self-esteem and to gain praise and approval.

How can each of the following qualities improve reputations, no matter how persons look?

- Kindness.
- Honesty.
- Patience.

● Courtesy.
● Dependability.

Write a paragraph. Jeans are like a second skin to some students.

On a separate sheet of paper describe your favorite article of clothing. Write no more than four sentences.

Include reasons why you like it so much.

DO NOT WRITE IN THIS BOOK.

Did you know? A uniform or costume can change a person's self-image. Also, some people react quite strongly to uniforms and costumes without even realizing it.

Make a list. On a separate sheet of paper, write the words from the following list on the left.

Then, after each word, write the emotion you would probably feel if you suddenly met each person in costume or uniform.

DO NOT WRITE IN THIS BOOK.

Fireman
Soldier
Cowboy
Ballet dancer
Police officer
Nurse
Doctor
Pilot
Clergyman or woman

What about me? Did you ever make a quick decision about a person on the basis of looks alone?

Did you then discover that you were wrong?

What happened to make you change your opinion?

To learn more. Select one idea or topic from this chapter that applies to you and the way you live your life.

On a separate sheet of paper describe your selection in one sentence.

In no more than three sentences explain why you chose it.

DO NOT WRITE IN THIS BOOK.

RECAP

Adolescence brings increasing interest in your self and your body. Body image means how you look to yourself

Natalie Leimkuhler
As the unsureness of adolescence fades away, most young adults begin to feel more satisfied with themselves.

and think you look to others. Self-concept means all your private feelings about yourself.

Body image and self-concept begin to build during infancy, mainly through the way others react to you. Children who are accepted for what they are as persons and neither praised too much or too little for their physical appearance grow up with good feelings about their bodies and themselves.

However, even normal boys and girls sometimes are not satisfied with their own looks. They often believe that others find them unattractive. The effects of occasional bad experiences are lessened just by growing older, and by being less sensitive and worried about looks.

Most boys wish for the ideal male body type—tall, well muscled and well developed, with broad shoulders and narrow hips. Early developing boys—those who add inches and pounds first—often gain extra attention from girls. They also take on increased poise and a sense of leadership. Late developers, on the other hand, seem to struggle more to reach their goals. They often believe that they must work extra hard to prove themselves. However, late developers can also achieve success.

Girls wish to be slender, not too tall, nor too well developed. For girls, rapid or slow rate of development in early adolescence doesn't seem so important. Girls who mature early tend to be larger, heavier, and menstruate sooner than others their age. Late maturers are more likely to have the shorter, thinner, build that is more admired.

In junior high school, most girls are taller than boys of the same age. However, boys grow for a longer time than girls. By the time they are adults, most males are larger and heavier than most females. Although not everyone grows into their desired height or body build, eventually growth rates even out and almost everyone falls within the range of normal or average.

All persons are one-of-a-kind when it comes to body shape and size. Inherited body builds tend to be like those of natural parents.

How a person looks at any one time may vary with weight gains and losses. However, the taller and thinner the build, the lighter are the bones and muscles. This makes it more difficult to accumulate extra pounds. Shorter, more rounded or muscular body types who mature early gain weight more easily.

Overweight is the most common body disorder of adolescence. Obesity can lead to many other health problems. Unnecessary body fat is caused by extra fat cells that often develop during infancy when a baby is fed too much or too often. Overweight can also result from eating the wrong foods. Although it's likely that everyone inherits a tendency to be more or less active, anyone can increase exercise and activity to help reduce extra weight. Less active people may gain extra pounds more readily.

Fat or thin, early adolescence is a time to grow and a time to eat plenty of nutritious food. If you are worried about being too fat or too thin, a physician is the best judge of the proper body weight and daily diet for your age and build.

Few people are perfectly put together. However, when something is really wrong with growth or development, a medical specialist can often correct or greatly improve the problem.

Daily attention to skin, hair, teeth, clothing, and posture soon becomes a grooming routine that can improve a person's self-concept. However, important as appearance is, too much emphasis on looks can make a boy or girl over concerned with self and therefore unattractive as a person.

Worry about appearance or body proportions is often part of teenage concerns. Unhappy persons often blame their misery or lack of popularity on some real or imagined flaw in their looks. However, total attractiveness as a person is measured in much more than weight, size, or facial features. Other values like concern for family and friends, generosity, and true interest in others count heavily, too.

TERMS

Body image	Early maturer	Hormone	Obesity
Self-concept	Late maturer	Growth rate	Plastic surgery
Maturity	Normal	Growth spurt	
Puberty	Abnormal	Overweight	

CHAPTER 4

Life Will Never Be the Same

So far you've read about the physical, mental, and emotional growth and development that rapidly change you from child to adult during the years called adolescence. Still, many other kinds of change also shape life at your age. Some of these changes are beyond your control.

You are one individual person, complete in yourself. However, "people need people" goes an old saying. You depend on others for love and companionship, for guidance and education, for protection, food, and clothing. In the same way others need you.

A VIEW OF LIFE

Depending on just how much detail you want to see, you can study a beautiful painting from a distance or up-close. From a distance you see the complete picture, as the artist intended. Move closer and you will notice small details, like the brush strokes that make up a fold in a dress or the crease in an ear.

Before taking a close look at the subject of relationships with family and friends, you are invited to step back for a big-picture view. You will read how the past affects you today, and what it means to be an adolescent during the last quarter of the twentieth century. Then you'll move in for a closer glimpse

Rohn Engh
Many persons living in North America still carry on the traditions of their own culture.

of some parts of your environment that keeps changing. You will also read how the world around you affects your life and your relationships with others.

CULTURE

One of the best ways to get some idea of how people lived hundreds of years ago is through archeology. *Archeologists* (ar-kee-OL-uh-jists) are scientists who study man-made things left by people who lived long ago. The scientists learn about persons from the past by looking closely at old pots, hunting weapons, eating tools, and scratches on cave walls. Archeologists also piece together a picture of the past by using chemical and physical tests. They learn how people spent their time and what they cared about. The information that archeologists collect tells them about a society's culture.

Culture is part of every civilization. Culture includes all that relates to the thought and activity of a certain group of people—their language, arts, laws, politics, work, money, war, and play. Watch a movie about ancient Romans. The buildings and battlefields help you imagine what life was like two thousand years ago. Costumes such as togas and tunics for both men and women make the story seem more real. Chariots, shields, and swords add to the illusion. In much the same way, a true-to-life cowboy picture tells you something about the culture of the western United States 100 years ago.

Along with your mental, emotional, and physical self, you also inherited a North American culture that you share with many others. The words you use, the clothing you wear, the type of building you live in, the food you eat and even the way you eat it are all part of your culture.

Children learn about their culture very early in life. Everywhere in the world boys and girls go through the same stages of physical growth and development. In addition, each culture helps mold its young.

Adults teach children what they believe to be important. This early training is so thorough that it stays with you wherever you go. Even if you moved to another part of the world your culture would remain part of you. You would still think, talk, and eat the way you do now. You might try to use chopsticks in a traditional Chinese setting, but you would not handle them as skillfully as someone raised in the Chinese culture.

If you stayed to live in another culture, you would gradually learn new ways. However, the effects of your past learning would never completely leave you. For example, you might learn to speak in French or Spanish, but you would probably still think in English.

There is never a single culture for everyone, even in the same country. Small groups of people live differently from other small groups—even in the same town. In the U. S., for example, many children of migrant workers miss the chance to go to school regularly. Life on an Indian reservation differs from living conditions on farms, in suburbs, or in big cities. Southerners may have different accents and points of view than New Englanders or Californians.

Look up the word. An encyclopedia (in-SY-kluh-PEE-dee-uh) is a reference book that contains information about many subjects. Most ideas are explained in one paragraph.

Look up the word *culture* in the encyclopedia in your school or local library. If you have an encyclopedia at home, use it.

On a separate sheet of paper, write a paragraph about culture. Include points not mentioned in this chapter.

If you discover something unusual, ask your teacher for a chance to tell the class what you discovered as a result of your research.

DO NOT WRITE IN THIS BOOK.

Make a list. Family customs, such as decorated cakes to celebrate a birthday, help make up the traditions of a culture.

Celebrations of national holidays like Independence Day, or the Fourth of July, usually include picnics, parades, and firework displays. Because "the Fourth" recalls the founding of the United States in 1776, Independence Day is an important part of the national culture.

Canadians celebrate their Dominion Day on July 1.

On a separate sheet of paper make a list of all the special occasions that your family celebrates. Some celebrations will honor relatives. Others may recall patriots and religious leaders. Ask your mother or father for help.

DO NOT WRITE IN THIS BOOK.

PAST HISTORY

Did you ever get the idea that life was easier in the past? Or that people got along better, or cared more about each other? Or that everyday life was simpler and more enjoyable?

Until very recently in human history, life was grim and hard for all but the wealthy. Even the rich were not protected from epidemics of smallpox, typhoid fever, diptheria, polio, and other killer diseases.

Immunizations during childhood and booster shots during the teen years protect Jean from the many killer diseases of the past.

Natalie Leimkuhler

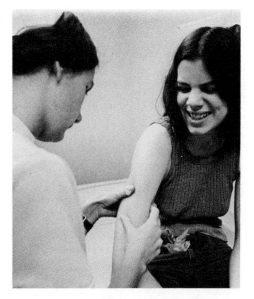

Living history. To help Americans get a better idea of their past culture, the National Park Service set up an exact copy of a colonial dirt farmer's life-style. Located a few miles from the nation's capital in McLean, Virginia, tourists walk a long winding path that gradually leads back into a mini-version of life during the last quarter of the 1700s.

Male and female actors work the eleven-acre farm. Visitors stare at their wrinkled clothes and muddy shoes. The house is another shock. It is small, only

Don Morrow, Bureau of Indian Affairs

These men are moving earth the old and slow way—with shovels. They are working at the site of a very old Indian pueblo in New Mexico.

eighteen by twenty feet. With a dirt floor and a single window, the tiny dwelling is built of unsplit logs, chinked with clay and lime. A large fireplace provides heat and a place to cook. There's not much furniture: a chest, a table, a spinning wheel, a straw mattress stored on a high shelf. The make-believe farmer and his family eat salted fish. Sometimes they have animal meat, such as bacon, and fried potatoes. The wife bakes corn bread in a pot called a Dutch oven that sits in fireplace coals.

Two hundred years ago, families settling this country wove their own cloth and made their own clothes. They raised gourds to use as bowls, and flax for linen. The farmer's survival depended on his hoe. His wife and children helped him with a staggering work load that brought only a meager existence. They knew that if they didn't work constantly, they wouldn't eat.

Life in early American and Canadian cities wasn't much easier. Fearful epidemics of diseases like smallpox and polio killed or maimed thousands each year. Newly discovered records of New York City reveal problems of drug abuse, murder, suicide, and divorce. Punishment was quick and harsh.

On October 17, 1795, the city coroner reported this about Susannah Tarf: "Having been intoxicated a few days previously . . . of her own voluntary will [she] did purchase and drink a quantity of laudanum [a drug made from opium] so as to cause her to sleep and expire [die] on the morning following."

About the same time, Catherine Shakell threw herself out of a window. Somebody killed Ann Bell with a brick.

A twelve-man jury found one Henry Thomassen guilty of burglary. He broke into the home of William Cox "with an intent to steale and spoile the goods and chattles of the said William." Thomassen was sentenced to be branded in the forehead with the letter B (for burglar) and be whipped with eleven stripes on the bare back.

In November, 1805, the coroner reported the discovery of two dead newborn infants, abandoned on the street. Daniel Carr committed suicide in debtor's jail. Three other suicides and six drownings were noted—all in a city with a population under 75,000.

Divorces were common. Between 5 and 10 percent of all chancery court cases were divorce actions.

It's almost 200 years later, but in some ways things are much the same today.

PRESENT

Some things will always remain as they are. Trying to understand and care about each other, and trying to get along without fighting—these challenges never change. However, there are some parts of life that keep shifting. These

Don Morrow, Bureau of Indian Affairs

These men drive heavy earth-moving equipment that represents the latest advances in modern technology.

changes have impact on how people get along with each other.

Technology and automation are two words that are now in common use. Together they sum up the remarkable changes of recent decades.

Technology (tek-NOL-uh-jee) refers to equipment developed to help humans do more than they could without the new invention. In this case, machines operated by humans do the work of many. For example, one piece of earth-moving equipment may dig a larger hole in one hour than a hundred workers with shovels could dig in a day.

Automation (aw-tuh-MAY-shun) means using a machine to do work automatically. In this case the new inventions not only replace the labor of people but also decide when to start or stop a process. For example, swiftly moving machines fill and seal bottles and cans with food at lightning speed. Computers do routine office work, like preparing bills for customers. With automation, workers maintain the machines and program the type and amount of production in advance. The complicated computers do the rest.

> *Look up the word.* Look up *technology* and *automation* in an encyclopedia.
> On a separate sheet of paper write a short report of no more than five sentences on either technology *or* automation.
> Look for details not mentioned in this chapter.
> DO NOT WRITE IN THIS BOOK.
> *To do more.* Look up the word that you did not research and write a short report about it.

Swift changes. Sometimes social change is like a snowball rolling downhill. As it moves, it grows larger and goes faster. As a result some old, familiar, and useful things may be wiped out. In Monticello, Iowa, a piece of the American past has died just that way. The last company to manufacture turkey feather dusters is now out of business. Turkey feathers pick up dust like a magnet. However, spray-on furniture polish and special vacuum cleaner attachments made feather dusters so old-fashioned that few housekeepers want or need them anymore.

Each new major discovery opens the way to others. Change in one area speeds up other new discoveries. Sometimes, still useful products like the feather dusters get pushed off the market because a recent invention is better or easier to use.

As you probably guessed, the people employed in the feather duster factory lost their jobs. A computer circuit company, employing a different crew, moved into the empty building.

Values. Automation and technology touch the lives of those involved in more personal ways. Lifesaving machines, for example, can take over the functions of a kidney or force a reluctant heart to beat. So today we have the strange situation of one machine putting a person out of work and another machine available to save that person's life.

Yet along with these major advances in technology come new problems about human values. A respected scientist recently suggested that when people die their bodies should be kept "alive" with the help of life support machines instead of being buried. Even after the brain dies, some body activities can keep on. The scientist suggests that these bodies could serve as "spare parts" for persons who need organ transplants.

> *What about me?* How would you feel about such a plan for some beloved family member? For yourself? You may be asked to make such a decision some day.

In a few years you will be faced with other important questions that need answers because of advance in technology. You may even invent or test out some new idea that no one has yet imagined.

A LOOK TO THE FUTURE

In the next pages are examples of some of the ways that automation and technology have changed and will continue to alter and shape the lives of persons like you, your family, and friends.

Changing work. You probably will never labor as hard physically as your ancestors did. That's one obvious change of the last fifty years. Work has changed in other ways, too. For example, child labor laws now protect children from being put to work at the cost of their health and education. Almost half of today's work force is composed of adult women. Few families turn out a product or carry on a business at home anymore.

Once it was natural and expected for sons and daughters to learn and carry on the work of their parents. Skilled craftspersons like the silversmith, carpenter, or seamstress taught fine handwork to their children. Each generation knew and appreciated the work of older family members.

Today, work is separated from family life. You may never see a parent on the job. It's a rare father who works for pay at home. In fact, men often disappear at one part of the day and show up nine or ten hours later. Children get only a faint idea of "what daddy does" or "where mother works."

Adults whom you admire often serve as *models* for you to imitate. It's hard to decide what kind of work you want to do when you see only teachers, clerks, police, and garbage collectors earning their living. Also, the lawyers and doctors of TV shows seldom follow the normal work schedule of a real professional.

As mentioned, the rate of change grows even faster. Workers are sometimes replaced by machines that work faster and better than people. Your parents may work in jobs like turkey duster

Natalie Leimkuhler
Almost everyone has more lazy time these days.

assembly, or do bookkeeping by hand. By the time you are ready for a career, such positions may no longer exist.

As a result of such changes, it won't be easy for you and your friends to plan for the kind of work you hope to do some day. Careful thought and special study may be necessary.

Changing leisure. In the past, the struggle to stay alive and grow enough food to eat was a full-time job. Free time or leisure was a rare treat. However, automation and technology not only cut down the need for hard human labor, but they also introduced great luxuries and more leisure time for all.

Research. To get a glimpse of how greatly machines influence human life, count the lifesaving devices that may be in your home. Washer, dryer, garbage disposal, dishwasher—all make life easier. Then add inventions often taken for granted—electric light and power, central heating, running water, automobiles. Now try to estimate the human

Although women are still not welcome to participate at most male rodeos, young females now have their own events. They ride the same bucking broncos, rope the same calves, and throw the same steers.

time and effort saved in using any *one* of the laborsaving devices and you'll begin to get an idea of what the "new leisure" really means.

With increased amounts of leisure, new challenges arise. Not only must you decide how to use your free time, but the extra time together puts new strains on all family members. Where once they labored side by side, today's parents and children must learn how to get along together peacefully without the common interest of work to help them.

Changing roles. A *role* means a particular person assigned to a particular job. In the past, fathers found the food or earned the family living. Mothers stayed at home. These traditional roles for adult males and females no longer apply to everyone today. Members of both sexes are capable of doing the same thinking and, to a great extent, the same work.

Human liberation invites each person to be free and to discover and use their special talents for the good of the community and self. In effect, you do others a favor when you use your natural gifts. As the laws that provide females with equal wages and work benefits take hold, favoritism on the basis of sex is changing. Fewer jobs are just for men or women.

Women, in increasing numbers, drive trucks, dig ditches, repair telephone lines, and mine coal. In a recent edition of the Labor Department's book of job titles (names of positions persons might hold) 3,500 jobs were renamed to make them more available for both males and females. A busboy is now called a dining room attendant. Foreman became supervisor. Stewardess became flight attendant. Salesman became salesperson.

The ancient, traditional role of woman as housekeeper and child raiser is also changing fast. Most women still marry. They also take the main responsibility to manage the home and bring up the children. However, modern women tend to bear fewer children and have them earlier. After her last child starts to school, a woman may find herself ready for a second career in the work world. If you have a working mother, you know how roles and responsibilities can change. Often, fathers and children take on some of what used to be considered "mother's work." Family relationships between husband and wife and between parents and children change when mother leaves home to work for pay.

To learn more about me. To check your present attitudes about "men's work" and "women's work," take the following quiz.

Write on a separate sheet of paper. Indicate your decision with (M) for male, (F) for female, and (B) for both.

Almost half of all workers today are female.

No answer is right or wrong. The purpose of this exercise is to help you discover your current attitudes about this subject.

DO NOT WRITE IN THIS BOOK.

Which Sex Works Best?

Male Female Both

- City mayor
- Artist
- Scientist
- Telephone installer
- Nursery school teacher
- Professional dancer
- Garbage collector
- Taxi driver
- College professor
- House cleaner

Something to think about. In some homes the work of running the family is shared or divided according to skills, preferences, or simply who's around when the work has to be done.

In other homes chores are divided according to sex: dads and sons do certain tasks, mothers and daughters do others.

For example, males may do major repairs like painting, plumbing, or car upkeep. Females usually cook, clean, and take care of children.

How do such things get done in your family?

Who pays the bills? Who decides on major purchases? Who fixes things? Who has the last word about how and where to spend vacation time?

What about me? Looking ahead a few years to your own marriage, how would you prefer to divide responsibilities between yourself and your spouse someday?

The modern family often scatters in many directions. These grandparents are happy with retirement life in Sun City, Arizona. Yet they miss their children and grandchildren who live in New Jersey and Indiana.

Is your answer based on what your observe in your own home today? Is it based on what you want in your own home-of-the-future?

Try to think of at least two reasons for each of your answers.

Changing family life. Just as the roles of men and women are not the same as years ago, the roles of parents and children are also changing. Parents are still very important and necessary, but what they do for and with their sons and daughters is very different from the past.

Because family members don't depend on each other as much to survive, more and more of them move farther and farther from home. Bonds between close relatives loosen. Parents, grandparents, and grown children often live many miles away from each other. This distance cuts off a sense of family closeness and dependence. It is no longer as easy for all relatives to gather together for a family reunion.

In the past, parents were convinced that they knew the best way to raise their children. Today, many parents are much less sure. During these times of rapid social change, many good, thoughtful mothers and fathers are not so certain that they know what is best for their children.

All this adds up to a definite switch, even from the years when your parents were young. Advances of automation and technology reach into all parts of family life. So you can see that these new changes are not limited to the farms, factories, and offices where the modern machines are located.

Changing education. Once the family was the center for education. Children learned practically everything at home from parents, grandparents, and older siblings. Today you must leave home and go to school to get the education and learn the skills you will need to earn a living. Few parents could teach you all the things that you need to know, like the metric system. In fact, today's youth may instruct their parents on the way a gadget like the pocket calculator works.

Natalie Leimkuhler

A reunion brings three generations together for a family portrait.

There's another great change in education that has already affected your life. Recent regulations from the Department of Health, Education, and Welfare in Washington, D.C., require all school boards to offer classes and programs equally to males and females. The old practices that put only boys in industrial arts and only girls in home economics are now against the law.

Other practices no longer permitted are summer programs limited to one sex, boys only as school crossing guards, counseling materials that favor one sex, and different standards of conduct expected from boys and girls.

In addition, the new law now requires that females will receive equal opportunities in athletics. Sports equipment and facilities like gym, track, and pool are to be shared equally.

All these changes are designed to do away with rules that favor members of one sex while depriving members of the other sex. Males are not to be barred from activities or careers once considered women's work. Nor are females to be shut out from athletic programs,

Natalie Leimkuhler
A carpenter learns her trade.

Natalie Leimkuhler
The kitchen crew at work.

Josie Lundstrom

Today's teens spend more time with friends than they did years ago.

scholarship aid, or anything else once reserved "for men only."

What about me? What do you think about ending all favoritism based on sex?

As a girl, would you want to join the Boy Scouts?

As a boy, are you eager to learn to cook and sew?

Changing friendships. At your age friends are more important than they would have been in the past. In 1835, in the *Mother's Book*, a magazine of the day, one writer scolded parents for the new custom of holding parties exclusively for children in their teens. The

lady author reminded her readers that parents are a child's closest friends.

Today, more and more teens live in a world made up of friends from their same-age group. As you are at home less, you spend more time with friends in school activities and recreation designed for adolescents.

As you will read in the chapters on friendships, in some ways friends take over for parents. You tell friends secrets. You talk openly with them about who you are and what you hope to be. Friends encourage you. They warn you against some actions and certain other persons. They give you praise and approval.

83

They cheer you on in your struggle for independence. You do the same for them.

Changing adolescence. You are growing faster physically and learning more than any generation of adolescents before you. Improved nutrition and control of killer diseases like polio and smallpox mean that you will live a longer and healthier life than your ancestors.

At the same time, however, you are not free to join the ranks of adults any sooner. Just the opposite may be true. You may need money from your parents for much longer than you would have 100 years ago. You may be encouraged to stay in school and then have to wait for privileges reserved for adults.

On the other hand, some fifteen-year-olds look like grown men and women. However, few employers hire them for full-time jobs. Even if you have a part-time job, you are almost sure to need some kind of financial help until you complete high school. If you attend college you may need money from your family for another two to four years, depending on how long you study. It almost seems that today, with more new knowledge and better education open to you, you must prepare yourself longer for the job market. And you might need similar help if you start a small business.

Change and you. Change can be good or bad. In the past many teens were forced into roles they didn't want. A boy might have been tied to work in his father's store, even if he wanted to be a sailor. A girl was encouraged to marry early and raise a family, even if she yearned to stay single and live and work away from home.

Female or male, opportunities to be yourself and to follow your own interests today are greater than ever before. If you haven't considered how you will use your special abilities to reach wished-for goals, *now* is a good time to think about what you would like to do with your life.

Hand-me-down clothing often fits poorly. In much the same way, many of yesterday's methods do not solve today's problems. Cultural changes can be so great and happen so fast that many parents and children feel they have nothing in common. Adult experience may seem outdated and useless.

Even so, each generation has much to offer the other. No change in a culture is so great that parents and children can find nothing to share. To shut each other out because experiences and opinions are not exactly the same means that those on both sides lose. Challenges of growing up and understanding yourself and others are not new. This is the challenge you face as a growing adolescent. The more you make use of your brains and special talents, the more productive and happy will be the rest of your life.

In the chapters that follow you'll read about how to understand and get along better with brothers, sisters, friends, enemies, parents and other adults. You'll consider more serious problems, like rejection, parent divorce, death, mental and physical illness.

Something to think about. This chapter is about the subject of change. It includes these general points about the idea of change and the world you live in.

● Today's family is smaller than in the past.

- Today's average family moves more often than did those in the past
- Training for a career today takes longer than it did years ago.
- Sons no longer learn trades from their fathers.
- The traditional role of woman as mother/homemaker is changing fast.

Of course, there are always exceptions to trends. Even so, for each point listed, try to think of one real-life example that you know about.

Do you know of any families that these general statements do *not* apply to?

For example, are you aware of a son who learned his father's trade or joined him in business?

Is there a large family in your neighborhood that seems to enjoy their constantly full and busy household?

Did you know? Military academies like West Point and Annapolis now admit females as cadets.

To learn more. Select one idea or topic from this chapter that applies to you and the way you live your life.

On a separate sheet of paper describe your selection in one sentence.

In no more than three sentences explain why you chose it.

DO NOT WRITE IN THIS BOOK.

RECAP

Culture means everything that makes up the life of a particular group of people. The culture of modern American youth includes music, pizza, soft drinks, motorcycles, and jeans. Every nation has "pockets" of people with somewhat different ways of living. Culture helps decide what members are like and how they act.

For thousands of years all families were tied to farming or hunting in an effort to provide enough food to stay alive. Most parents and children worked together. Later they developed handcrafts, making things to sell or trade for food or other household needs.

In Western countries today, life-styles are quite different. Automation and technology changed our culture. Increasingly, factories or machines took over work formerly done in homes. It's less expensive and more efficient to mass-produce most items. In some cases, one piece of heavy machinery can do work faster and better than hundreds of workers using hand methods.

As change happens faster, persons as well as machines get outdated. New problems about human values puzzle the world's greatest thinkers.

Because of automation and technology, your life is and will be quite different from what your parents and grandparents knew. Machines relieve you of hard labor. You will enjoy more leisure, and get more freedom than ever before to choose a way of life that does not separate the work of males and females.

Bonds holding families together are no longer so tight because the members don't have to depend on each other so much to get along. You may need special advanced education to earn a living. However, the need for education means that you may stay dependent on your parents longer than in years past.

You spend more time away from home and family. Friends play an important part in your life. Getting along together is more important than ever before. Families may not work side-by-side as much, but close relatives can develop a new level of love and trust to enrich the lives of all concerned.

Learning to build skills in human relationships may be the "new frontier."

Now is the best time to begin to decide what you will need to know in order to earn enough income for the kind of life you want for your adult years. Now is the best time to establish the kind of person you will be in a changing society.

TERMS

Archeologist	Migrant	Computer program	Obsolete
Culture	Automation	Input	
Model	Technology	Leisure time	

UNIT II
Parent and Adolescent

CHAPTER 5

Understanding My Parents

Parents are adults who take care of children until the younger ones can make it on their own. Although other relatives, teachers, and friends may provide help along the way, parents have the most influence of all.

Teens talk a lot about their parents. However, do you have any idea what your parents are really like? What they think about? What they talk about when you're not around? What is most important to them?

It's surprising how little most children understand their parents—mother, father, or both. For example, it's easy to forget that all adults were teens once. Parents enjoyed many of the same kinds of hopes and dreams that you have today. They felt just as eager to mature and be accepted by others. They, too, wanted to do something exciting and important with their lives.

Conduct an interview. Many adolescents do not know what life was like when their parents were younger. Boys and girls who urge their fathers and mothers to talk about their own teen years often discover some surprising information.

As a way to get to know your parents better, interview one or both of them. Pretend that you are the host on a TV talk show.

Natalie Leimkuhler
These parents invest much effort planning good times for their six children. Even so, like most mothers and fathers, sometimes they get tired, become impatient, and make decisions that don't please everyone.

To get the dialog started, ask either your mother or father to complete these sentences.
• The most important thing that happened to me during my teen years was . . .
• When I was fifteen, I wanted to grow up to be . . .
• If I were an adolescent again I'd like a second chance to . . .
• When I was a teenager my biggest disagreement with my parents was usually about . . .

ALL KINDS

Parents come in all sizes, shapes, and colors.
• They may be young, middle-aged, or old.
• They may live with each other or live apart.
• They may live together in love and peace, or be caught up in what seems like one continuous fight.
• They may be steady and reliable, or disappoint their children and repeatedly let them down.
• They may expect too much or ask too little.
• They may seem too interested in what you are doing, or not interested enough.

In short, parents are just like everyone else. They do some things right and some things wrong.

Parents who don't help. There are two kinds of parents who either *do* not or *can* not provide love and care for their children. Those in the first ("do not") group don't seem to care about their

89

offspring. They may be cruel. They seem indifferent, or angry and accusing. Sometimes they walk out and never return.

Those in the second ("cannot") group want to raise their children well. However, they are unable to show love and concern because they are old, sick, or have too much to do. In both cases the children suffer.

Parents who do help. In this chapter you'll meet normal parents who love their children but also complain, get tired, say the wrong things, and make mistakes. Sometimes they run out of money or patience, or both. It takes a long time for younger persons to realize that mothers and fathers have interests and worries other than just taking care of children.

First you'll read how mothers and fathers help influence the personalities of their children. To a great extent, your parents decide how you feel about yourself as a person.

Then you'll read what it's like to be a parent, from a parent's point of view. By trying to learn more about your parents as individuals, you'll find it easier to understand some of the things they do. You will also begin to understand yourself better by learning more about the adults who got you started in life.

Something to think about. Humor often helps persons of different generations get along better. Many years ago Mark Twain said, "When I was fourteen my father was so stupid I could hardly stand to have him in the house. At age twenty-one, I was amazed to see how much he had learned in just seven years."

More recently a modern father expressed the same idea in a little different way. He said, "It's hard for my teenagers to understand that in another twenty years they'll seem just as dumb to their kids as I seem to them now."

These comments invite adolescents to look at themselves in a new way.

Is it possible that you don't ever try to see things from your parents' point of view?

You may want to compare your answer to this question with that of a friend.

GOOD FEELINGS

As you know, an *attitude* is a way of thinking about someone or something. All persons *learn* attitudes about bodies, about selves, and about others.

You probably know people who seem to feel good about themselves. They don't brag a lot, but they seem comfortable in most situations.

Suppose that every day your parents, brothers and sisters, friends, and teachers told you things like these:

"Thanks for being a fine son (or daughter, or brother, or sister, or student)."

"Want to borrow my new jacket? You are always generous with your things. I'd like to pay you back."

"You were just great in the game. You always keep trying."

How would you feel about such remarks? Over a long period of time, how would such remarks affect your self-concept?

If you hear enough good things about yourself you'll probably come to the conclusion that you are a pretty nice person. In fact, sincere praise has some potent side effects. When others notice and comment favorably on good behavior, fine work, or an attitude of cooperation, you are likely to repeat the things that caused you to win the applause in the first place.

Good times together build bonds of love that last a lifetime.

Approval, encouragement, and sincere compliments help you to trust yourself and to gain strength and confidence. Even if you have some bad experiences later in life, you will be more capable of handling them when you feel valuable as a person.

BAD FEEDBACK

Of course, you know that no one gets only praise and approval. In fact, most persons probably hear more bad and critical things about themselves than nice words. Great numbers of people find it easier to notice a fault than to praise a virtue. As a result, fine young

perons get the idea that they aren't worth very much.

Thinking badly about yourself can begin early in life. The negative feelings may take a stranglehold during adolescence. Such an attitude can take the joy out of living. It can shut you off from others. After a while you may think, "What's the use of trying. I'd only fail anyway."

Almost everyone knows how it is to feel no good and not wanted. Men and women, boys and girls, don't seem to mind insulting or hurting each other. Words like *stupid, clumsy,* and *ugly* seem to flow more easily than *smart,*

David Snodgress, Journal and Courier, Lafayette, Indiana

When you hit the bull's-eye it makes up for those times spent wondering whether you could ever do anything right.

charming, and good-looking. This is caused partly by the fierce competition that is part of life.

From the time they are little, boys and girls are faced with mental and physical ratings, grades, contests, races, prizes, and awards. Those who don't win anything are made to feel no good. By the time the teen years arrive, competition for achievement gets more and more intense. So do feelings about self.

Adolescents may come to believe that they don't measure up. Or their negative feelings may be limited to special weaknesses. For example, you may feel confident with members of your own sex.

However, you may feel awkward when with the other sex. You may be capable when washing windows or mowing the lawn, but clumsy when sewing on a button or using a hammer and nails.

THE AUTHORITY FIGURE

CASE EXAMPLE

A teacher of home economics received two notes the same day. The first was not signed.

"Dear Mrs. Kelley:

You know that you are very mean. All you do is tell us nice girls to shut up. That's why we hate you so much. Please (you'd better) be nicer to us from now on. And stop those stupid questions. They are gross.

Sincerely *not* yours,"
The second note also arrived unannounced:
"Dear Mrs. Kelley:

We heard about the note you received and we just wanted you to know that we don't feel that way. You are one of our favorite teachers.

7th period girls: Katy, Mary, Liz, Janet.

P. S. We didn't have time to get the names of all the others who feel this way too."

The teacher explained that the notes came because she had to get tough with the class. The students had become hard to handle. Despite her warnings, they persisted in giggling and whispering. Result: Mrs. Kelley sentenced the entire group to remain after school.

One group of girls resented her action and told her so. They were afraid to sign their note. The second group not only considered the punishment well-deserved, but also tried to make up for the remarks of the first group who sent the unsigned note. They told Mrs. Kelley that she was a good and fair teacher.

This example is used to help you think about something that you observe in school everyday: attitudes toward teachers and other authority figures. (People *in charge* are called "authority figures.")

Some people seem to bump through life not even willing to take signals from their own quarterback. For no clear rea-

Kathy Tuite
When children are raised in a loving home they grow up trusting parents and others.

son they seem to resent all rules and directions from anyone. It doesn't make any difference whether the person in charge is fair or unfair, younger or older.

Other persons have not learned such negative attitudes. They can tell when treatment is fair or not. They react in a healthy and cooperative way to reasonable limits and directions.

What makes the difference? Although there is no one simple answer, attitudes toward authority figures are *learned* early in life—mostly from parents. Later, during childhood, adolescence, and adulthood, these same attitudes tend to spread to other parent-like people: teachers, principals, bosses, police officers, and public officials.

Trust. You know that young persons are more likely to develop attitudes of openness and trust when they have been loved and treated fairly most of the time. They grow up expecting that older, stronger, and more powerful people will be fair and kind. This basic attitude of trust usually continues through the years because it was learned so early and well.

Distrust. What happens between you and your parents decides to a great extent how you will react to other persons in charge. Unfortunately some children learn *not* to trust at home. Then later as adolescents and adults they continue to cart around the heavy resentments learned when they were young. They expect to be misjudged or treated unfairly by authority persons. They may spend a lifetime fighting anyone who has some kind of control over them. Anyone bigger, stronger, or in charge is to be feared, avoided, or resisted.

Differences. Parents have different ways of expressing authority, depending on:

- What kind of personalities the parents have.
- What they believe.
- What they see, read, or hear.
- What the neighbors or other close groups think and say.

However, most of all, parents are influenced by *the way they were treated by their own parents.* A parent often seems to be saying, "If it was good enough for me, it is good enough for my kid."

Authority's influence. Sometimes you can get a better idea of just how parents' authority influences their children by taking a look at extreme cases not so close to home. In Uganda, Africa, lives a group of very poor people called the Ik. Colin Turnbull, a social scientist who studies people in other cultures, spent some time with the Ik. He found that Ik parents throw their children out at three years of age. Somehow the children manage to get enough to eat and survive. The tables are turned when the parents are too old to take care of themselves. The children just sit and watch their elders die of hunger and thirst. Turnbull reports that it is not unusual to see a young Ik force open the jaws of an older person and take food right out of the mouth. In this example of the Ik, the selfish and unfeeling attitude of the parents produces selfish, unloving children.

To learn more about me. Following are some statements about parents and other adults who may be in charge of children.

Which sentence seems to explain your attitude best?

DO NOT WRITE IN THIS BOOK.

- Teens need older and wiser adults to both help and guide them.
- Most adults in positions of authority are both just and fair to those under them.
- Teenagers can take care of themselves. They don't need any help from adults.
- I don't like anyone telling me what to do, no matter who it is.

If none of the statements applies to you, how would you describe your viewpoint?

Do you have any idea *where* and *from whom* you learned your present attitude?

BEGINNINGS

Influences of parents on their children are not always as easy to see as with the Ik. Parents are complicated people. So are children. Each influences the behavior of the other.

Some babies seem to fit into the family right from the start. In other cases it

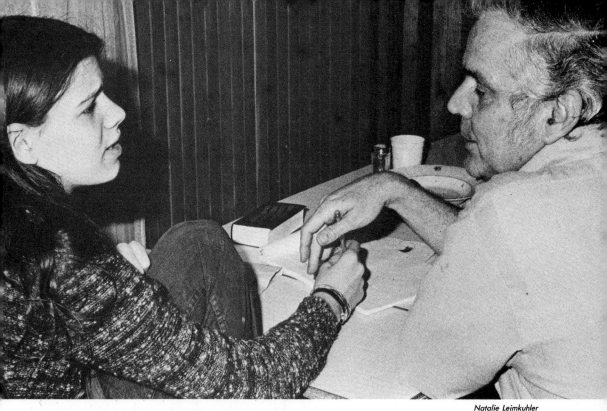

Natalie Leimkuhler

Jean and her father have different views on many things. Even so, he always considers her opinion. Over the years she has learned to respect his judgment.

seems as if the baby arrived at the wrong house because it is so unlike the parents. Yet in most cases parents want their children to be just like them.

Two active parents who love sports would probably be very happy with a tough little baby who is all over the place. You can imagine their reaction if they have a thin, sickly infant who cries a lot.

Of course, hospitals don't have an Exchange Department where a new baby can be traded in for a new model. In fact, most parents soon change their thinking about what a child "should be like." After a short time they learn to enjoy their child as an individual.

Sometimes, however, parents who are not satisfied try to "make over" their child. Such parents sacrifice to give

their children more than they had themselves. However, in many cases, they seem dissatisfied with the results.

CASE EXAMPLE

Sam's parents love their son. They welcomed his arrival and planned carefully for his future. They wanted the best for their boy. Yet, as you will read, the results turned out to be quite different from what they had hoped. Sam explains it this way.

"I was raised in the small town where my mother and father grew up. Both parents are very successful in their jobs, local politics, and small-town society.

"As the first child on either side of the family, and a boy as well, I got a lot of love and attention. Great expec-

react before I dare open my mouth. I am afraid to sound foolish in front of a class. I can't talk unless I know that what I have to say is absolutely right.

"I disappointed everybody. My sister, younger by two years, is only a year behind me in school. She turned out to be really intelligent, active, outgoing, and popular. This was often thrown at me as we grew up.

"By the time I was about thirteen, even my parents had to admit that I had grown into a quiet person. But they never stopped pushing me. I didn't learn to make friends fast enough to suit them. They thought that extra activities would change my personality, so they signed me up for church choir, pony league baseball, 4-H Club, Boy Scouts, and a paper route, besides all the school work.

"When I started high school, my parents added Hi-Y, Photo Club and band as 'nice activities for a young man.' When I complained, they'd say, 'Other boys can belong to these organizations and enjoy them.' I always tried to live up to their dreams for me, but I never could change into the type of person they really wanted.

"The more attention I got, the more my parents tried to force me out in the open. Then I became more shy than ever. I know my parents wanted to help me, but I think I was meant to be a quiet person. Instead of changing me, I think my family and teachers actually made me worse."

tations were placed on me. "Little Pres," they called me.

"Even before I started school, I can remember my parents trying to teach me how to talk, write, read, color—anything to make me smarter. After all, I was going to be president someday.

"When I started school my teachers expected me to be outstanding just like my parents. They pushed me along, too. Only it didn't work. Today I think of any simple mistake as really bad, even though I know no one is perfect.

"Even in school, I stick my neck out only when I'm sure I'm right and not likely to be picked on. As a little boy my parents told me that others must have a perfect image of me. Even though I fought against their attitude I became used to it. I still try to be perfect even when I know others don't expect it of me.

"I'm extremely sensitive about criticism. I must be certain of what I'm going to say and how people will

Sam feels like a puppet—his parents pull the strings and he is supposed to jump. His reaction is really not surprising. Sam says, "I've felt angry and resentful ever since I was old enough to be told what to do. When they order me around now, my first reaction is to walk out. My father thinks that mistakes are not forgivable. He always wants just a little more than the best out of me. I want to be myself, Sam, not some idol of perfection. I just want to be me!"

CASE EXAMPLE

Betsey's case seems just the opposite of Sam's. Her parents seem against her doing anything for herself. She is almost fifteen, but she thinks of herself as a clumsy third-grader.

"My mother does everything for us. She never let me cook because I'd mess up the kitchen. She thinks that I can't pour milk without spilling it or walk across the carpet without tripping.

"She tries to make us clean our rooms, but if the room is messed up for more than an hour she straightens it herself. In fact, if we don't do our chores immediately, she jumps in before we get a second chance. Then she makes me feel guilty for being a slob.

"My friends laugh at me because there are so many things I can't do for myself. They joke and ask me if I was raised in another country. And all of them seem to know how to do simple household things. Last week I spent the night with a friend, and I broke a bottle of popcorn oil. It splattered all over and I didn't even know how to mop the floor.

"I have the feeling that my mother thinks I am helpless. She probably stays up nights worrying about me, even when I'm safe in bed! I don't mean to sound bitter, but a too-helpful mother can ruin a child growing up."

Parents aren't perfect. You have just read how some parents try to shape the future lives of their children. Following are some reasons *why* mothers and fathers act that way.

What about me? Consider Sam and Betsey. They both went to a counselor because they were so mixed-up. How did you react to their problems? Did you feel anger toward their parents for not understanding them better?

Of course, parents are not perfect. They make mistakes. Parents like Sam's expect too much of their children. Others, like Betsey's, expect too little.

The parents' side. Sam puzzles his parents. They admit that they don't understand him. His mother says it this way.

"Sam is a very quiet and private person. He never tells us what he feels about anything, even though we try to talk with him. We give him every advantage, but he never seems pleased or excited about anything. His sister is outgoing and involved in things. We'd be a much happier family if Sam were only like her."

Sam and Betsey are quite honest about how they seem themselves. They didn't try to lie or fool the counselor. As far as they are concerned, their parents are to blame.

However there are always *two sides* to any story. If adolescents understand some of the reasons why mothers and fathers need to act the way they do, there might be fewer fights and hurt feelings. Children might be able to explain themselves better so their parents could understand.

CASE EXAMPLE

Read what Betsey's mother went through when she was young.

"No one cared much about me as a child. My mother had to work to support us because my father died when I was six. I never had nice things. Mother tried hard, but she couldn't stay home to do things for me. Even as a little girl I determined that my children would get all the attention I missed.

"I admit I probably do too much for my girls, but why shouldn't they be free to enjoy life as I never did? As for Betsey, she's quick enough to criticize me but she rarely offers to do anything around the house. I must always ask her for help. Then she usually finds an excuse to get out of work. So it's easier to do things myself. I've tried to get her interested in

helping me prepare dinner, but she wants to cook only after I've cleaned the kitchen."

The story of Betsey's mother is reported here to help you see things from the other side. If your parents still do things today in terms of the way their parents treated them years ago, the way they act may be easier for you to understand.

There are countless other examples of how parents' attitudes shape children's lives. A father who got into trouble with police as an adolescent may keep a close watch on his son. He may refuse even reasonable requests for independence from his son. Or, the father's attitude may be just the opposite. "I survived, let him have his fun."

A mother who never had pretty things as a child may think that her daughter's requests for new clothes are outrageous. Another mother who came from a poor family may go to the opposite extreme. She might spend so much money on her daughter that the girl is embarrassed when her friends see her closets stuffed with clothes.

Sometimes parents and children share the same goals. For example, it often happens that a mother or father might wish that a child would become a doctor, lawyer, musician, or scientist. When the child shares the same ambitions, everyone works together to achieve the common goal. And they all enjoy the successes together.

Success. Most people value success. For many different reasons, parents want their children to do well. Sometimes mothers and fathers see a second chance to undo their past mistakes or old feelings of failure. They believe they can change the effects of the past through their children. When a child succeeds where the parent failed, an old score is settled.

The father who never made the football team tries to raise a halfback hero. The mother who struggled with schoolwork tries to raise an honor-roll daughter. Each parent feels a special and personal victory at such times. That's one reason why some parents get so excited at Little League baseball games.

The effects of a parent's past are often felt in the area of achievement. There's an attitude that says: "A person is as good as what has been done."

A grown woman tells a story of her longtime ambition to become a psychologist. However, her father always wanted her to become a medical doctor—a goal he wanted, but was never able to reach. After years of study she earned her psychology degree.

In a proud mood she visited her parents, expecting praise and approval. Instead, her father sighed and said, "*Now* you can go to medical school."

What about me? If you were the psychologist-daughter, how would you feel? What would you want to say? Can you explain the father's attitude?

Of course, it's natural enough for a parent to want a child to do best in the areas the parent thinks important. After all, a successful grown child is living proof that the parents have done a good job.

Parent hopes and dreams for you can help a lot if they are reasonable, if they are in areas in which you have talent, and if the hopes match yours. In fact, the rewards of parent praise are very strong. Many children actually learn to do things well just to please a parent. For example, a child may stick with piano lessons just for the smiles and approval

Kathy Tuite

After disappointing your parents, it is normal to feel depressed, guilty, or even angry.

that are almost sure to follow. In time, playing the piano can become enjoyable just for itself.

Different goals. However, things don't always work out so smoothly. Sometimes young people like Sam feel pushed to bring their parent's dreams to life even though the child wants to do something else. As with Sam, feelings of guilt, resentment, and anxiety usually develop. He felt the pressure to become something that he was not. He felt conflict within himself, between what he was and what his parents wanted him to be.

When a child simply cannot or doesn't want to meet parent hopes, and when parents won't change their goals, three things can happen: (1) the child is almost sure to feel like a failure, or (2) the child ends up resenting pressure from

Parents have hopes and dreams for their fast-growing children. Even so, it takes time to decide what you want to do now and what kind of person you want to become later.

the parents, or (3) the child simply doesn't care either way.

Problems also develop when parents try to *use* a child to gain satisfactions just for themselves. For example, adults compete with friends and neighbors with questions like, "How did your kid do—in grades, in honors, in sports?"

In time, most young persons discover what they like to do and what kind of person they want to be. Parents usually go along, even though they may have had bigger dreams for their growing children.

It is important to remember that no single bad or unhappy event can destroy a personality. In the same way, no one good experience can guarantee a happy life.

To a great degree you become what you have been taught to believe you are. The daily give and take between parent and child helps decide whether adolescents think of themselves as valuable or not. Remember, all through adolescence many other experiences will pile on each other. They all add up to influence your total personality.

Something to think about. Recently, on Mother's Day, some famous persons were asked how their mothers helped them to become successful in their careers.

Walt Frazier is an all-star basketball

100

player. He said that he was driven by a desire to "do something my mother could be proud of me for."

Virginia Capers is an actress. She won a Tony Award for her part in a play called *Raisin*, the story of a black family. She said that her mother taught her that "hope to succeed comes from within."

Edward Villella is an outstanding male ballet dancer. He has to do strenuous exercises every day to keep in shape for his performances. When a young boy, he was knocked out by a thrown baseball. The next day his mother dragged him to dancing school with his sister.

Write a paragraph. It may be too soon for you to know for sure what career you will choose some day. However, it is not too early to think about it.

On a separate sheet of paper write out the ways that your future life may be shaped by advice and encouragement from one or both of your parents. Include all the "little things" they may have done to help you decide a type of work for life.

DO NOT WRITE IN THIS BOOK.

MISTAKES

In Wueppertal, Germany, a man won a bet by climbing a local church tower. Unfortunately, he couldn't get down. Firemen had to rescue him. The rescue cost the man $68 in charges from the fire department. He made an expensive error in judgment.

It seems a common human failing in all age groups to stretch one's own abilities and powers. Persons who "bite off more than they can chew" often wind up in a mess of their own making, just like the tower climber.

Parents also make mistakes. Yet they may demand responsible behavior or constantly insist that you "grow up."

What about me? Of course, you probably have made a mistake or two of your own. Did you ever barge in, sure you could fix something, only to make it

Natalie Leimkuhler

Teens may not understand why adults behave as they do. Sometimes parents worry about things that their children don't even know about.

worse? Or have you offered to take on a job that turned out to be more than you could handle? Or go along with the crowd someplace, only to discover it cost more money than you had with you? Adolescents who end up calling their parents from a police station often wish they had made a different decision earlier in the evening about where to go and what to do.

PARENT PROBLEMS

Sometimes parents are faced with overwhelming problems. In Chapters 18 and 19, you'll read about such family crises and how to meet them. Here, a few "parent problems" are mentioned to help you understand mothers and fathers a little better.

Every child of every age wishes that parents would love and honor each other. Yet about one marriage in three breaks up. Parents who stay together

101

Natalie Leimkuhler
A parent argument sets the mood for everyone else.

may still tear each other apart emotionally by fighting or cheating.

Divorce brings special problems both for parents and for adolescents. Suppose a close friend brushed you off or told you not to phone anymore. How would you feel? Surprised? Angry? Bitter? Confused?

Divorced parents often have such feelings. Some of them work hard to get rid of their resentments. They may remarry, or try to build a new life by remaining single.

Others work to keep hate alive. They may say mean things that aren't true. One spouse may tear down the former partner in front of the children. Or he or she might make visits difficult.

Some divorced parents try to hurt each other through the children. They say things like, "Ask your *father* (or mother) what happened."

Mothers without husbands often worry about money and new expenses, if they are not used to supporting themselves. Fathers must often support two homes for years, till all children are educated. Many single parents feel concerned that they cannot be both mother and father. They may feel depressed, lonely, helpless. They miss adult companionship and affection. During such times children who are patient and understanding can be a big help.

NEWCOMERS

During the early years of the United States, family members often included several generations or age groups. Everyone lived under one roof. One home often included grandparents, parents, children, an unmarried aunt, or a stray cousin. Sometimes boarders and servants lived in. Many families in an area were closely related.

Today's *typical* American family has shrunk in average size to a mother, father, and two children. They may live miles from their nearest relative.

Of course, there are many other kinds of family groups. For example, about one-fourth of all families in the U. S. have only one parent. Divorce splits and rearranges families. Long-staying relatives, guests, stepparents, and adopted and foster children still move in or out.

Any new ingredient changes a recipe—sometimes for the better. Any new arrival (even a baby) changes old family patterns. Some newcomers are welcome. They ease in, find a place, help with the work, and share the fun. Soon they become part of the family.

Other newcomers bring major family crises. They may get sick, or be hard to get along with. Bossy, or unwilling to change old ways, they can cause conflict and unhappiness in the family.

Even in the best of situations, shared bathroom schedules and crowded sleeping quarters may cause irritation and bad feelings. Jealousy and resentment bubble up when "old" family members compete with "new" arrivals for the love and attention of parents.

Next you'll read about what can happen when stepparents and grandparents move in. Remember, the same kind of problems can develop with any newcomer.

Stepparents. When divorced or widowed parents remarry, the children are sometimes very happy to get a new father or mother. Of course a lot depends on the circumstances and the kind of person the new parent happens to be.

To a widowed mother, remarriage may mean a new husband, a new father for the children, and a regular income. Very young children and those age twenty or older seem to adjust to stepparents best. Adolescents seem to have the biggest problems getting used to a new adult in the home.

In fairy stories, stepmothers are always witches. (Stepfathers are rarely mentioned, possibily because they had much less to do with child rearing.) In real life, stepparents can be just as warm and loving as natural parents.

A stepparent can do all the things expected of a good parent. Most stepparents want to succeed in their new role. They want to like their new children. They also hope for love in return.

Even though stepparents are not perfect, sometimes they are blamed for things not their fault. For example, if a child is angry at a real father for leaving

Natalie Leimkuhler
Love can flow in both directions when a stepparent joins the family.

when needed most, the youngster may direct that 'anger to a stepparent and deny any bad feeling for the real parent who has left the home and family. Sometimes adolescents make a steely decision to reject the intruder in the home no matter what.

When a divorced parent marries a new partner, a child who is still hoping that the real parents will remarry each other may feel betrayed.

Feelings of jealousy and competition are also common right after a parent marries for the second time. The stepparent may seem like a rival for the attention of the natural parent. Often a single parent and the children have grown close and depend a lot on each other. Then a stranger enters as stepparent. A child of any age may feel either pushed out or just left out of the new marriage.

Of course, it takes time and good will to adjust to any newcomer. True friendship and real love need to grow slowly and naturally. Sometimes a stepparent seems too pushy or eager to win acceptance and to join the inner circle.

With good will on both sides and desire to make things work, problems can often be solved. Love always can stretch to include one more person who needs it. Consider the following case.

CASE EXAMPLE

Cheryl has a fine stepfather. She loves and respects him. Yet she feels very mixed-up about loyalty to her real father who is gone.

"My mother has been married three times. I have a sister, Carol, twenty-two, whose father was my mother's first husband—before my dad. I was born during Mom's second marriage. Her present husband is the father of my younger sister and brother, Susie, ten, and Kevin, eight.

"Everyone tells me that I look like my real father, although I really don't know. My folks were divorced when I was four years old. All I remember about Dad were the screaming and the fights. After that, my mother tried to turn me against him. For a while he came to visit me, but then I saw him less and less. I haven't seen him in six years, although he lives just a few miles away.

"My mother still says bad things about him. But I'd like to see and talk with him anyway. Mom says that I can't. She claims it would hurt my stepfather if I did. My stepfather has been so good to us. He adopted my sister and me, and he's given us everything that we wanted or needed. I love him—I think I love him even more than my mother. I don't want to hurt him—I just want to see my real father. Is that too much to ask?"

What about me? How would you answer Cheryl's question? Can you put yourself in her place? Can you understand the pinch she feels even though she has no control over things? If you were her best friend, what advice would you give her?

Finish this case. Melody lives with her father. They get along with each other just fine. Melody shops and cooks. She enjoys the independence and responsibility that her father gives her.

After five years of being a single parent, her dad announced recently that he wants to marry again. The woman he plans to marry seems like a kind and pleasant person.

Put yourself in Melody's place.

How would you feel about the idea of your father taking a new wife? What would you consider advantages of such an arrangement? How about disadvantages?

Now test your attitude in reaction to these possibilities. Suppose:
• Melody's mother had divorced her father to remarry?
• Melody's real mother had died in an accident?
• Melody lived with her mother instead of her father?
• Melody was an only child?
• Melody was a boy instead of a girl?
• Melody had several brothers and sisters?

Grandparents. You read earlier of generation gaps between parents and adolescents. Today, there's also a trend toward separating older people from middle-aged and younger folks.

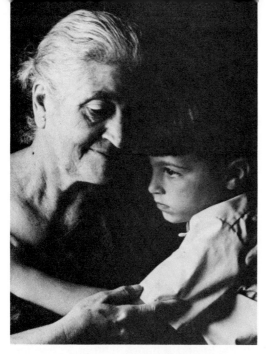

Photographed for Eli Lilly & Company by Duane Michals

A grandparent can be a close friend.

Grandparents may choose to live by themselves. Some retirement villages sell homes only to older people. Or the elderly may be left on their own because there seems to be no other place for them. However, the old and the sick are often placed in nursing homes even when they could live comfortably outside. Life has changed so much that there may seem to be no work and no place for the aged. In the past, everyone had a job to do. Older persons helped to raise the children and prepare the food. They mended clothes. They planted gardens and preserved what they grew. Grandparents were respected both for what they knew and what they could do.

Today, there are smaller families and lighter housekeeping chores. Many of the jobs that were done by the elderly in the past have disappeared. Without important family work to do, even a grandparent may seem like an intruder or outsider.

However, many families settle the problems caused by having three generations in the home. Grandparents often enjoy grandchildren greatly. In turn, children may find grandparents good listeners, helpers, and close friends.

Margaret Mead is a famous anthropologist (AN-thruh-POL-uh-jist). Anthropologists study persons of different races and cultures. Her grandmother lived with the family from the time Dr. Mead's parents married until her grandmother died.

A trustworthy woman who commanded respect, Grandmother gave no silly orders. When she said, "Do it," things got done. Grandmother served as a model of what a female should be. She could teach, tell stories, and keep secrets. She was a link to the past. She had plenty of good influence on the children in the house. Now a grandmother herself, Dr. Mead sees great value in closeness between young children and their grandparents. She describes how grandparents know the world isn't going to end because a child doesn't do everything perfectly.

What about me? In your thinking, jump ahead fifty years. In what type of place would you like to spend your old age? How would you prefer to spend your time each day?

MIDDLE AGE

Middle age—the years from about forty to sixty-five—can be a wonderful time of life. Parents who keep good health and a happy marriage often feel very satisfied.

Most parents are pleased and proud to see their children grow up and become independent. However, adolescent children also serve as living proof that parents are growing older.

Even when a long way from old age or retirement, parents often feel the pressures of middle age. You can make life easier for yourself and more pleasant for your parents if you can understand how things seem to them. For example, following are some of the special concerns of the middle years. As you read, think which examples apply to your family.

Problems of middle age. After thirty-five an age of development sometimes called "the second adolescence" begins. Fathers and mothers become less confident about just how much they will be able to accomplish during the rest of their lives. The dreams of childhood and adolescence fade. The weight of family responsibilities gets heavier. To many parents in this situation, life may seem a never-ending list of things

Kathy Tuite

Middle age can be a good time of life.

to pay for or get fixed. For them the middle years are all work and no fun.

• Middle age offers everyone a last chance for change. It is a time to examine old values and decide to keep them or not. Marriage to the same partner may seem less attractive. Unfaithfulness and divorce both increase during middle age.

• Middle age makes parents the "generation in the middle." That's a way of saying that parents often carry heavy burdens. On one hand, they must be concerned about their own children. On

the other, they may also be responsible for their aging parents.

• Middle age brings worries about growing older. Mothers and fathers may fear the loss of youth. Wrinkles and bulges make them see less attractive to themselves and others.

• Middle age brings worries about health. Strength and endurance slack off. Good health of earlier years may change. Heart problems, overweight, digestive miseries, diabetes, and the everyday wear-and-tear of living all take a toll during the middle years.

• Middle age brings worry about money. How to pay for the children's education? How to meet the rising costs on a stand-still income?

• Middle age brings disappointments. Parents may feel bored with their work. Fathers—and working mothers in many cases—may worry about good deals passed up, or chances gone by. They may also worry about the threat of young and eager persons at work. Men who have hoped to become a big success learn that some dreams just won't come true. They may feel depressed and let down. Such feelings make it difficult for them to be perfect parents.

You'll read more about conflict in families in Chapter 6. Meanwhile, many day-to-day squabbles could be caused by reasons that are never mentioned. If your parents seem unreasonable, grouchy, or otherwise hard to get along with, they may be worrying about some thing you don't even know about.

CASE EXAMPLE

Tracy and her mother argue all the time. Tracy's mother was going through menopause. During menopause, or "change of life," the female body enters a new phase. Between the ages of forty-five and fifty-five the supply of female hormones slows down and the woman is no longer able to become pregnant. Menopause is both natural and normal for all women. Many women feel no special problems. However, Tracy's mother admitted that she is more cranky than before. She dreaded an "empty nest" after Tracy left home. Already she felt useless and neglected. Without meaning to, she picked on Tracy and criticized her friends.

Things worked out fairly well for Tracy and her mother. Both really wanted to change and recapture their old closeness. Like many other women who feel uncomfortable, depressed, and upset during menopause, Tracy's mother decided to see her doctor. He prescribed medicine that helped Tracy's mom to feel better fast. Soon, she took a part-time job.

With less to do at home and fewer children to raise, many mothers turn toward second careers. They polish up old skills like typing and nursing to get a new job. They return to school to learn a trade or enter a profession. Compared with the number a few years ago, many more women now want to live a full and rich life after their last child has left home. They are aware of the problems of middle age, and they want to make plans ahead of time to keep themselves busy and healthy.

Something to think about. There are many cases today of men between the ages of forty and fifty-five turning to a new type of work to make a living. Many are engineers, businessmen, and teachers who decide to do something completely different.

Suppose your father decided to change his line of work. Would that concern you? If yes, any idea why?

In some home situations a temporary or even permanent role reversal takes place. In such cases the husband-father may cook, clean the house, and even raise the children while the wife-mother goes to work or school.

If you were a husband, how would you like that idea?

As a wife?

Write a paragraph. On a separate sheet of paper write out your reasons in favor of such a plan. Then give your opinions against it.

You may want to compare your work with that of a classmate.

DO NOT WRITE IN THIS BOOK.

Competition. No one really enjoys getting older. Yet some men and women seem to handle aging a lot better than others. Many adults feel an honest envy at the wonderful opportunities of youth. They may regret things they missed when they were younger. Sometimes such feelings get expressed in unpleasant rivalry and competition.

It's natural for a boy to yearn for the day when he is stronger than his father. Young girls look forward to the day when they will be more attractive than their mothers. Such "friendly rivalry" helps children to want to grow up and become complete men and women.

Sometimes, however, competition gets heated and hostile. For example, most adolescents want their parents to look and act young and modern. However, they may draw the line at adults who copy teen fashions or behavior.

Most parents take great pleasure in watching their children grow up. They settle back and enjoy the show, sitting quietly in the audience. For other adults, it's hard not to jump on-stage with their children and try to relive their teen years. Youth receives lots of attention and approval in our culture. So adults may try to join in.

Of course, no one can go back in time. *You* can't retreat to childhood. Adults can't recapture adolescnce. No adolescent expects a middle-aged parent to be the life of a teen party. It's one thing for a mother or father to serve as chaperone. However, it's quite another for the parent to grab the spotlight. You probably want your friends to like your parents. At the same time you would rather not compete with your folks for the attention of a boyfriend or girlfriend.

Simply, most teens want their parents to act like parents, not rivals. They may want to imitate their parents, but not compete with them in the teen world.

Be kind. Of course, there's always a happy medium, a meeting ground of kindness and compromise. Any girl who knows what it means to try to look pretty won't ridicule her mother's experiments with new makeup or hair color. Any boy who finds joy in testing his strength and endurance won't poke fun at his father's efforts to stay in good physical shape.

In the following chapters on improving communication and solving conflicts with parents, you will learn how attitudes can be changed, how compromises can be developed. Whether parent or adolescent, you can help to heal old hurts, change old ways, act differently for everyone's benefit.

Something to think about. When the time comes for you to be a separate and independent person, you may not want to be exactly like your parents. Even so, parents and children almost always have some things in common.

Make a list. To discover in what ways you agree with your parents make a list on a separate sheet of paper.

DO NOT WRITE IN THIS BOOK.

Organize your list in terms of these issues:

- Attitudes toward spending money.
- Favorite types of entertainment, like TV, sports, books.
- Food favorites.
- Humor: jokes or situations that amuse you.
- Values: religious beliefs, attitudes towards other people.

Now make a second list that includes ways that you are different from either or both parents in each of the previous areas listed above.

To learn more. Select one idea or topic from this chapter that applies to you and the way you live your life.

On a separate sheet of paper describe your selection in one sentence.

In no more than three sentences explain why you chose it.

DO NOT WRITE IN THIS BOOK.

RECAP

Although you spend time with your parents almost every day, it's not easy for growing children to see parents as individuals. Emotions get in the way. You learn attitudes and feelings about yourself from brothers and sisters, friends and teachers. However, you learn to respect yourself mostly from your parents.

What parents say and do has a great effect on their sons and daughters. The way that children treat their parents has a great effect on the parents. Each side influences the other.

You can take some of the arguments out of family life when you understand more why your parents do and say the things they do. Perhaps you can also help them understand your need to become a separate person.

Parents raise children in reaction to the way they were brought up.

Even very loving parents with the best intentions make mistakes. Sometimes they expect too much, sometimes too little. Either attitude causes the child to wonder or doubt self-worth. After a while, children begin to think of themselves the same way their parents have treated them. The stronger the parent attitude, the stronger the sense of worth for the adolescent.

In general, good feelings about self develop when a child is accepted and approved. Bad feelings are learned when a child is constantly rejected and criticized.

No single bad experience can damage a person for a lifetime. However, a number of them can make a person feel unwanted and unworthy.

It's possible to love your parents but feel angry and impatient with them at the same time. Parents often disappoint their children. They may not inspire respect and affection. Parents make mistakes, just like their children.

When any new person moves into the home, some things must change. Whether the changes are for better or worse depends on both the new arrival and the family members. If parents and children like the newcomer, things will be easier. When there's goodwill on both sides and everyone works to avoid conflict, the results are usually good. When everyone pitches in and no one holds grudges, newcomers and mixed generations can still live together in peace.

Middle age can be a rewarding time for parents. It also brings special problems, like heavy money problems and worries about health and approaching old age. When earlier dreams of success and accomplishment don't come true, parents often feel let down. Conflicts, rivalry, and family upsets are also common during middle age.

After children grow up and leave home, mothers may feel useless and neglected. Such women often look for new things to do. Both parents may worry about younger competition in their work.

In spite of such problems, most parents love and care about their children very much. In spite of their differences, most parents and adolescents would like to work out disagreements and become good friends.

Many problems in family life can be solved by stopping to think at the time they happen. Later, when the tensions of the teen years fade away, parents and their grown children enjoy each other's company more than ever.

TERMS

Feedback	Trust	Success	Middle age
Authority	Distrust	Goals	Rivalry
Authority figure	Criticism	Anthropologist	Competition

CHAPTER 6

Communication Is More Than Talk

In a recent opinion poll, more than 3,000 parents of North American families were asked what they thought about their teen children. The greatest number reported that they were very pleased.

Only 7 percent claimed that they never enjoyed their sons and daughters. These few were mostly parents of runaways, drug victims, and other youth in serious trouble.

Most mothers and fathers thought their adolescents were just great. The satisfied parents said they admired traits like these:

- Lack of prejudice and phoniness.
- Sense of fair play.
- Eagerness to be involved.
- Hope for a new world morality.

"We love to see how well they can carry on without us," said one mother. "This generation's attitude is more responsible than ours."

Another said, "We sneaked; they don't."

A father wrote, "We love their fresh insights, their maturity, their idealism, and eagerness to learn."

Private and personal. Suppose your parents had been interviewed in the survey described at the beginning of this chapter. What would your mother and/or father like most about you?

If you were asked to list the things your folks do right, what would you report about them?

Natalie Leimkuhler
"You were right, son. All it needed was a little gas."

Suppose that you are pleased with the way that your parents treat you. Then the next question becomes: have you told them lately?

If you haven't expressed your appreciation in some time, you may want to say thanks for the help you like most. Most parents don't get much praise.

MAIN PROBLEMS

In spite of such good comments overall, parents admit that they worry a lot about their teens managing problems with drugs and sex. However, the two main concerns of mothers and fathers were:

- *Lack of communication* (parents and children don't talk together about important things).
- *Rebellion* against the parents' authority (arguments over family rules and regulations).

In this chapter you'll read about communication—honest, face-to-face talks between parents and their adolescents. Chapter 7 deals with the struggle for independence.

CASE EXAMPLE

Kris yearned for a racing bicycle. Her father worried because she selected a tricky model that would need special care and upkeep. Gears could be easily damaged. But she begged and pleaded. Finally, for her fourteenth birthday she got what she wanted: a shiny, yellow, ten-speed beauty.

Actually, Kris surprised both herself and her father. She took excellent care of her bicycle. She oiled it regularly, put it into the family garage at night, and locked it when at school.

Then one evening she rode to the library and left her bike in an outdoor rack. Later she returned to find the light smashed and the gears twisted. Someone had crippled the joy of her life. Squeezing back tears, she pushed her bike home and thought about what she would say to her folks.

Kris lived in a happy home. She and her parents were honest and open with each other. Love and respect flowed in both directions. Yet she felt scared and defensive. She knew that her father would be disappointed and possibly very angry.

From past experience, Kris also knew that her folks expected a prompt and truthful report. So she told them exactly what happened, and fought back a strong urge to whine, "It wasn't my fault."

It would make a neat case example to report that Kris's parents smiled without comment and promised her a new bicycle. However, that's not what happened. Even in close and loving families, feelings of impatience, anger, and the desire to get even can take over.

Her mother's first remark was a sharp reminder that Kris should have selected a sturdier bike. Her father was grim and silent. He thought of the original cost of the bike, and the repair bill to come.

However, everyone kept reasonably cool in a tense situation. Kris was in low spirits and felt guilty. For the first time she understood the common sense of her father's warnings. In turn, both parents swallowed their great desires to remind Kris of the money they'd spent, or to taunt her with "We told you so."

When the initial shock of the crisis passed, the facts were clearer. Kris really had followed her father's directions. The damage to her bike was not her fault. Her parents did not scold. However, they believed it was important that Kris accept her share of the responsibility to keep the expensive bike in working order. Kris agreed to pay for repair costs out of her babysitting money.

Time out. Pause awhile to think about this case. Notice how Kris and her parents handled a minor family crisis. Even though they felt tempted, no one blamed anyone else. No one used the situation to get even for old hurts. No one used put-down words like "stupid" or "careless." *Time in.*

It's difficult to handle a crisis well. It takes good will, flexibility, and lots of practice to express honest feelings without blaming another person, or trying to escape personal responsibility.

Actually, thinking about it later, Kris's dad wished that he could have matched his daughter's bitter disappointment with words to let her know he understood her feelings: "You must have felt terrible when you saw what happened to your beautiful new bike." In turn, Kris regrets that she was not enough aware of her parent's feelings to say: "I know that you and Mom spent a lot of money. You must feel sick about the damage."

What about me? How would you feel if you were Kris? If her parents?

In what other ways could this case have ended? For example, suppose Kris decided to hide the damage? Or her parents blamed her for choosing a bike with expensive gadgets that invite damage?

Most parents are very pleased with their teenaged children.

This case study is a simple example of the give-and-take that can happen in any family. It is included so that you can think about some of the many ways that members of one generation can better understand members of the other. In this chapter the focus is on parents and children because it is with parents that you first learn how to share messages. More than anyone else, parents influence the way you think, act, and express yourself today.

Although "parents" means mother and father, many families have only one parent or a substitute, like a grandmother or a foster parent. Also, sometimes communication with one parent is far better than with the other.

However, the ideas presented here can apply to getting along with anyone. As you read, try substituting teachers, coaches, neighbors, brothers, sisters, and friends for parents in the examples and activities given.

Communication means to express yourself so another person can understand what you are thinking and/or feeling. Communication is a two-way process: one person sends a signal with or without words. The second person receives it. Communication includes talking, listening, observing, and understanding.

Look up the word "communication" in a large library dictionary. Note the many different meanings the word can have.

In this chapter you'll read about what can happen when parents and adolescents try to understand the other's point of view, and then discuss issues they don't agree on. Good communication is

Natalie Leimkuhler

Laura and her mother don't always agree. However, each tries to understand the other's side of the story.

the difference between a parent "laying down the law" compared to inviting discussion of all sides and the possibility of changes in parent decisions. It's also the difference between a teen's stony silence, and a willingness to talk about where you want to go and what you plan to do.

Finish this case. Good communication is absolutely necessary when parents and teens must solve a serious family problem. However, honest and gentle dialog is also needed for everyday issues at home. Consider the following example.

Fifteen-year-old Herb is planning his first girl-boy party. His biggest problem is what to do about his parents. He has thought of these options:

- Ask them to go to a late movie.
- Ask them to stay home, but out of sight.
- Invite them to join the party.

Which plan would you favor?

Can you think of other possibilities? How would you get your message across?

DIALOG

Families develop styles of talking to each other. Dialog means both sides talking and listening. Dialog in some families is excellent, others fair, in some poor. Habits of communicating seem to stick like glue. They may even pass on from one generation to the next.

Think of families you know well. Some may try to cover up conflict by pretending it doesn't exist. Some may shout and even swing at each other whether outsiders are visiting or not. Others may nag and tease a lot.

In many homes, parents and children treat each other with respect. They listen to each other. They realize that on occasion another person may have a better plan for solving the problem of the moment. In such homes the parents and children realize that they are not perfect and not always right.

Most parents and children care about each other. They want to talk simply and honestly to each other. However, there's usually room for improvement. Still, it isn't easy to imagine yourself in the place of another and to guess what emotions that person feels at the time. Sometimes it is hard enough to know your own emotions.

STRONG EMOTIONS

When people live closely together they discover that there are times when they like each other, and times they don't. Family members need ways to express honest complaints. They need ways to point out the annoying behavior of others without nagging and whining. They need ways to understand the emotions another person is feeling at the time.

You can't keep silent all the time. In fact, when hostile feelings are bottled inside, the anger boils and bubbles silently. Sometimes the strong negative emotions explode and cause a major family fight.

An anger-packed home is not healthy for parents or children. When persons old or young are reminded continually about their faults, chances are good that they will learn to feel unsure about their worth as persons.

Of course, it's not easy to express anger in ways that will not make things worse. In fact, it's sometimes difficult to express helpful, loving feelings. You have probably noticed that it's easier to cut down and criticize others than to praise, show thanks, or to offer affection and concern.

To learn more about me. Following is a short list of human emotions. At one time or another you have probably experienced all of them.

As you review the list, try to think of a recent event that caused you to notice one of them in yourself.

Some Human Emotions (I feel . . .)

Afraid	Happy
Angry	Helpless
Annoyed	Hemmed in
Blah	Impatient
Bored	Jealous
Bouncy	Left out
Confused	Nervous
Disgusted	Sad
Distracted	Scared
Dumb	Shocked
Excited	Shy
Frustrated	Sick
Foolish	Suspicious
Furious	Tense
Glad	Tired
Great	Uptight
Grouchy	Used
Guilty	

Make a list. On a separate sheet of paper write three negative emotions from the list.

Then write three positive emotions.

Now try to think of one of each not on the list in the book. Add them to your written list.

DO NOT WRITE IN THIS BOOK.

DIFFERENCES

Honest and unhurried dialog can lead to good communication. Without a chance to talk things over, sons and daughters often feel cut off from their parents. The adolescents begin to think that there's little to be gained in even trying to get their parents' attention. They start to believe that adults won't understand or trust them no matter how carefully they explain a request, nor how good their reasons for asking in the first place.

On the other side, parents may assume that adolescents will only ignore what the adults say, so why bother explaining? Trust and understanding disappear. The emotional climate of the home gets cooler—even though everyone may still act like everything is just fine.

In the ideal home parents will try to break the ice first. Parents will listen longer and with more patience. Parents will reconsider and even change some of their attitudes.

However, you know that the ideal situation often does not happen. Sometimes parents just won't change, or they can't. Regardless of the reason, children don't like that. Here are some typical differences between the generations of parents and adolescent children.

• *Different rules.* Some years ago the rules for right and wrong seemed clearcut and easier to understand. "Do *this,* but don't do *that.*" Today there is a trend

Even though years and different experiences separate them, adolescents and their parents can still find ways to talk easily and openly.

to relax such strict standards. Also, some growing children discover that their parents aren't always certain what they believe themselves. Or when they do know, mothers and fathers don't always stick to what they claim they believe. For example, parents may say, "Go to church," but stay home themselves. Parents may say, "Don't lie," yet their children hear made-up stories and untrue excuses.

Also, parents and teens may not believe that the same things are important. In some families elders value thrift, hard work, and the family reputation. In the same home adolescents may prefer having a good time and buying status symbols like stereo sets and high-powered cars. To them, saving money seems a waste of time.

• *Different experiences.* Because they grew up when things were quite different from what they are today, many parents have not had your experiences. For example, maybe they never saw drugs at school or in the street. So when parents pretend to be know-it-alls about topics they know nothing about, they make fools of themselves in the eyes of their growing children.

• *Different attitudes.* Most adolescents would like to talk openly and honestly with their parents. However, the teens may keep quiet about important matters if they fear that their parents will blab to the neighbors. If parents tell others what was revealed to them in private, make jokes of it, or use confidences as a weapon against the adolescent later, sons and daughters will resent it, feel betrayed, and clam up. Every time that happens, the so-called generation gap gets a little wider. Later these same parents wonder why their children won't confide in them.

• *Different types of talk.* If you've ever had the experience of starting a conversation only to discover that the adults have suddenly taken over and changed it into a question-answer session, you'll be more careful about what you say next time. The same is probably true if adults change the give and take from a conversation to a lecture, or if they dodge the issue completely when you want their honest opinons about whether something is right or wrong. It's no fun to be treated like a child when you are trying to act like an adult.

MISUNDERSTANDING

Unspoken and distorted communication. As a baby you could neither say words nor understand them. Yet you received messages through your senses—particularly touch, sight, and sound. In turn, you communicated your delight or dissatisfaction with coos, grunts, and yowls.

Later, when you learned language, you discovered puzzling differences between spoken words and unspoken messages. You may have heard that "spinach is delicious." Yet you found it gritty and gruesome. You may have observed adults exchanging nice words with each other. Yet later, in private, you may have overheard one ridicule or criticize the other. You may have seen people smile and pretend "everything's fine," when you knew that they were terribly unhappy.

A mother may insist that she has a happy marriage, when her children know it isn't so. A father may claim that he doesn't drink too much, when the children see him sneak his booze every night.

Parents may *need* to change their stories to protect their own self-image, or for some other reason. Some adults may even insist that others see things their way. Or they may almost seem to call their children liars if teens don't agree with the adult version of a family story.

When the truth hurts too much, adults may try to change it. Yet, in such homes, children wonder if they are seeing and hearing correctly. Boys and girls become confused and wonder if they can

Kathy Tuite

From the time he was old enough to hold a hammer, Brian's dad taught him how to repair things around the house. Now they work so smoothly together that each often knows what the other needs before a word is exchanged.

trust their own impressions. They have good reason to feel that way.

No words. About 90 percent of all human messages travel to the receiving person without use of words. Expressions of the face and body transmit "hidden" messages. So do gestures and voice tones.

Take a familiar example. Your mother says, "I want you to do this now." The way she says it means that there's no big hurry. The same words said in a slightly different way let you know that she means *right now!*

Long before their first birthday, little babies can detect anger or joy in others. As children grow older they learn to recognize many other emotions.

Everyone needs to learn how to decode unspoken signals. Being aware of directions without words is the only way to know if others are really angry or just kidding, if they are really interested or just pretending.

In every family flows a secret river of communication. After years of studying

119

your parents, you are probably sensitive to changes of voice and attitude.

You may not know the words to explain the messages sent to you, but you sense the *feelings* well enough. You may even understand the reasons why your folks do certain things. In fact, some teens are such sharp readers of adults that they get what they want by taking advantage of indecision in a parent or teacher.

Whether family communication is spoken or unspoken seems less important than whether each family member knows exactly what the other really means. When one parent is mentally ill, for example, communication can be badly distorted. Children grow up confused and uncertain because the family rules seem to change from day to day.

Sometimes adults practice "split level" communication. They disguise messages by saying one thing but meaning another. For example, some mothers say "no" in such a way that it's hard to tell whether they mean "yes," "maybe," or "I don't care." If you notice enough mixed messages like that you may doubt your own ability to understand the words you hear.

Other mixed messages. Some parents act permissive—they let the teenager make the decisions. However, such parents don't always feel permissive inside. They really want to be firm and strict, but they don't dare say so. Result: unclear instructions.

For example, a parent may say, "Make your own decision," but the unspoken message is, "Make the decision I want, or I'll be disappointed." Parents may be unaware of the big difference between the signals they send and what they really mean. They may not intend to confuse, but they do. Even so, their children usually get the intended message that lurks behind the spoken words.

From a mental health point of view it would be better for parents to say, "This is what I'd like you to do. But if you make another decision I'll try to live with it." Some teens would even prefer parents to make a clear and definite statement such as "I know best," and then really mean it. You may not agree with adults who take such a position, but at least you know what they mean and where you stand.

Mothers and fathers don't always agree with each other when it comes to raising families. For example, it sometimes happens that a teen receives a different message from each parent. A mother may tell her son to respect the girls he meets. A few minutes later the boy's father may give him a big wink which seems to say, "Don't take Mom too seriously. Boys will be boys."

Even where serious family problems exist, communication can still be open. When parents hide dark secrets, children are forced to imagine what's going on.

Most teens would rather know that father may lose his job or that Mother is sick than be forced to wonder why everyone seems so touchy and upset. When something is seriously wrong in a family, even younger children get the message. Without the facts, minors may imagine terrible things, feel disloyal to one or both parents, or even believe that they caused the problems. Perhaps you've had such experiences during your childhood.

FOR PERSONAL GROWTH

You can't force other persons to be more open and honest. However, by

Sometimes the best communication happens without any special planning.

modifying your own behavior, sometimes you can show others how to change. Following are some suggestions that may help you become a more effective communicator. Although the suggestions are directed to parents and children, you can use the same ideas to improve exchanges with brothers, sisters, friends, teachers and other adults.

Guidelines for living.

For Better Communication

• *Learn causes.* Next time you are part of a breakdown in communication, try to figure out the words or actions that set events in motion in the first place. Most persons play a very human game of "blaming others." However, every family member shares responsibility for what happens at home. Who hasn't started something by teasing a younger sibling (brother or sister)? Or, when feeling ill-tempered, who hasn't spit out a nasty remark? When you learn the causes for poor communication, you will be able to change what you say and do during family fights or disputes.

• *Learn solutions.* Study others who seem to communicate well. What do they say or do that seems to open an exchange of feelings and ideas? Think about your own response to a breakdown in communication at home. For example, almost everyone has hidden hurt feelings or said "I don't want to talk about that." On the other hand, almost

everyone has soothed troubled waters by saying, "I'm sorry," or "let's talk about it."

• *Learn to consider advice you have not asked for.* Many adults really want to give children the benefit of their mistakes and experiences. They want you to grow up better, stronger, more successful than they. However, at times they may not be too gentle when they send such messages.

When someone attacks you with words or fists, the normal reaction is to defend self or to counterattack. When parental advice is full of sarcasm and rejection, it's hard to listen. Instead of bristling with counter-offensives like "You do the same thing," or "Why are you picking on me?" adolescents who try a different approach such as "Thanks for the feedback," or "Let me think about what you said," improve chances for healthy family give and take. It's always possible you'll hear something really helpful, even if it hurts.

• *Learn to listen.* Listening means more than just not speaking. Ever notice how adults and adolescents talk at each other and completely or partly close out what the other person says until it's their turn to speak again? Few persons know how to listen carefully. The fact is that others can offer us important information. They may see us more clearly than we see ourselves. However, if the person uses listening time to plan a sharp counter-attack, the chance to learn something important about self is lost.

121

Listening is required for good communication. When someone pays close attention to what you have to say, it is natural for you to feel good about it.

Listening to praise is always fun. However, listening to negative criticism is not quite so easy.

Using the following checklist, rate yourself as a listener.

Which of the guidelines do you use now?

Which have you never used?

Which could you begin to use?

DO NOT WRITE IN THIS BOOK.

How Do I Listen?

• When someone tells me about my faults, I try *not* to answer with a lot of excuses, even though it hurts to hear the truth without saying something.

• I try to look at the other person to show that I am willing to hear and consider the negative comments about me.

• I don't make jokes about the other person's comments.

• I don't try to change the subject, even though I may want to.

• I don't try to even the score by finding fault with the other person.

• Even when I can say something to defend myself, I wait my turn to speak.

FEELINGS FIRST

Many older people are like children in that they do not understand how to manage their own emotions. You may know adults who use angry, accusing words or have temper tantrums a lot. What you might not know is that there are several ways for unhappy persons to get rid of disturbing feelings without hurting themselves or others.

Psychiatrists (sih-KY-uh-trists)—physicians who work with persons emotionally upset—sometimes use a method known as catharsis (kuh-THAR-sis). Catharsis means to let out locked-up emotions by talking about them.

Like releasing air from an inflated balloon, people who talk about their angry feelings drain off built-up pressures. Sometimes they are encouraged to work off negative emotions by punching bags or breaking dishes (instead of punching people or breaking heads).

Persons who are not terribly upset or mentally ill can also release their emotions without harm to self or others by giving a correct label to their emotion-of-the-moment.

"I feel angry."

"I feel frustrated."

One of the advantages of practicing "feelings first" is that you get a chance to talk about your real emotions without using them to hurt others. Acting out angry feelings often gets people into trouble. Learning to control anger and aggression and finding nonviolent ways to drain such negative emotions helps people of all ages.

PRIVATE AND PERSONAL

Good communication always depends on the adolescent and adult who are doing the talking. If both are honest, open, and trusting, the quality of the communication improves.

Of course, good communication doesn't mean that parents and children talk about everything that is private and personal. For example, most teens won't want to discuss the rushing excitement of falling in love. Or they may resent an adult who says, "I felt just the way you do now when I was a kid."

From your point of view you are different, and your emotions are one-of-a-kind between you and your special friend. Everyone has a need to be treated like an individual person and *not* like a carbon copy of parents.

Another private area may be daydreams. All persons have secret fantasies. Teens often daydream about becoming very rich and powerful, about becoming a hero or a TV star, or at least a big hit with the other sex. Such daydreaming is a normal part of adolescent development. However, some thoughts are just too personal to share with others.

Did you know? Daydreams are flashing mental pictures that are often behind another person's blank look. However, daydreams can be very useful. For example:

• Daydreams can help you pretest something you want to do. By thinking about your plan in advance you can avoid making a serious mistake.

• Daydreams also help you notice other possibilities of your plan that might have missed your attention the first time around.

Private and personal. What are your daydreams about?

Have you ever daydreamed about a project that actually came true later on?

OTHER PROBLEMS

Even if you want to encourage openness in the areas that concern family members and how they get along, problems can still arise. For example, teens don't always make it easy for parents to talk with them. Sometimes they decide that all older people, including teachers, couldn't possibly understand what it's like to grow up today. Therefore what's the use of talking?

Of course, times, customs, and attitudes change. However, basic human problems and needs do not. The Bible reports acts of human love, hate, greed, and generosity that happened many years ago. Such emotions remain much the same today.

Natalie Leimkuhler
Parents may stay clear of touchy topics. If you are willing to talk first, communication can be improved for all involved.

Parents often have useful advice or information to offer. Even when they've made mistakes themselves, they want their children to have a better life.

Many parents are sensitive about the feelings of their children. They may hesitate to open a discussion about a touchy topic for fear of embarrassing the younger person or intruding too far into their private lives. In such cases, a word of invitation or a smile from the adolescent may open the door to better dialog.

Guidelines for living. Some phrases serve as helpful "door openers" to improve communication. These Openers invite you and the other person to explain yourself better and to release emotions without damage.

Other phrases serve as "door slammers." The Slammers almost guarantee ruined chances for understanding between the persons involved. Consider these examples.

DOOR OPENERS
Tell me more.
Do you mean that . . .
I'm not sure I understand . . .
Tell me if I'm wrong.
Are you feeling . . .

DOOR SLAMMERS

Shut up.

You're wrong.

I don't want to listen.

You're too young (or old) to know anything about that.

That's a stupid thing to say.

If you had any sense . . .

That's not the way I see it.

You don't know what you're talking about.

Something to think about. Which of the Slammers or Openers have been used on you?

Which have you used on others?

What emotions do you feel when you get Slammer messages?

What emotions do you feel when you get Opener messages?

Private and personal. Would life be easier for you if you used fewer Slammers and more Openers?

IF PARENTS CAN'T HELP

Some parents are not able to help. They may be sick, absent, uninformed, or simply unable to offer sound guidance. As a result, they may give their children the silent treatment when the teens need help immediately.

Sometimes parent-like substitutes such as school counselors, teachers, or older friends and relatives may be the persons you need. If you have a bad problem and can't find help at home or school, try community agencies. Family Service agencies, a mental health center, or an adolescent clinic based in a hospital often offer information and counseling to teens.

Teens and parents who have grown so far apart that they can no longer talk to each other can benefit from professional help. A third party can help remove the roadblocks to family communication. You'll read more about where troubled families can get help in Chapter 19.

Guidelines for living. There may be times when it seems necessary to "clear the air" by saying what you need to say.

At the same time you would probably prefer to express your negative emotion in such a way that you don't hurt the other person in the process. Also, you probably don't want to ruin the relationship you share now.

The suggestions following can be helpful. Notice that they recommend saying what you feel at the time rather than calling the other person a dirty name.

As you read the suggestions, rate yourself.

Which of the guidelines do you use now?

Which have you never used?

Which could you begin to use?

DO NOT WRITE IN THIS BOOK.

Clearing the Air

- I describe my emotion-of-the-moment directly to the person whose behavior upsets me.
- I do not acuse the person of wanting to harm me.
- I do not complain to someone else first.
- I try not to express my negative emotions in front of a third party.
- I don't compare the other person's annoying behavior with anyone else's.
- After I describe my emotions and make my point, I don't repeat them over and over.
- I try to limit my suggestions to certain types of behavior that I believe the other person can actually do something about.
- I try to avoid sarcasm.
- I make only one negative comment at a time.
- I try to say nice things about the other person whenever I can.

Private and personal. As a result of reading this chapter, what one change could you make today in order to improve communication with your parents?

With your teachers?

With your friends?

To learn more. Select one idea or topic from this chapter that applies to you and the way you live your life.

On a separate sheet of paper describe your selection in one sentence.

In no more than three sentences explain why you chose it.

DO NOT WRITE IN THIS BOOK.

RECAP

Children learn to express their thoughts and feelings at home from parents or other adults. Even in the best of families, misunderstandings, angry feelings, and breakdowns in communication happen. Everyone—especially close relatives—needs to find ways to express both bad and good feelings and still stay friends.

Communication is like a wheel with many spokes. One spoke stands for open, honest talk. Another could represent the shared exchange of ideas. Other spokes may represent hidden meanings, double meanings, unspoken messages, and high-quality listening. Much communication takes place without any words at all.

When children reach adolescence, straight talk between parents and off-spring sometimes dries up. Younger family members often develop different personal values. They use different rules for living.

One generation may shortchange another. Young people fail to credit older ones with useful wisdom and valuable life experience. Older people fail to notice how mature and capable younger ones have become. Both sides shut the others out and fail to notice needs to communicate and stay close.

Each generation can work to improve communication. Taking an interest in others helps. Listening for what the other person really means helps. Holding back the tendency to criticize helps. Labeling your own emotions and saying them aloud can relieve inner pressure. Using "feelings first" by stating the emotion you feel at the time helps others understand you better.

In every family there are some touchy topics. Family members may either steer clear of such issues or try to discuss things openly.

Good communication doesn't mean that parents and adolescents must discuss every fact, every experience, or every idea. More important is that the door stays open for discussion and exchange of opinions. Even disagreements need not lead to accusations, anger, or the silent treatment.

Not all parents can offer a strong personal model for their children to imitate. Still, good communication can also take place with a relative or adult friend such as a teacher. More and more community agencies offer counseling services to adolescents.

TERMS

Communication	Status symbols	Disturbed families
Discussion	Communication without	Listening for meaning
Dialog	words	Feelings first
Differences	Mixed messages	Touchy topics

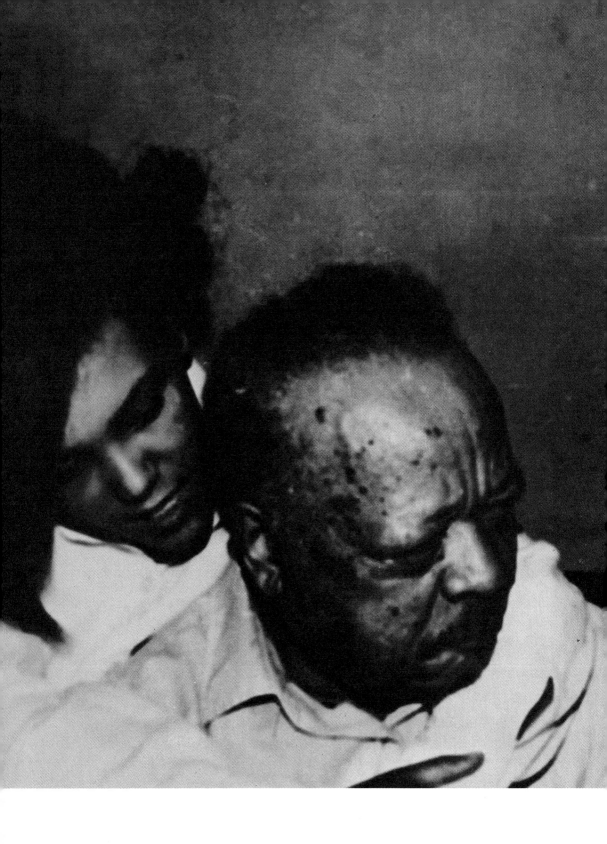

CHAPTER 7

The Struggle for Independence

Almost every teen wants more freedom to make personal decisions and choices. Some adolescents consider rebellion, anger, harsh words, and stubborn resistance all necessary for their struggle for independence.

However, many other young persons don't feel the same need to fight for their rights. In fact, when parents and teens take time to talk about their disagreements and then find compromises that all can live with, there may not be any need for a battle.

However, it's a rare family that completely avoids struggles for independence. No matter what it's called, parents and their adolescents usually go through a tug-of-war before the teens mature and move out on their own.

Teen opinion. Part of the preparation for this book included talking to adolescents about their parents. In spite of disagreements, most teens also feel warm affection and respect for their mothers and fathers. Following are opinions of four young persons who are pleased with the way their parents raised them. As you read, look for comments that match your own opinions.

CASE EXAMPLE

"My parents are great. They try to help me and set me straight on things

Eric Johnson
Sometimes a conflict can be settled quickly with a simple "I'm sorry."

I'm not too sure about. They aren't strict or old fashioned. They give me a certain time to get home. If I don't make it, I can't go out the next night. Their rules are fair, even if I complain once in a while. At least I know what they expect of me."

"For as long as I can remember, my parents gave me a lot of freedom. But they also taught me about responsibility. They are always willing to discuss my problems and help me see if I'm headed in the right direction or not. They praise the good things I do. Their attitude helps bring about respect and trust on both sides."

"My parents help me work things out. Last month my boyfriend and I broke up. He was the only boy I ever went with. I got so used to him that I thought my whole world had collapsed. My mom helped me realize that I still have plenty of time to date boys. The most important thing is to finish school and do something that will help me make a good life. When I can't work out a problem for myself, I go to Mom and we always get things straight. Even if it's not the way I want, she helps me find an answer."

"My parents, my brother, and I sit down and talk things out. We don't always agree but we don't fight either. We never have arguments like a lot of families I know. But when my parents say no, they mean it. It wouldn't do any good to beg because they don't change their minds."

Natalie Leimkuhler

In spite of minor conflicts about rules and limits, most adolescents feel affection and respect for their parents.

A special ingredient? The fact is, happy and healthy adolescents the world over grow up in an amazing variety of homes. Some parents are easygoing. Others are strict. Some persuade in a soft voice. Others shout orders.

In turn, some teens seem willing to listen, to talk, and to work with parents in finding solutions to disagreements. Others turn away and shut themselves off from the family.

As you will read, some methods really do make for less conflict and better

relationships between parents and children. However, even if such ideas fail or never get tried, most teens still turn out to be healthy adults.

CONFLICT

In Johannesburg, South Africa, an old man named Sam Spector died recently. Authorities needed twenty-six truckloads to clear his home of more than a million newspapers. Sam left old papers stacked everywhere. Under a big mound in the garage they found an ancient automobile. A lot of parents worry that their sloppy adolescents will turn out just like Sam.

Conflicts between parents and teens differ in size and severity. Many fights flare up like a match and die quickly. No damage is done. Other scraps are like brush fires. They smolder for days, then flare up suddenly and pollute the home environment.

Conflict between parents and children may start with issues like unmade beds, messy rooms, dirty clothes dropped on the floor, and soiled dishes in the sink. At about age eleven, most children start listening less and arguing more. They start skipping their chores and begin protesting assignments. Parents often complain that their once reasonable and agreeable sons and daughters are now more difficult to live with.

Something to think about. The following list includes issues that can cause conflict between teens and parents.

Possible Conflict Issues

- Selection of friends.
- Disagreement about late hours.
- Areas of responsibility.
- Work habits.
- Spending patterns.
- Clothing styles and grooming.
- Attitudes about language.
- Willingness to listen.
- Opinions about schoolwork.
- Amount of time spent away from home.
- Overuse of the telephone.
- Amount of attention from parents.
- Importance of values and morals.
- Use of drugs and alcohol.

Private and personal. Which of these issues cause tension between you and your folks?

Keep your personal problems in mind as you read how to solve conflicts in this chapter.

Rebellion-type conflict with parents usually peaks between the ages of fifteen to sixteen for girls and fifteen to seventeen for boys. Younger and older offspring seem to have less need to struggle with their folks.

Even so, battles don't have to happen. Some boys and girls seem to glide through adolescence a lot more smoothly than others. Even in the same family, some teens may get along with parents better than others.

In the best of homes, however, there are differences of opinion. Minor squabbles erupt over who carries out the garbage or who walks the dog. More serious conflicts over the use of drugs or choosing the wrong friends can tear families apart. Whatever the conflict, the basic issues in the struggle for independence usually are:

- How soon should freedom and independence be granted?
- Who makes the rules?

Following you'll learn why independence is so important to fast-growing adolescents like yourself. You'll think about independence from two sides: (1) the way you see it, and (2) the way your parents see it. You'll examine some of the typical problems that arise when adolescents start to become adults.

INDEPENDENCE

What does the idea of personal freedom mean to you? To a thirteen-year-old, independence may mean staying out an hour later at night. To an eighteen-year-old it may mean moving out of the house.

The meaning of independence for you also depends on how close you are to living on your own. A few fifteen-year-olds are capable of supporting themselves completely. However, many

David Snodgress, Journal and Courier, Lafayette, Indiana
From the time they are very young, children gradually range into the neighborhood and community, farther and farther from home.

eighteen-year-olds have never held a paying job.

Defined. Independence, as discussed here, means boys and girls splitting from their parents and other adults who have helped them grow and learn to make decisions. This distance between parent and growing child develops a little at a time. It is normal, healthy, and necessary.

Independence means freedom. However, freedom demands responsibility. It has been said that the measure of maturity is what a person does when no one is looking. According to that standard, how grown up are you?

Making decisions. No matter what your age or your level of skills, during adolescence you must begin to make important decisions. You must begin to manage your own life. You must learn to put controls on yourself when there is no adult standing by to say what's right or wrong.

Right now there is probably a strong link between you and your parents. It can't be measured or touched. Yet you can feel this invisible connection, sometimes strong as steel wire. Although this tie between parents and child is rarely broken completely, it must be made looser so you can become an independent adult.

As you grow older you become less close to your parents. This increased distance is not measured in miles or kilometers but in "psychological space." This increasing distance means you don't need your parents so much any more. It means that you are beginning to function more as a one-of-a-kind person. It means that someday you will be able to live your life, your way.

Gradual. The greatest degree of independence comes gradually. Using home as a safe base, in ever-widening circles, you venture out to friends, school, and more distant places. Knowing you can return home offers you strength and encouragement to try out your new freedom. After a bad experience, the protection of your home and your family probably feels warm, good, and comfortable.

As you observe older friends and siblings, you see that some people mature faster than others. It may take you less or more time to mature than persons you know.

Timetables. In most families, the question of whether or not adolescents will get independence is much less important than how *soon* the freedom begins. "When can I begin to do things on my own?" becomes the important question for teens.

Adults usually hold out for a slower, more gradual approach. They often try to slow down the pace with guidance and supervision. (To some teens, such overconcern seems like *snoopervision*.)

Young persons usually want freedom and independence at a faster pace.

"If I don't fight for my rights, I'll be a baby forever," mutters the adolescent.

"If I don't say no, what will they demand next?" worries the parent.

Much like airline or bus schedules, no one single timetable pleases everyone.

PARENTS ALSO FAVOR TEENAGE INDEPENDENCE

In successful families, parents help children become self-reliant and free. In fact, so powerful is the adolescent drive for independence that few parents could hold it back even if they wanted to. Of course, poor health or other problems may slow things down, but a great force of nature helps adolescents in their struggle. Just as baby birds grow too big for the nest and are shoved out for their first flight, children "outgrow" the house or become too much for aging parents.

Believe it or not, few parents want to keep their offspring "jailed" at home. Almost any mother or father hates the idea of a thirty-year-old "child" still asking for movie money.

Few normal, healthy adults remain dependent on their parents for money. Yet you probably know of some married persons who still are not emotionally free. They may be unable to make a

Although mother helped out at first, Leslie and Laura agreed to take over responsibility for their paper route.

Natalie Leimkuhler

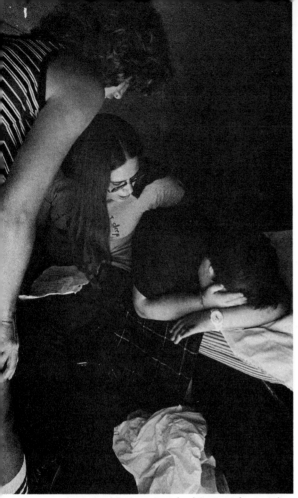

David Snodgress, Journal and Courier, Lafayette, Indiana

Independence doesn't happen all at once. Marie enjoys summer camp, but a letter and a package from her family bring a flood of homesick tears.

decision or afraid to act without their parents' approval.

In extreme cases of stunted emotional growth, adults continue to act like children. They never leave home, never start their own family, nor carve out a life of their own. *Physical* growth is measured in inches and pounds, centimetres and grams. *Psychological* growth can be measured by observing changes in what people say and do.

Mixed feelings go along with gaining independence. For example, at times you want the freedom to do as you please. Once in a while you may also want the feelings of protection and safety that go with remaining a child. You may protest that you don't need or want parent guidance. However, down deep you may yearn for proof that parents still care about you.

Parents feel uncertain. Parents suffer mixed feelings, too. They worry about whether to hold you back or to let you go. They are not always sure whether to *ask* you to do something or to *demand* it. Parents want their growing children to become responsible and independent. Yet mothers and fathers also enjoy the feeling of being needed.

Parents feel good when you make wise decisions. They also worry that your lack of experience may lead to bad choices and hurtful mistakes. Therefore they may keep on making decisions for you, out of habit, even when you prove you don't need help. For example, some mothers select clothing, order food, even answer questions for their teens long after the youths are capable of doing such things for themselves.

Although teens do more on their own and are at home less, for many years parents continue to be blamed for the mistakes of their growing children. For example, if you damage property or injure someone, your parents can be held legally responsible. That's one good reason why parents seem cautious in granting new privileges.

WEAPONS OF REBELLION

Of course, not every teen must battle for independence. In many families parents generously give increasing freedom as adolescents demonstrate in-

132

creasing responsibility and maturity. However, the words of war can be helpful in understanding the heated struggles, temporary truces, and the permanent stand-offs that so often happen in families.

In the battle between parents and adolescents, the arsenal of weapons and the strategy of the generals can become fearsome. Parents own the big guns. They have the power. They can take away privileges like late hours or spending money. However, teens are not without weapons of their own. They scare parents with psychological warfare that includes sniper activity, refusal to talk peace, and the threat of all-out rebellion.

Psychological warfare. Very young children often think that their parents know everything and can do anything. As they grow older, adolescents become more critical of the same parents who seemed without fault just a few years earlier.

Part of growing up includes the disappointing discovery that parents are not perfect. Worse, what adults say is not always what they do. Sometimes grown-ups insist on rules that they don't practice themselves.

In turn, young people seem to own radar-like antennas in discovering adult flaws. They catch parents in mistakes or lies. Picking on parents and criticizing them seems the popular thing to do. Finding fault with adults also gives you an opportunity to test your own view of life and to convince yourself that you don't need adult advice, attention, or direction any more.

Sniper activity. Sometimes little "hit and run" shots substitute for big battles. Low-grade conflict is a form of sniper activity that wears down the "enemy,"

even though no big fight is in progress at the time.

During this stage practically anything that parents suggest suddenly becomes exactly what you don't want to do. In fact, you may feel obliged to disagree even if you think a parent is right. For example, mother asks you to wear rain gear to school or to turn down the volume of the stereo while you study. Even such reasonable requests may seem like nagging criticism or an intrusion into your personal life.

Sometimes the need to criticize and to disagree may override everything else. You may wonder why you act so. You may even feel guilty about your behavior, knowing that your lack of cooperation destroys family peace. You may feel the need to get even—exchanging volley for volley. Yet you don't know how to change things for the better.

The pot-shots of the sniper might be comments like these:

"Your hair (or clothes, or makeup, or weight), Mom! Honestly, don't you care how you look?"

"Really, Dad! This isn't the year 1900!"

Something to think about. List other "pot-shot" phrases used by teens and parents. What kind of feelings do such "attacks" cause? What kind of replies do they invite?

Withdrawal. Some family skirmishes end in a stalemate in which nobody wins and everyone loses. Neither side will give in. Each withdraws to an armed camp. Frosty silence and dirty looks are the main weapons.

Withdrawal is a serious kind of resistance. Members of each side pull back in hurt or anger and won't discuss anything with the other. Sometimes parents and children both refuse to state honest

Natalie Leimkuhler
Daydreaming is one way to shut out painful family conflicts.

differences. They also refuse to admit emotions or anything that might leave them open to more criticism or to a new attack.

Even though things may seem normal to an outsider, there are many ways to withdraw.

- Daydreaming can be a way to escape conflict.
- Sometimes reading a lot or watching TV for hours puts up a protective wall.
- Pretending to be sick, overeating, or turning to drugs are ways to withdraw and show contempt for family rules.
- Running away is the most direct form of withdrawal from home problems.

In more extreme kinds of withdrawal, parents or children may feel depressed and discouraged. They become quiet and no longer care about arguing. Either side may act cold and uncaring. Life at home becomes even more tense and difficult.

HEALTHY DISAGREEMENTS

During early adolescence the fight for personal independence usually begins with words. Actions follow later. When teens grow big and strong enough, conflict with parents may flare up with fights that include yelling and hitting.

Sometimes the best way to clear the air is for both sides to state what bothers them. Such showdowns can be helpful if all concerned take turns spelling out their honest disagreements. Then, if each is willing to work for a peaceful solution, problems may be settled on the spot.

Not all conflict can be avoided. Yet control of attacks and counterattacks helps prevent constant bickering. Fights that seem to go on and on can't make things better.

Sometimes teens are harder on their parents than they mean to be. They may hurt their folks deeply with cruel words or the silent treatment. Sometimes they do just the opposite of what they are asked.

You probably don't like being teased, insulted, or coldly ignored. Parents feel the same way about mean, cruel words or the silent treatment.

WHAT'S MOST IMPORTANT?

"I'll never do that to *my* kids!" exclaims young onlookers who disapprove of how some parents treat their children. Suppose you were in charge. How would you treat adolescents? How would you raise younger children?

The world over, parents try all sorts of approaches. Some mothers and fathers set out to raise their children the way they were brought up. Others use methods *they wish* had been used on them. In some countries parents train their children as the government tells them.

In China, children are taught to behave and not ask questions. In West Germany, more than half of the parents responding to a survey considered it useful to hit their children. "I don't mean just a cuff on the ear, I mean beating with a stick or even a board," reported K. H. von Rabenau, child psychologist at the University Clinic in Frankfurt, Germany.

Many Europeans think of the United States as a place where parents let their children get away with anything. Of course you know that's far from the truth. If you think about the families you know, you'll probably discover some stern parents whose attitude seems to say, "Do as I say, no questions asked!"

Others seem to take no stand at all. Instead they shrug off responsibility as if to say, "Make your own decisions."

A third group of parents can't make up their minds. One day they take a hard line. The next they permit almost anything. As a result their children don't know what to expect next.

Some wise parents say, "You are a person. You have rights. But as your parents, we are responsible for your behavior. Let's discuss our disagreements and find a set of rules that we can all live with."

Sometimes parents disagree with each other openly about what their children can or cannot do. Or one parent may cut the other's authority by changing the rules after the first parent has laid down the law. Obviously such undermining can cause conflict between parents. Adolescents are often caught in the middle of parent struggles. In such

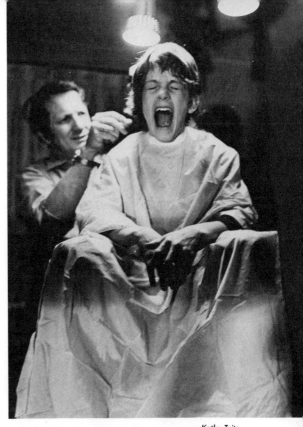

Kathy Tuite
As youngsters mature they seek more independence. Preteen Paul just told his dad that next time he wants to go to a "real" barber.

cases teens can lose respect for both parents.

Attitudes that count most. Many experts agree that good, successful parenting always includes one adult who loves and accepts the child (or adolescent). Whether Russian, German, African, or American, children seem to gain strength, dignity, and feelings of personal value when parents care about the youngsters and try to act in their best interest.

As you know, such attitudes are not present in every family. Sometimes even good parents put their own interests first. In other cases, unloving parents are nice to their children once in a while.

135

Basic intentions and day-to-day attitudes seem to make the main difference. Parents can make a lot of mistakes as long as they show their love for the child and as long as the child knows it.

"Love me, care about me," seems to be every child's message to every parent. However, an old saying goes, "Love is not enough." That means if you really care about someone, you'll find ways to show it.

That's why loving parents must demonstrate their consideration, interest, and concern with words and actions. Even in strong, steady families, there's usually room for improvement from both generations. Problems can always pop up. Such conflicts must be settled.

LIMITS

The big battles in the war of independence often erupt over the question of *limits.* Limits are the foul lines that decide who you spend time with, where you go, what you do, and how late you stay out. Both parents and teens share the responsibility for setting reasonable limits to avoid conflict over these questions.

Of course, some problems can't be solved with limits. For example, marriage difficulties between a mother and father can cause conflict over which you have no control. If a parent drinks heavily, or is mentally ill, there may be no way for you to help. If a child has a physical handicap that prevents participation in sports, there may be no way to change that, either.

Who needs limits? When you think about it, everyone needs limits. Young or old, each persons needs to know how far to go without getting into trouble or hurting someone else. When you know what your parents or teachers won't ac-cept, you can avoid the things that bother them most.

Even though teens may feel tied down by rules, limits seem to be a necessary part of life. In fact, when there are no limits on what people can do, and those persons refuse to put limits on themselves, trouble usually develops.

Not all rules are good rules, even if they are made by wise parents. Some limits make sense and are necessary. Others seem unfair and not needed. The best limits can be discussed, changed, or removed when they no longer serve a purpose.

CASE EXAMPLE

"I want you to care about me, but not too much," Betty Sue explained to her parents. What she meant was that she liked the feeling that her parents were strong and dependable, ready to help her if she needed them. On the other hand, she wanted more freedom to go out with her friends, make more decisions on her own, and practice independence without her parents butting in.

CASE EXAMPLE

Dennis is moving out of adolescence. He's far enough away from his own battles for independence to look back and see family conflicts in a different way.

Dennis can see the virtues and faults of his parents with the clear eyes of youth. However, he also understands that sometimes he's just like them. He wants to understand how they helped to make him the kind of person he is. He wants to pause for a moment on the brink of becoming an adult. He wants to pull his thoughts together, to think about the

Limits help you to understand how far you can go without hurting yourself or others.

past, and to learn from his experience.

Dennis talks freely and understands himself well. His story is here to make you think and to serve as a preview of what lies ahead for you. As you read, notice where you agree with him. Are your experiences similar to his? Different? How? Ask yourself: are these my feelings too? Could I be so honest about myself?

As in most families, Dennis and his parents really love each other. Yet they had plenty of conflict, too. Here is his report.

"Power is a familiar tactic in our home. My parents use it a lot. I often find myself trying to use power, too. For example, my parents and I usually end a disagreement by yelling at each other.

"I'm beginning to wonder if things might be better if I changed and used some nonpower tactics. Instead of screaming, 'You be different' at them, I might try to accept them just as they are.

"My parents still try to use power to deal with me. When I was younger they had all the authority. I had to do what they said. As I grew up and took more independence, fights happened more often. At times they still try to settle our differences by using force. Finally it dawned on all of us that force doesn't settle anything.

"I think my parents yell at me because they see their faults in me. They want me to overcome their drawbacks. Yet it's hard for them to see me succeeding in some things they'll never be able to do.

"To me the main goal of adolescence is for kids to work for independence. It will be easier for my parents when I show them that I not only want to be independent but that I can manage freedom as well.

"Growing up is hard work. It's much easier for me to put all the blame for my problems on my parents. Many things about them bother me. I'm beginning to find out that I have many of their faults. After all, they raised me. It stands to reason that I'd be like them.

"I can't change my parents but I can still change myself. Maybe the way for me to really grow up is to admit my own faults. Then I can try to change the things I do wrong. Actually, change will be difficult for me. I always want to look good and come out on top. If I want to change, it means that I have to let my parents and other people be right once in awhile.

"The more I understand myself, the more I discover how much I still have to learn. My parents must know a lot of things I haven't learned yet. They're nice enough not to force all their knowledge on me. They let me learn at my own pace.

"When they do offer me advice, I'd like to stop acting so touchy. They're

not out to get me. They just want to make my life easier. Listening to their side doesn't mean I have to give up my independence. Actually I'm learning that my parents are fair and reasonable. They would probably have more respect for me if they saw me handle conflict in a more mature way. Maybe then it would be easier for them to let me live my own life."

What makes Dennis different is he admits that *he* also plays a part in family problems. He is beginning to understand the causes for the bullying power plays used in his home. He also realizes that he uses the same tactics on his parents and others. Dennis didn't stop at just blaming his parents for all his own problems. He began to change himself.

Dennis has discovered that one of life's greatest challenges (inside the family and out) is to find ways to get along with others despite occasional disagreements and differences. He is also learning that he doesn't have to be a carbon copy of his parents.

Something to think about. Insight means new understanding about a continuing problem. Some insights happen in a flash, as when the person says, "Aha!"

As he grows to maturity, Dennis has gained insights about the way his parents get along with each other. He's beginning to understand that one person never deserves all the blame for family troubles.

Private and personal. After reading about parents and teens, what new insights have you gained into the way that adolescents and their parents get along?

On a separate sheet of paper make a list of your insights.
DO NOT WRITE IN THIS BOOK.

OK to test limits? Once, adults believed that children should be "seen but not heard." It's hard to believe that only a few generations ago some youngsters got to talk in the company of adults only when the grown-ups approved.

Today adolescents enjoy more freedom to offer opinions and have a say in family matters. When you get a chance to question decisions, you sharpen the ability to think for yourself. You learn to trust yourself and to depend on yourself.

Almost all adolescents test the limits set for them. In fact, unless you do question adult authority once in a while, it's hard to know just how far you can go or how competent you really are. At times you may push against boundaries set up by parents *just to discover the limits.*

In building muscle power, professional boxers slug away at heavy bags. Boys and girls do something like that when they argue, protest, and struggle against parents. They build "psychological muscles" that help them become capable, independent adults.

Some adolescent demands are made to find out just how much freedom parents are willing to give at the time. Few teens expect to get everything they ask for. Nor are they too upset when a refusal is reasonable and firm.

When limits are welcome. Have you ever felt secretly relieved when told no to something you really didn't want in the first place? Parents come in handy at times to protect you from things you don't yet feel ready to handle. Their refusal takes the pressure off you when telling your friends why you can't join the group in the current project.

CASE EXAMPLE

Bob asked his parents if he could ride along with friends to an out-of-town game. The older brother of his best friend was to do the driving for the two-hour trip.

Bob did not tell his folks that the boys planned to take along a case of beer. Also, the driver had been fined twice in recent weeks for speeding.

Bob felt uncertain and afraid. He really hoped that his parents would say no. That way he could avoid the dangers the trip seemed to promise. At the same time he could grumble and complain to his friends about his parents not letting him go along.

What about me? Have you ever wished that someone would make an important decision for you? Can you think of a time when you wanted your parents to tell you what to do when you felt unsure to decide for yourself? Compare your experiences with those of classmates.

Finish this case. Let's return to Bob. As it turned out, his parents didn't let him go to the game. And he decided not to complain about their refusal.

Now, a few weeks later, he feels thrilled and excited. He has a chance to attend a rock concert in that same distant city. A chartered bus will take a group from school. Teachers and parent chaperones will ride along. Bob really wants to make this trip.

What's different about this second request?

What differences of opinion might Bob and his parents have about this plan?

Something to think about. What emotions will Bob probably feel while asking his folks?

What emotions will his parents probably feel when they realize what Bob is asking?

Defensive reactions. Some adults—parents, teachers, and others in authority—welcome questions and testing as a way to keep everything out in the open. Others may feel angry or afraid when teens challenge rules and test limits.

In a compromise each person gives a little and each person gets a little.

They react with loud protests as if to say that youth have no right to question things.

You read about psychological defenses in Chapter 1. Defensive persons act as if they are under personal attack, rather than try to understand the cause of the conflict or to settle the disagreement.

Adolescents can also be defensive. Such behavior usually happens when parents inquire about personal lives, or how and where the teens spend their time. In both adolescents and adults, defensive attitudes can destroy good dialog and lead to conflict.

Compromise. Adolescence has always been the time when youth begin to test the authority of older persons. Such challenges need not damage parent-child closeness. The important factor is how members on each side of the argument carry on the debate. Each generation must "win" something to avoid a knock-down, drag-out finish. Members of both sides must give a little and get a little. That's what compromise is all about.

Parents win a little when they say, "All right, you may go (to the party, game, dance), but please be home by eleven."

Teens win a little when they say, "Yes, I'll clean (my room, the windows, oven). But I promised the guys I'd be at team practice this morning. I'll do the work right after lunch." When each keeps the bargain struck, good faith and good feelings grow stronger.

Inner controls. Perhaps the best reason for seeking limits is to learn just how far you can go without supervision from someone older. Limits from the outside are not the same as learning to say no to yourself. The best limits are *inner controls.* Inner controls put you in charge of yourself. You learn how to manage inner tensions and to make decisions about how you will act. You become responsible for you.

Conscience is a mental reminder to use inner controls. You read about conscience in Chapter 2. Conscience helps you do what's right for you and others when on your own. When parents and teens agree on limits that are fair, those who cheat often suffer a guilty conscience.

Parents also have responsibilities. When parents are clear and reasonable about what they expect of their children, both sides benefit. When parents consider your opinion and help you develop a set of personal values to cover issues like lying and stealing, your life becomes easier.

You may not always do exactly what your parents want. However, at least you know what they expect of you. When parents are fair and consistent, children develop their own inner controls. As teens, they become increasingly responsible for their behavior when away from home and parent supervision.

Too many limits. Limits start with the very young. If too few limits can confuse a child, so can too many.

"Don't touch!"

"Don't cross the street."

"Don't leave the yard."

"Don't go anywhere with strangers."

Young children need plenty of reminders and supervision because they haven't yet learned what is best for them. However, when parents keep the same tight childhood controls on their sons and daughters into the teen years, problems are almost sure to pop up. Too much protection can do just as much harm as too much freedom.

Too few limits. Many young persons believe that happiness is "no one telling you what to do." Yet, with no one to say no, adolescents seldom feel really free at all. They are more likely to feel ignored and neglected.

With no limits, guidelines, or boundaries to help them, some teens even feel frightened and lonely. They are so scared that they seem unable to act. Others use the freedom to act on impulses whenever pressure builds. They fight, steal, take drugs, and test each new situation in a search for controls. They wish someone would tell them just how far they can go.

Because adolescents so often look and sound confident, and insist they can handle their own lives, few adults guess that the teens are often scared. Not all youth want as much freedom as they ask for. Most are quite content with a compromise.

SHOWDOWN

Sometimes teens try to force their parents into a showdown by causing a fight, or getting into serious trouble. They try to get parent attention by forc-

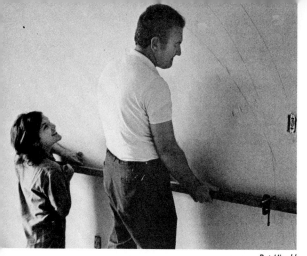

Pat Hirschl

Working together can lead to more closeness and improved communication. Here Maida and her father cooperate on a project to paint a rainbow on her bedroom wall.

ing the adults to say exactly what the teen can and can't do.

CASE EXAMPLE

A mother says: "Our daughter, Linda Lee, is pleasant and easy-going—except when she's home. Here she's rude and mean, and won't do what we say. She picks on her sister and ignores her father. She says she gets along with everyone else so it must be our fault.

"She seems to hate me. Nothing I say or do pleases her. When she's asked to help around the house she sulks and argues.

"She treats us all like dirt. When I tell her it isn't necessary to say everything she thinks, she insists that its phony not to express an honest opinion.

"Every day there is a family fight, and she is always the cause. At times I don't feel much love for her. In fact, I can hardly wait for her to grow up and move out!"

Joe says: "My parents and I can't agree on anything. They give me ad-

vice, but I never take it. They never follow up on anything. I want to do the things I want. I don't want any help from them.

"I don't drink or smoke or cuss in front of my parents because my father is going to give me $100 when I'm twenty-one if I say I didn't smoke. It won't bother me to lie to him. He's got plenty of money, and he sure is tight with it.

"I want to roam around when I want and do what I please without anyone holding me back. Eventually I'll get married and live a straight life. I want to live today. Who knows if there will be a tomorrow.

"My father says I care only about myself. It is true that I might be upset if he was hurt or killed, but I don't think anything else happening to him would bother me."

You be the counselor. Linda Lee and Joe are angry, rebellious, unhappy teens, caught in a pattern of conflict and battle. Although they may sound uncaring, both would really like to improve things at home.

As a counselor, what suggestions would you make to the adolescents in these cases? What would you say to the parents?

TRUCE AND PEACE

Parents aren't perfect. Even the best mothers and fathers make mistakes. They set the wrong limits, or don't set any at all. They feel unsure about when to say yes and when to say no. Sometimes they ignore the really important issues. At other times they worry about dinky little things.

Whenever a group lives together, gripes, complaints, and conflicts are sure to flare up. Conflicts happen because people are different and not perfect. Even close relatives have different goals, and prefer different life-styles.

Conflict and fighting can destroy a family. Yet conflict isn't always bad, especially if it helps family members to say what they really think. When disagreements are brought out in the open, problems are often solved.

In some families, even though they disagree from time to time, parents and adolescents learn how to manage conflict, settle problems, and live together in peace. When there's fairness, affection, goodwill, and no need to have someone to blame, family members can settle their differences. However, some ways to solve conflicts work faster and better than others.

A method that works. Following you'll read some ideas about how to settle differences between parents and teens. This plan is not the only way, nor is it guaranteed to work in every family. As you read, think about how the suggestions might work in your family.

• Both parents and teens must pay close attention to the words of the others in order to hear what is really being said.

• All persons get a chance to explain their viewpoints.

• When it's your turn to talk, don't accuse the other person of mistakes and faults. Instead try to state your emotion-of-the-moment in a nondestructive way.

• When something bothers you, state your complaint at the time without later accusing or blaming someone else.

By using such suggestions, you can help your parents understand your side of the story. You also can learn the reasons behind their preferences. You also cut down the need for defensiveness and counterattacks on both sides. Mutual respect and understanding re-

place blame, fear, faultfinding, and punishment. Conflicts with brothers and sisters, friends, and teachers can also be settled this way.

Improvement. After bucking the wild rapids of the Colorado River, persons on rafts float into tranquil pools. They are often amazed and relieved that they made it through the fast-running river safely. Looking back, parents and grown children often comment with similar wonder that they all survived the adolescent years.

In most families, disagreements and conflict begin to fade by late adolescence. Parents discover that their grown children really can stand alone. Late teens discover that parents are important people whose affection and admiration are valuable.

Most grown children don't stop loving their parents. They simply love them differently. Strong and lasting ties develop. Love and respect continue to grow. Friendships of this type can last a lifetime.

Make a list. On a separate sheet of paper list three issues on which you have gained some independence during the past year at home.

List two more ways that you are getting closer to indpendence.

Now list some areas where you hope to achieve independence some day.

Compare your list with that of a classmate.

Look for differences and similarities.
DO NOT WRITE IN THIS BOOK.

Something to think about. The text suggests that both teens and parents share some of the responsibility for getting along together.

What one thing could you say or do that would increase understanding between you and your parents?

To learn more. Select one idea or topic from this chapter that applies to you and the way you live your life.

On a separate sheet of paper describe your selection in one sentence.

In no more than three sentences explain why you chose it.

DO NOT WRITE IN THIS BOOK.

RECAP

Even parents who admire and enjoy their children admit that they can't always talk together about important things. Also, parents worry about adolescents who rebel against authority.

Conflict at home usually peaks when adolescents are between ages fifteen and seventeen. Although the battles are often over little things, the basic issues are independence and freedom. What parents call rebellion, teens usually see as their necessary fight for independence.

Independence can mean different things. It depends on your age and maturity. Basically, independence means separating from parents, standing alone, and accepting the responsibility to govern yourself.

Few parents want to hold back the growing independence of their adolescent children, but many are concerned about the timetable. Parents usually prefer a slower, more gradual schedule. Teens want freedoms more quickly.

Some sons and daughters ask for more independence than they really want. In other cases parents hold them back too much. Parents have to feel needed and wanted. Also, parents are still responsible for you in some ways even after you are able to take care of yourself.

Open warfare is hurtful to both sides and often destroys family harmony. The battle for independence may become a full-scale war when parents use power and force to get their way. Adolescents respond to such tactics with hit-and-run attacks. Or sometimes both sides withdraw and refuse to have anything to do with the other.

Parents and adolescents can find ways to get along better when at least one parent or other caring adult shows love and concern for the teenager. However, even with love, disagreements about limits or boundaries still pop up from time to time.

Teens want to know what parents think. Even though they are eager to get along better with parents, and to earn their respect, teens also need to test the limits put on them.

Limits help you to build inner controls. However, rules and regulations that are too strict can make adolescents too dependent. Or they may become angry with the rules and break them.

Too few limits aren't much better. Without any foul lines it's easy to feel unloved, neglected, scared, and worthless.

Although some disagreement between generations is sure to occur, conflict need not be unhealthy or destructive. Dissent does not have to erupt into all-out warfare.

Life is better for all when parents and children express their real feelings and concerns, then listen carefully to hear the words of the other.

TERMS		
Rebellion	Psychological warfare	Testing limits
Independence	Withdrawal	Defensive reactions
Conflict	Limits	

UNIT III
Brother and Sister

CHAPTER 8

Getting Along Together

CASE EXAMPLE

When he was a boy, former President Dwight D. Eisenhower carried the family nickname of "Little Ike." He and his older brother Edgar, "Big Ike," were close throughout life. However, intense feelings of competition reaching back to childhood often pitted them against each other.

Edgar was almost two years older than Dwight. He had a big advantage when the boys had fist fights for the sheer joy of slugging one another. Dwight's goal in those days was "to lick Ed."

In later years, when Edgar was a lawyer in Tacoma, Washington, and Dwight was president, there were times when the older brother still thought he knew best. Once Edgar publicly criticized a proposed national budget as too big. The President smiled wryly. He said, "Edgar has been criticizing me since I was five years old."

Even so, Edgar and Ike were also close friends. When fourteen-year-old Dwight got blood poisoning after skinning his knee, Edgar wouldn't let the doctor amputate his brother's leg. After high school, each agreed to work for a year at a creamery to pay for the other's college education.

Little Ike and Big Ike combined the fierce rivalry and close friendship of many family members.

SIBS

Brothers and sisters are called *siblings*, or *sibs* for short. Having sibs or not always influences your own personality. Sibs help decide your interests and feelings about yourself. They also determine how well you get along with others, and perhaps even the person you choose to marry—or not to marry. In this unit, you'll read about some of the ways siblings shape your life, and how you affect theirs.

Siblings may remain close friends for a lifetime.

Natalie Leimkuhler
Brothers and sisters can be good friends.

147

Like many brothers, Ben and Tom are often together. At the time, each may follow his own special interest.

Sibs share food and bedrooms. They borrow money and clothing. They confide secrets and daydreams. They help each other. As with the Eisenhowers, they often remain loyal friends throughout life. However, some brothers and sisters do not grow close. Their sex and age differences, likes and dislikes, keep them apart.

ADVANTAGES

"Blood is thicker than water" is an old saying. Ties of family loyalty and affection usually develop before any closeness with persons who are not relatives.

In families where parents keep the peace, don't play favorites, and protect each child from too much hurt, siblings can toughen one another against some of the bumps and bruises of life. For example, consider these advantages. As you read think about how they apply to you.

● Brothers and sisters introduce you to the real world of cut-throat competition. Parents often act soft. They let you win in games, or give you an extra turn.

Sibs are true rivals who insist that you play by the rules (but don't mind cheating a little themselves). Then they wipe you out in a game of checkers without showing any mercy.

● Brothers and sisters help keep each other from spending too much time with adults. Siblings treat one another more like equals. They prepare each other for the strict rules of getting along with persons in their own age range.

● Brothers and sisters draw the fine line of "what's mine and what's yours." They teach you to respect the property of others if you want the same treatment in return. In the sibling scramble, you learn to give a little in order to get a little.

● Brothers and sisters often understand each other and their problems. In fact, many siblings continue to confide in, advise, and help each other throughout life.

● Brothers and sisters stimulate each other to do a little better or try a little harder. The struggles of sibs to outdo each other can lend zest to life. Rivalry produces winners of Nobel peace prizes and Olympic gold medals around the world. At home, an older child may set an example that the younger ones imitate. In some families all the children work hard to complete high school, attend college, and succeed as adults. Each competes to match the model set by an older child. In other families, younger children try to keep pace by being leaders in street struggles or by making money in odd jobs.

● Brothers and sisters provide the other with a clear picture of what each is really like. Siblings are keen observers. They know each other's weaknesses and strengths as well. You may fool a parent into believing that your intentions are good when they're not. However, it's mighty hard to trick a battle-hardened sib. Years of playing, trading, and working together develop a sharp knowledge of the other's tactics. Each builds a "you can't fool me" attitude.

Private and personal. Have you ever had an ongoing argument with a brother or sister that no longer seems important to you?

Are there any disagreements still going on?

Can you recall when one of your sibs was really helpful or kind to you?

During the past week in what ways have you been sincerely generous or loving to a sibling?

If not at all, do you wish that you could have been more friendly and helpful?

Any idea what keeps you from doing and saying the things you would like to?

JUSTICE FOR ALL

Many brothers and sisters try to work out their own disagreements and let parents "break it up" only when the conflict gets out of control. Actually, parents can be mistaken about "who started it." Adults often assign blame and even punish the wrong child (to the delight—or shame—of the real culprit).

Sibling justice is often rough, but it's usually swift, direct, and fair. Brothers and sisters seem to know, often better than parents, what sort of things are out of line. Also, sibs may punish each other without "telling." In fact, sibs use parent-like rules to control each other.

Brothers and sisters often accuse each other of their own worst habits, such as lying or stealing. Claiming that someone else has your own weakness is a defense used to deny that a fault exists in you. If you do blame others for your

Natalie Leimkuhler
"Mother said it's my turn!"

own drawbacks once in a while, you are quite normal. Once you become aware of such habits in yourself you can begin to change them.

FAMILY SIZE

The number of children in a family helps decide the role assigned to each and how the members treat each other. The average American family includes two children. In theory, at least, everything gets divided in half. In smaller families children have more contact with parents. Often the sibs get better grades in school and show more ambition than those from larger families.

In larger families, children spend a lot more time with each other and less with parents. With six or more family members, children tend to gain independence earlier. In turn, however, they usually carry more responsibilities. Parents run the family, but they expect older sibs to help out. Firstborn children are assigned to look after younger ones. Sometimes the oldest might have to keep house, shop, or do other chores.

Rohn Engh

When love and warmth fill the home, members of large families feel comfortable with each other.

As any group grows larger, a need to be organized and have leaders grows, too. Rules tend to be stricter. Parents of large families often use force more than reason.

CASE EXAMPLE

The D family is larger than any you may know. There are eighteen children ranging from as old as twenty-two years to as young as five months.

Their case shows how one very big family keeps going. As you read, think about how things differ in your home.

The D's are a close, efficient group. The parents are strong, stable people who delight in their children.

Mrs. D estimates that in one week the family consumes sixteen extra-large loaves of bread, twenty-six gallons of milk, five boxes of cereal and the giant size of everything else. "If I wasn't organized," claims Mrs. D, "we'd have a madhouse. Fortunately there's enough money to meet everyone's needs, although careful management is essential. We even go to church in shifts. None of our children have been in trouble.

"We have a dishwasher. One child clears the table and stacks the dishes. Another cleans pots and sweeps. Jobs rotate. Chores are done because you live here. The girls usually fold the clothes and put them away. The boys do the yard work, clean the basement and garage.

"Even bedtime is organized into three shifts. The older kids help the younger ones to get washed and into bed."

Something to think about. In the D family the girls did the laundry. The boys took care of the heavier work in the yard. However, both helped with kitchen clean-up.

In your home, do chores get divided according to sex?

If yes, give reasons why.

Could all housework be done just as well by members of either sex? Explain.

What about me? Knowing what you know about brothers and sisters, explain how it would feel to be the oldest in the D family. The youngest? One of the sixteen in the middle?

BROTHER OR SISTER

The sex of your sibs will affect your interests and abilities. Boys with brothers nearly always play rougher and tougher. Girls with sisters are more likely to enjoy gentle pastimes.

In one study, children were asked to choose their favorite activities. Boys with sisters often showed less interest in sports than did boys with brothers. Preferring planning to win more than playing, the boys with sisters seem to enjoy plotting the strategy more than the action of the game.

Girls with brothers were more likely to develop active outdoor skills like tree-climbing or fort-building. Boys with brothers more often favored baseball, football, camping out, building things, and "cops and robbers" type games. Girls with sisters preferred dolls, playing house or school, acting, and handcrafts.

What about me? The sex of your sibs may help decide the kinds of interests and special abilities you develop. Think of your own experience. If you are a girl with sisters, what games did you play together as children? If a boy with brothers? If you are a girl with brothers, or a boy with sisters, what kinds of games did you play? How might an only child learn to enjoy many different games and activities?

AGE

The greater the age spread between sibs, the less competition and jealousy they are likely to experience. When

Natalie Leimkuhler

As the number of years between siblings increases, the amount of jealousy and competition decreases.

more than six years separate two sibs, each grows up more like an only child.

Especially if they are the same sex, sibs close in age get thrown together, like it or not. They share meals and toys, trips to the doctor and the dentist. They may even get punished together for causing trouble.

What about me? Think of one way a brother or sister has influenced your life. Imagine that you have a sibling six years older. You share neither the same school nor the same friends. Now suppose that same brother or sister is just one or two years older than you. What would be the same or different in the way you get along? For your interests? Your friends? Your school life?

151

MORE ABOUT ROLES

Depending on whether it seems attractive or not, a successful actor either accepts or rejects a role in a play or movie. Family members get no such choice. Roles may be assigned because of age or sex even before a child is born. The larger the family, the more likely each child will be expected to act or behave in a certain way.

The number of roles in a family increases with each new arrival. As you know, the first child usually gets the Assistant Mother role. The youngest may get the Spoiled Brat role.

What about me? Following are some roles that sibs either inherit, take, or get assigned. Notice that each role may have an opposite held by another sib. Or it may stay unfilled. Which roles, if any, fit you? What other roles could you add to the list?

DO NOT WRITE IN THIS BOOK.

Some Sibling Roles

Most affectionate . . .Least affectionate
Best liked . . . . Least liked
Most responsible . . . Least responsible
Most studious . . . . Least studious
Most ambitious . . . . . . Least ambitious
Most spoiled . . . . Least spoiled
Loner . . . . Most sociable
Most generous . . . . Most selfish

As noted before, roles get assigned early. Also, they tend to stick even after sibs get much older. Sometimes a child gets put in a role that doesn't fit very well.

For example, a boy assigned a certain role in a family (such as The Smartest) may get an unpleasant surprise when people outside the family don't treat him the same way. You might be the brightest one in your family but meet stiffer competition at school.

Children can also get pigeonholed into unattractive or unwanted roles. Things usually go better if a role fits

right and makes you feel good. If you are called The Brain and you really do enjoy books and study, getting assigned to a bookworm role may spur your interest in reading.

However, suppose you hear over and over that you are The Slow Poke, or Lazy Bones. In time you may begin to wonder about your own abilities. You may suspect that others know more about you than you know about yourself. In such situations, role assignments can cause a damaged self-concept.

CASE EXAMPLE

Sidney is called "The Moody One" in his family. Anytime he chooses to be alone in his room, or whenever he growls at his sister, everyone nods as if to say, "Sid is in one of his moods again." Sid may prefer quiet, or like to read. However, the family treats him as if he must grump from one mood to the next. In time Sid may begin to think of himself as 100 percent moody, and actually become more glum than ever.

Or Sidney may resist the role assignment and protest, "I'm not moody!" However, deep inside he is forced to wonder and think, "If that's what they believe me to be, I might as well act moody." The opinions of others can shape not only a person's actions but also the self-concept.

Roles are assigned in other ways. In some families, the oldest son often inherits a name, a position (first, second, third), and an expectation. John Smith III may be destined for the law or medicine if his ancestors were in the same professions. John may prefer to teach, farm, or start a business, but the pressures to follow the assigned family role are

Every sibling is part of a larger
family group.

strong. Roles get passed from generation to generation, just like a piece of
jewelry. If one person becomes outstanding in a family, a talent search may
go on in the next generation to find
someone to take the same role.

CASE EXAMPLE

Sometimes, the Black Sheep role
gets handed down in much the same
way. In one family, Kitty, the oldest
girl, was often criticized for her selfish behavior. Actually, she often did
act self-centered and uncaring about
others. Her younger brother resented

her the most. When the brother grew
up and became a father, he often
found himself greatly annoyed at any
sign of selfishness in his firstborn
daughter, Helen. "You're selfish, just
like your Aunt Kitty," the father would
scold. Helen dreaded such criticism
because she always wanted to be
seen as kind and generous. Even at a
very early age, the child sensed how
deeply her father resented Aunt Kitty,
his older sister.

Of course, words like "selfish" or
"generous" never fully describe anyone.

Natalie Leimkuhler

Big sister's birthday is fun time for everyone in the family. Even though siblings grow up and leave home, parties like this strengthen lasting bonds of love and friendship.

Each person has many different qualities. Also, you grow and change in many ways as you mature.

If you get stuck with a role you don't like, try to remember that adults sometimes assign them because of their own needs or past experiences. The adults may be wrong or unfair in the labels they hang on you.

Simply because someone says you are selfish or moody doesn't mean that you must act that way. Suppose there are some things about yourself that you don't like. If you get assigned to a role that doesn't fit, you can change things. No one must stay locked into an unwanted life-style.

CHANGE

Many things change in families, even though ties remain close. Parents grow older. You mature. An older sister marries. A brother moves out. Roles change, too. For example, when an older sib leaves home a younger child probably will inherit new freedom and responsibilities. Young Sam describes it this way.

CASE EXAMPLE

"My older brother Jerry influenced me greatly for the good. He taught me how to share. Even though we fought a lot, we never had an argument that lasted more than a day. Now that he's married and I'm the oldest child at home, I understand what he went through. I used to wonder how anybody could be so patient with a goofy little brother bothering him all the time. Things are different when you become Number One with a goofy little sister to bother you!"

NOT EVERY FAMILY IS AVERAGE

Not everyone lives in a so-called average family. Parents lose jobs. Some get divorces or separate. Stepparents or new stepsiblings move into, or out of, the family home. Some life crises may tear brothers and sisters apart or force them closer together by making them more dependent on each other.

CASE EXAMPLE

Marilyn talks of such changes in her family. She says, "My mother just got her second divorce. My older sister is really a half sister. Mom divorced Sis's father to marry my dad. Then my brother and I came along.

"I can't express how much my older stepsister means to us. We love her and think of her as a second mother. She was about twelve when Mom divorced our father. Now Mom works evenings, so Sis started taking care of us after school. She has a lot of responsibility. When she wants to do something with her friends, one of us always tags along. She says she doesn't mind. She sure never shows any signs that we're pests."

Marilyn's experience shows that family problems can bring brothers and sisters closer. When parents are out of the home, siblings may help each other in many ways.

LEARNING TO MANAGE STRONG FEELINGS

The family is the place where you learn about love and loyalty and all the good feelings that help you enjoy being with others. However, the family is also the place where you get your first taste of strong negative emotions like anger and aggression.

Early in life, for example, you meet frustrations that lead to anger. Imagine that a toy you want is out of reach. Mother says no when you want to hear yes.

Children soon learn how to control angry emotions or to hold them in check until they can be drained out with less risk. Every child learns early that parents are bigger, stronger, and more powerful people who can punish and withhold love.

Aggression. Brothers and sisters often use each other to express aggression (uh-GRESH-un). Aggression happens when one person attacks another with words or weapons. Aggression plays a big part in the give and take between brothers and sisters.

During early adolescence aggressive feelings develop. They can lead to arguments and angry challenges between siblings. For example, frustration often causes aggression. Think about it. Who can frustrate you so much as a sib? Who can find your weak spots so well? Who can cut you down more?

Brothers are more likely to show open aggression with each other. They might punch, wrestle, or shove. Sisters sometimes use the same tactics. They also pull hair, pinch, and push. Or they may attack with nasty insults. Whether male or female, when sibs are frustrated enough they are likely to act out their anger with aggressive tactics.

Siblings often take out their aggressive emotions directly. Brothers and sisters are natural and handy targets. It's not a good idea to take a poke at a parent. There are fewer risks in teasing or fighting with sibs. As a result, anger and aggression are often turned in full force on an irritating sibling. Brothers and sisters may try to punish each other for aggression, but they can't stay aloof for long while living in the same family.

Experience with siblings can help you to learn how to control aggression and how to use your anger in healthy ways. You can also learn how to stand up for yourself and state your complaints even if you are smaller and weaker. As you will read, younger sibs discover clever ways to upset older rivals.

PERMANENT DAMAGE?

"You're a big liar!"

"You're a phoney!"

Sometimes attacks like these hit home and force sibs to face up to their own faults. However, such accusations are often shouted in anger and stretched a

Charles Riker

Siblings close in age often share good times. It is easy to see that these sisters are enjoying a day at the beach.

little, even though they may contain some truth. Also, one child in a family can turn out to be the scapegoat—the sib who gets blamed automatically for causing trouble.

"Bill did it" or "It's Bill's fault" can be familiar battle cries on a home front where Bill wears the scapegoat label.

It's one thing to criticize how the other person behaves. Human actions can be changed. It's a lot more damaging to attack another's appearance or personality. For example, one sibling can deeply hurt another by sneering, "Your legs are too fat" or "Your ears stick out."

In some families, faultfinding of this type nibbles away at a person's self-concept. Continual criticism, unrelieved

by praise and encouragement, can make young children and adolescents both self-conscious and discouraged.

Competition and criticism are seldom sweetened with compliments and kindness. Fights and insults can be the standard methods of handling the frustrations of living close together in a family. In such situations siblings may learn to dislike and distrust each other.

Continual fighting or cutting remarks are harmful to both the victim and the attacker. Such learned ways of mistreating each other can last a lifetime.

You be the counselor. Terry is fifteen, her sister Heather, fourteen. They battle about everything, including who does the most housework. In fact, they rarely agree on anything.

One day Terry realized that she had some control over what happened between her and Heather. Since nothing else seemed to work, and she was sick of all the fighting, Terry made a decision that changed her life.

No matter what Heather said or did, Terry would not fight back.

At first it wasn't easy. Terry had to keep reminding herself how to play her secret game with her younger sister. Her basic rule was to ignore all of Heather's familiar attempts to start an argument.

After a few days, Terry added a second rule: whenever Heather said or did anything nice, Terry would be nice in return.

The results were amazing. Terry actually managed to change Heather's habit of teasing and baiting. When she got no reaction from Terry with her usual tactics, Heather began to change.

And, to the older sister's surprise, Terry also changed her own aggressive and nasty behavior. Together the sisters earned a fresh start with each other.

What do you think of Terry's method?

In your own words, explain what Terry did to change Heather's aggressive behavior.

Why did it work?

Although she hadn't planned to change her own tactics, Terry also discovered that she was no longer angry at Heather. How would you explain that?

If you considered it necessary, could the same plan work in your family?

The case that follows describes many of the influences and attitudes that flow between siblings. Sara's story shows just how complicated life with sibs can be. The case will also help you understand how family life forms personality development and the growth of relationships.

As you read, notice how each sister was assigned a certain role. Keep alert for the many emotions at work.

CASE EXAMPLE

Sara is a pretty and popular teenager, the youngest of three daughters. Jill is seven years older than Sara, making her more an Assistant Mother than an older sister. Jill is already living away from home and doesn't play a big part in this story. However, Lisa, the middle sister, is only a year older than Sara. The closeness of their ages has greatly influenced both their lives.

Here are Sara's own words: "I love my sisters, but Lisa and I are especially close. Yet when we were little we fought all the time. No matter who started the fight, I soon learned that I could run to mother and Lisa would get scolded. I took advantage of being the baby. Lisa got punished for many of the mean things I did.

"Our birthdays are a few days apart, so our parties were held together. We dressed the same. We looked alike. We were often treated as twins. I liked that because Lisa was older and I got to share her

Natalie Leimkuhler
These sisters look alike. Although they share much, each has friends and interests all her own.

157

privileges. But Lisa hated the equal treatment and felt cheated.

"I always knew Lisa was jealous of me but I didn't understand why. Now I can think of lots of reasons. We were constantly compared. Once, I overheard my third grade teacher ask Mother why Lisa wasn't as good a student as her sisters. I think Lisa heard, too. As she grew older she seemed to lose confidence in her intelligence. She gradually developed a negative attitude.

"When Lisa started junior high she began acting stupid. She'd play the part of the clown to get attention. Sometimes she is funny. Most of the time she's just a butt of a group joke.

"Lisa flunked two courses in junior high, but my parents didn't seem surprised. In fact, I remember hearing them say they didn't expect Lisa to graduate from high school. They'd often compare her to Jill, who is a real brain, and to me. I get better grades than Lisa but she is really smarter than I am.

"In fact, Lisa is pretty and intelligent. She has real depth. But she plays up her looks. She gets upset when she doesn't look perfect. Sometimes I wonder if she feels so second-rate in everything else that she tries to look beautiful at all times.

"Our competition started very early. Without meaning to, our parents encouraged our rivalry. We received everything in pairs. When I needed glasses, Lisa wanted them too. She has perfect vision, but when I got contact lenses, she sulked for days.

"Even today, if I need a new blouse, Lisa claims she deserves one too. This year my mother asked me to tell Lisa that I bought my winter coat with money I earned last summer. My parents actually paid for it. But they didn't want to have a fight about buying Lisa a coat she didn't need. No two people wear out clothes at the same time. I wonder why my parents don't explain that to us.

"I also wonder if our parents try to show us that they are very fair in giving us *things*. They divide up clothes and money to prove they are fair because they can't divide up love and favoritism equally.

"We all know that my father favors Jill, even though he's affectionate to Lisa and me. I am my mother's favorite. Lisa is nobody's pet.

"Even though I think it's unfair, I can't blame my parents entirely for their treatment of Lisa. She is very cold. Yet she expects them to be warm to her. I've seen her turn away from my father's hugs until he finally stopped showing affection. Mom still kisses us goodnight, but Lisa never smiles or kisses her back.

"When we were much younger Lisa accused my parents of favoring Jill and me. It's hard to say whether she is a naturally cold person or whether my parents caused her to be that way. I was always an affectionate child, so it seemed natural that my parents were more loving to me.

"I feel hurt when Lisa is mean to my mother and cold to my father. But I also get angry when my parents cut her down and make her feel inferior. I know Lisa better than anyone. She is so lonely. I am the only one she can talk to. I love my sister and I love my parents but I don't know how to make things better."

TALKING HELPS

As often happens in a family, the person who feels most upset about family fights looks for help. Even though it seems that Lisa had the real problems, it was Sara who spoke with a counselor.

After talking so openly about herself and her family, Sara understood many things better. She learned, for example, that children often receive role assignments, whether they like them or not. Although her parents never planned it that way, Sara was assigned a Good Girl role because of her sunny disposition. She enjoyed the praise and affection she earned for her pleasing behavior. Being sweet and nice brought many rewards, so Sara worked extra hard to fill her role.

Lisa, it seems, was born with a different temperament. Even as a baby she was known for her fussy tantrums and her independent ways. As she grew older she was often sulky and uncooperative. Gradually she seemed to fall into a role of Bad Girl. Her emotional behavior earned her a lot of attention, but most of it was negative.

Of course, the parents did not tell the girls to act as they did. The parents didn't have to do that. The combination of Sara's and Lisa's natural dispositions, plus the many times the parents noticed, talked about, and reinforced their roles, helped make the roles stick.

Sara's counselor encouraged her to think through such past events. One day she asked Sara if she had helped keep Lisa in the Bad Girl role. Sara was shocked. She protested, "No! I'm the only one who ever sticks up for Lisa!"

Yet Sara went away wondering about the counselor's remark. The next week she reported, "I was afraid to come here today. I had to admit that I was made to look good compared to Lisa. I liked that. I really thought I never did anything to invite the comparisons between us. But that's not true. There were times when I tried to make myself look better than Lisa. I still do. My parents brag about the good things I do. But when I disappoint them they say, "You're acting just like Lisa.""

There is no neat answer to Sara's story. It is simply one small part taken from her family's history. The case appears here to illustrate role types in one home.

Each family member sees things from a different viewpoint. It's difficult to sort out who influences whom and how much. All sibs affect each other. Parents in turn influence all brothers and sisters.

Something to think about. Suppose Lisa and Sara were six years apart rather than just one. How would the greater age difference change what happens between them?

Make a list. A TV show called "Brothers & Sisters" is in the making. You have been invited to be a paid advisor.

The director wants to record your family on film. What daily events in your family would be the most help to a TV audience in terms of understanding what goes on between the siblings?

For example, would you select any of the following?

If yes, write your reasons on a separate sheet of paper.

DO NOT WRITE IN THIS BOOK.

- Breakfast time.
- Use of the telephone.
- Sharing "family property," such as a hair dryer.

Make a list of other family events you would select to give a true picture of sibling give-and-take in your home.

Something to think about. In this chapter you read that some competition

159

between sibs can spur each to accomplish more in life.

What is "enough" competition?

What is too much?

Should parents set some foul lines for sibling behavior with each other?

If yes, describe what you consider to be limits that are both sensible and fair.

What about me? This chapter suggests that it is difficult to fool a sib about your true intentions.

In what ways can a brother or sister understand you better than anyone else?

In what ways do you understand your brother or sister better than anyone else?

To learn more. Select one idea or topic from this chapter that applies to you and the way you live your life.

On a separate sheet of paper describe your selection in one sentence.

In no more than three sentences explain why you chose it.

DO NOT WRITE IN THIS BOOK.

RECAP

Brothers and sisters permanently shape each other's lives. Affection, loyalty, competition, and jealousy are all mixed together in the early years.

The sibling scramble toughens young people for school and neighborhood contacts. Brothers and sisters help each other with problems. Often, sibs are forced to find ways to settle their disagreements so parents won't interfere. Learning to negotiate and to get along in the world are part of the human relationships that come from living with sibs.

Siblings feed each other important personal information. It's as though they hold up mirrors to each other, pointing out faults and flaws, and sometimes strengths and virtues.

The larger the family, the more time sibs spend with each other and the more complicated the relationships. Sex differences also help decide the interests and abilities sibs develop. Boys with brothers are usually more athletic than boys without brothers. Girls with sisters are less active and athletic in their interests. Boys with sisters concentrate on planning how to win. Girls with brothers are more likely to learn and enjoy outdoor skills and games.

The wider the age gap, the less sibs will have in common. The closer their age, the more sibs are thrown together in almost everything they do.

Children may get assigned to special family roles because of their particular personalities, talents, or place in the line-up. Because some sibs like their role assignments, they work hard to keep them. Those who dislike their roles may protest because the labels seem unfair or untrue.

If you get a role that you don't like or one that seems not to suit you, you need not stay in it. Roles often change as parents, brothers, and sisters grow older. A middle or younger sib may inherit a favored role when an older sib leaves home.

Even though family relationships change, sibling ties can remain close. In fact, when parents are divorced or absent from the home, brothers and sisters may depend more on each other.

Siblings use each other to learn how to express emotions, both positive and negative. In fact, learning to express and control anger and aggression is often learned from sibs. However, unless parents control full-scale hostilities between siblings, the children may grow up with permanent bad feelings about themselves and others.

Family life is complicated. Each member influences every other one in countless ways. Each, in turn, is shaped by every other member.

TERMS

Siblings	Role assignments	The Smartest	Scapegoat
Sibs	Black Sheep	The Brain	Good Girl
Competition	Aggression	Bookworm	Bad Girl
Jealousy	Criticism	Slow Poke	
Loyalty	Assistant Mother	Lazy Bones	
Sibling roles	Spoiled Brat	The Moody One	

CHAPTER 9

Siblings as Rivals and Friends

Sisters and brothers are like members of a marching band. When all members play on key, the band makes enjoyable music. If one plays at a different tempo, or loud enough to drown out the others, discord results.

Parents are like band conductors. They select the music and plan the line of march. Ideally, the family adults arrange for each child to play a solo once in a while.

Sibling rivalry is a common term that refers to the natural tug-of-war that takes place in families with children whose ages are just a year or two apart. These urges of rivalry and competition receive special attention in this chapter. The ongoing struggle between brothers and brothers, sisters and sisters, or brothers and sisters, is an important fact in your life. How you decide to handle the rivalry at home helps decide how you will get along with other persons outside your home. And the way you learn to build relationships with non-family members can last for a lifetime.

In this chapter you'll also read how the attitudes and behavior of parents influence how siblings get along with each other.

Being raised with siblings is a little like living on a rehearsal stage for adult life. You get a chance to act in many short plays of real human drama. You may struggle for recognition and power. Or you may practice love and generosity, and let others have their way.

FRIENDLY RIVALS

In every family, even the best-natured and most affectionate, brothers and sisters compete with each other. Each keeps an eye on "who gets what" in terms of money, privileges, clothes, and even living space.

The most intense, four-fisted rivalry happens when children are the same sex and spaced two years or less apart. The more years that separate children, the shorter time they live together. As a result they share fewer experiences and seldom develop into keen rivals.

The closer sibs are to the same age, the more they try to outdo each other. Although such attitudes don't show so much during middle childhood and adolescence, actions that say "Look at me!" are unmistakable in younger children. Parents often report that following the birth of a new baby, older toddlers already toilet trained now claim they need diapers again. Or the older child may demand a baby bottle given up months before. One teenager still remembers his hurt reaction (at age three) to the birth of a sister: "What did I do wrong?"

Sibling rivalry means much more than who ends up with the biggest piece of cake or the most ice cream. Brothers and sisters also compete for the love and attention of mothers and fathers.

Natalie Leimkuhler
"I'm gonna beat my brother this time, or die trying."

"Someday I'll be just like my big brother."

Of course, rivalry doesn't have to be bad. It's very much a part of life. Children compare school grades and little league scores. Adults eye each other's cars and homes.

One way to find out who you are and how much you can do is to match yourself with others. If you come out ahead you feel good. If you place second or third your reaction will be different.

Strong emotions, both bright and dark, exist in every family. Positive emotions usually bring brothers and sisters together in moments of fun and sharing. The negative emotions can cause conflict and turn these same sibs against one another. For example, one day you may love and admire a brother or sister. At other times you may feel jealousy, resentment, or intense rivalry.

Depending on the general mood at the time, reactions to each other can also change. Sibs who fight with each other at home often join together against threats from outside the family. The brother who torments his sister in the house may jump to her defense when a neighborhood bully teases her. The sister who thinks her brother is a brat may get upset if a classmate calls him the same thing.

POWER AND CONTROL

Brothers and sisters try out different methods to control each other. A technique that seems to work one time will be used again.

Studies show that older children tend to use their age, size, and bribes to control younger sibs. When threatened, younger children plead, beg, and cry. The youngest family members attack property—like clothes or a toy—rather than persons. Boys often use force to get their way with someone of equal or smaller size. Girls most often try to make the other sib feel guilty.

One research study of siblings discovered forty different ways that brothers and sisters influence each other. Techniques range from a punch in the nose to gentle, skillful compliments.

How Siblings Try to Influence Each Other

Beat up, belt, hit
Promise to change
Boss, power, pressure
Scratch, pinch, pull hair, bite
Bribe, blackmail
Ask, request
Flatter
Wrestle, sit on, chase
Bargain
Seek parent's help
Get angry (shout, scream)
Play tricks
Cry, pout, sulk
Take turns
Break things
Explain, reason, persuade
Ask other sibs for help

Ignore

Hide things

Do something for other person

Ask for sympathy

Take things

Make other feel guilty

Annoy (change TV channel)

Pretend to be sick

Tease (name-call, pester)

Threaten to hurt

Be stubborn, refuse to move

Threaten to tell

Make a wish

Keep other from phone, bathroom

Exclude or lock out

Give things (money, clothing)

Give others a choice (TV show)

Be nice, sweet talk

Make a list. As you read the ways in which siblings try to change each other, make a list of the methods you have used at home. Use a separate sheet of paper.

DO NOT WRITE IN THIS BOOK.

When you have finished, make a second list of the methods you have never used with your siblings.

Something to think about. In your opinion, which of the tactics listed in the book have the best chance of making siblings change?

Which ones are the least effective?

Teasing is a common way that sibs let off steam and mask negative feelings for each other. Teasing is a way to needle someone without getting into a serious feud. The teaser can always protest, "I didn't mean it."

CASE EXAMPLE

Ned and Cliff fought at times but shared affection for each other and their younger sister Sally. Although both boys liked Sally, they also resented her crybaby tactics of running to mother every time they made a fuss.

Aware of Sally's fear of the dark, they joyfully used it at every opportunity. For example, they'd lie in wait at the top of the dark stairs to scare their kid sister as she came up. The great delight they shared in hearing her terrified screams helped to drain some of the annoyance they felt because of her special position in the family. When their mother scolded them, the boys would innocently protest, "Aw, Ma, we were only playing!"

Without parent supervision and intervention, teasing can get out of control. When teasing becomes mean and causes damage to persons and their property, the "kidding" is no longer harmless or innocent.

Something to think about. A lot of people tease others without ever considering the feelings of the person who is the butt of the jokes.

Make a list. On a separate sheet of paper make a list of the things that members of your group get teased about most.

DO NOT WRITE IN THIS BOOK.

SPECIAL FRIENDS

Sometimes brothers and sisters become very close. They share their talents and money. They work together, play together, trade dreams, hopes, and projects.

CASE EXAMPLE

Randy and Douglas are typical of many brothers who are close in age and interests. Sometimes they argued and fought, but more often they enjoyed a special sibling closeness. One summer they decided to pool their boundless energies and limited money to build a tree house.

It took three years and $400 to build the three-room home in the tree

Brothers Randy and Douglas work on their treehouse.

branches. The boys' hideaway was equipped with a propane heater, running water, electricity, telephone, a TV, and hi-fi.

Randy, the elder, was no raw beginner. He knew how to motorize go-carts by age eleven and could assemble a motorcycle at thirteen. Douglas was a super-scrounger. The younger brother would prowl the neighborhood early each day, beating the garbage truck to such usable treasures as broken furniture and old rugs. He also collected beams and other building parts by bargaining,

trading, or offering his labor in exchange for something the brothers needed.

The boys did most of the planning and building. Generous friends and neighbors contributed brains, muscle, equipment, and even money.

The brothers raised the bedroom with a block, tackle, and winch—using the family car to hoist the room into place. An old rickety ladder that was great for keeping parents out was later replaced by a staircase. An architect who was a family friend checked the place for safety by jumping and stomping about. He declared the tree house structurally sound.

During one period, the boys lived in the house from March to October. Their home became a favorite hangout for classmates. Each weekend as many as thirty-five kids visited. Randy and Doug had created a real teenage dream house where adolescents could get away from adults.

The total building effort called for tremendous energy and careful planning. Despite their disagreements and a natural tendency for sibling rivalry, the boys grew closer as brothers. They shared the praise and publicity they got, and they felt good about themselves and their project.

This story has an unhappy ending. The local building inspector ordered the structure torn down, perhaps because of complaints about noisy parties. However, Randy now plans to become an engineer and go on to bigger projects. He was neither angry nor bitter about the official's decision.

However, Douglas feels let down. "I was supposed to move in alone after Randy went to college," he said sadly.

Something to think about. Randy and Douglas are normal brothers. During their three-year project they often disagreed about how to build their tree house.

However, they usually settled their arguments quickly and got back to their "high-rise apartment." By working together, they accomplished far more than either could have done alone.

Are there projects that you have completed with the help of a sib that you couldn't have finished by yourself?

Have there been times when you needed some help from a sibling, but refused to ask?

If yes, do you have any idea *why* you did not request help?

You may want to compare your answers with those of a classmate.

PARENTS AND SIBLINGS

Important as the presence of each is during the growing years, brothers and sisters don't raise each other. Parents or parent substitutes pay the bills, hand out rewards and punishments, and make the major family decisions.

Even when mothers and fathers aren't around, their influence remains. Parent attitudes, preferences, and rules always affect the way that sibs get along.

Ground rules. Mothers and fathers help build the lifelong attitudes that sibs form toward each other. Parents set the ground rules. They decide how to enforce them. Some adults refuse to listen to tale-telling. Others encourage squealing to learn what really goes on when they aren't watching.

Some parents permit fighting and try not to interfere. "Settle it yourselves," they say. They may even hand out boxing gloves. Other mothers and fathers refuse to permit punching, kicking, or destruction of property. Yet they may allow verbal blows—insults and merciless teasing.

In the case that follows the family rules included:
- No shouting and screaming.
- No hitting and fighting.

As you will see, forbidding negative emotions won't make them go away. Instead, the resentments go underground. The ugly feelings may surface again later, disguised as secret plans for revenge or blackmail. As you read about Sherry and Felice, think what you would do if you were in their places.

CASE EXAMPLE

Two sisters played darts one rainy afternoon. What started as a friendly game soon turned into a heated contest with shouts of, "You cheater!" and, "You're standing too close!" Finally Sherry, the older sister, bent so far forward that she lost her balance and fell. Felice, the younger, couldn't stand the cheating any more. In a burst of rage she threw her dart into Sherry's bare foot.

Felice was filled with immediate regret. She was really afraid that she'd hurt her sister.

However, after the initial shock, Sherry quickly checked the damage: not much. The dart barely pierced her skin. It didn't even hurt. However, it dangled dramatically from her foot. Sherry saw her opportunity.

With the evidence of the offending dart in her foot she threatened, "I'm calling Mom right now to show her what you did to me—unless you let me wear your new red sweater tomorrow."

Felice quickly agreed to the truce terms. Anything was better than to be caught wounding her sister, an act forbidden in their family. Yet even while she silently turned over her

Natalie Leimkuhler

Only an hour ago Leslie and Laura had a big fight over whose turn it was to do the dishes.

precious new sweater, Felice plotted dark revenge. Her day to get even would come.

The case of Sherry and Felice shows that aggression and anger don't disappear just because parents forbid fighting. More likely the negative emotions get hidden and show up later in ways that are not so noticeable. The sisters' case also illustrates that a lot goes on between sibs that parents never see nor learn about.

You be the judge. The case of Sherry and Felice shows how parents' rules don't work all the time.

Consider the following questions. DO NOT WRITE IN THIS BOOK.

If you were Felice, how would you react to Sherry's blackmail?

If you were a parent to the girls, what ground rules would you set?

Would you forbid *all* physical acting out?

Would you permit some rough-and-tumble with no hitting? If yes, how much?

Would you tell them to settle their own arguments?

Do you have any idea why you favor the rules you would choose?

Would you like to live under the rules you have set for Sherry and Felice?

Compare your reactions with those of a classmate.

Private and personal. Sometimes parents' rules are not spelled out. Even so, everyone in the family knows exactly what they are.

Think of one rule in your family that affects the way that brothers and sisters get along.

Does the rule work?

Give reasons for your opinion.

You decide. Wendy says, "I come from a family where the first rule is to get even. If my brother broke something of mine, I was allowed to destroy something of his."

How do you like that idea for a family policy?

As a parent would you set such a rule for your children?

As a child, would you want such a rule?

Any idea why?

Write a paragraph. If you had to make one rule that would help siblings get along better, what would it be?

On a separate sheet of paper, write your proposed rule and give reasons for your choice. Write no more than four sentences.

DO NOT WRITE IN THIS BOOK.

Parents' past history. Parents were children once. Things that happened to them years ago help decide how they treat their own children today. Past events may also influence an adult to side with one child against another.

Watching a new generation of scrapping rivals can awaken old jealousies and forgotten resentments. So parents may sympathize with a child who holds the same position in the family that the mother or father held while growing up. For example, a mother who was always "second" when she was little may feel a special sympathy for her own second child.

Such influences from a parent's past may be remembered or not. In either case, parent behavior can be formed by relationships with siblings that happened years ago.

FAVORITISM

Real or imagined favorites appear in every family. Other than the only child, who is an automatic favorite, every brother or sister watches closely to discover what parent likes which child best.

A normal kind of favoritism helps each child feel special at times. Suppose, unasked, you sweep the garage, or clean the windows. Your mother expresses surprise and gratitude. For that moment you really are a favorite.

Another kind of favoritism often blossoms when a child indicates love or appreciation for a parent. "You are a very good father," said one. It's a rare parent who wouldn't like to hear such a compliment.

Normal parent favoritism shifts from day to day, from child to child, according to moods and events. Fathers and mothers may deeply love all their children, yet prefer one today and a second tomorrow. "My favorite is the one who's not a pest right now," explained one busy mother. If you think about it, you'll probably discover that there are times when you deserve to feel favored and other times when you don't.

Fortunately, most parents can find something lovable in each child. When parents are aware that they tend to favor one sib over another, they can often control their feelings and refuse to play favorites.

Of course, parents can be fooled. Sometimes they pick the wrong offender or protect the wrong victim. "Remember the time you punished Greg for hitting me?" a younger sister asked her mother. "It really wasn't his fault. I teased him until he hit me. Then I cried and ran to tell you. You punished him instead of me!" With a huge, satisfied grin, she added, "It was worth it!"

Favoring "baby." Parents sometimes side with younger children because they are smaller and less experienced. Adults listen more readily to their complaints and cries for help. At any age, a younger child—especially the baby of the family—is less likely to be scolded or punished. Such treatment doesn't escape the eagle-eyed vigilance of older sibs. In fact, older children often complain about such favoritism that seems unfair to them.

The arrival of any new baby also reduces the amount of attention paid to older children. Older sibs may feel left out or replaced. Such attitudes may linger for a lifetime.

Even though older children compete with a younger sib for parent attention, this rivalry need not be harmful. Much depends on the way problems are handled.

Something to think about. Some parents claim that they treat all their children the same. No one child is a favorite.

Natalie Leimkuhler
"Hey Sis, how do you spell 'nature'?"

often find it hard to assert themselves in a family of older sisters.

A girl with older brothers stands a better chance for special treatment than a girl with older sisters. The same holds true for a boy with older sisters rather than older brothers.

Simply, after one or more sons or daughters, parents usually hope for a change. If an infant of the wished-for sex arrives, the new baby may be treated almost as an only child.

What about me? How has the sex of your sibling(s) influenced your life?

For example, if you are a girl with a brother, how has your experience been different than if your sib had been a sister?

Sibling favorites. If parents influence what goes on between brothers and sisters, so do siblings themselves. If parents play favorites sometimes, so do children.

Have you ever preferred one parent to the other? Siblings are often quite open about a favorite brother or sister. When there are more than two children in a family, two will often team up against one.

During early adolescence, most girls prefer a sister to a brother. As they grow older, sisters often switch to brothers, and to older brothers rather than younger ones. Older brothers are less likely to tease or insult them.

Adolescent boys also prefer the company of brothers. However, they tend to favor ones that are younger rather than older because younger boys are more likely to hero-worship. An older brother may act too important or bossy.

Of course, in any family, the personalities of brothers and sisters make a big difference. In families where there are several children of the same sex, girls

Such parents claim that no child gets more attention, love, or privileges than any other.

In your opinion, is it possible for a parent to treat each sibling exactly like all the others?

If so, explain how.

If not, give your reasons.

Sexism and favoritism. Another kind of favoritism may arise in a family. Siblings of the same sex compete more, fight more, and feel more jealousy toward each other. However, the more children of the same sex in a family, the less likely it is that parents will show preference to any particular one. Yet when a girl is sister to both an older and a younger brother, or if a boy arrives after two or three girls, each may get extra attention.

An only boy born after two or three girls may not find life so easy in spite of extra parent attention. Younger brothers favor sisters whose interests are similar and who show the most affection and acceptance. Both brothers and sisters often show a special fondness for a handicapped child, no matter the age or sex. Siblings may also feel protective to a child they think is picked on by parents or teachers. However, any "parent's pet" is rarely a favorite among the rest of the children.

Following is a case of sibling favoritism. As you read, ask yourself if you would react as Tim does to his three sisters. Put yourself in the place of each sister and try to imagine the attitude of each toward their older brother.

CASE EXAMPLE

Tim is both firstborn and the only boy in his family. He often feels like a third parent. He says, "I feel responsible about how my sisters turn out." Yet Tim also admits his impatience with the girls when they refuse to listen to him, or they don't learn as fast as he'd like.

Tim's give-and-take with each sister is different. He fights most with Christie, the oldest girl. They are real rivals. Christie challenges Tim's authority and often refuses to accept his advice. With a hint of embarrassment, Tim admits that he once punched Christie in the mouth. Most of the time they settle for insults and threats, he reports.

"Christie, fourteen, never does what I say. Jenny, who's eleven, sometimes listens to me. Kate, who's seven, always does." He openly admits he favors little Kate, who in turn adores him. Yet, he quickly adds, "I feel close to all my sisters. They all rely on me.

"I feel under a lot of pressure to be

Kathy Tuite
The early stages of a solid friendship.

as good as they expect me to be. Last summer, when I went to camp, Mom said that Kate slept in my bed for the first three nights. She missed me so much. When I got home, they all treated me like a king, even Christie. The first morning, Kate climbed up in my lap to watch cartoons on TV. I guess I love them all a lot."

Something to think about. In terms of what you already know about feelings between brothers and sisters, why does Tim favor Kate? Suppose you were speaking for Jenny or Christie? How might either describe their older brother? Why does Christie seem challenging and competitive to Tim when the younger girls do not?

Sudden change. A serious illness or a sudden accident may also change the ways that sibs are expected to relate to each other. In the case that follows, the oldest boy, Ralph, was resented by his younger brother, Vic. Ralph was not a bossy or bullying older brother at all. In fact, Ralph spent much of his early childhood either in hospitals or in the house watching his younger brothers play outside.

CASE EXAMPLE

Vic says, "I resented my older brother Ralph. He got so much extra attention. He was a crybaby and temperamental. He got sick with asthma a lot. We always had to let him have his way so he wouldn't get upset and start wheezing. Sometimes he faked his breathing just to get us to do what he wanted. Finally, things go so bad that my folks went to talk to a shrink [psychiatrist]. He told them they should be tougher on Ralph. It took a while, but now they aren't so easy on him. They don't make the rest of us give in to him so much. When he has an attack they just give him his medicine and leave him alone for a while.

"I think Ralph learned that he must cooperate, too. Things are better all around at home."

Finish this case in another way.

Suppose the parents ignored the psychiatrist's advice and continued to cater to Ralph.

In that case, how would Vic describe his feelings toward his sickly older brother?

How about toward his parents?

Later life. Brothers and sisters grow up and part company. Yet their influence lingers on. Attitudes learned in childhood carry on into adult life. Take a common example: You know the experience of liking or disliking someone at first sight. You might make such a judgment before the new person says a word. Reasons for such swift decisions often lie in sibling experiences from years ago.

CASE EXAMPLE

One grown man found it difficult to work for older women. He bristled in the presence of female supervisors. Even bank tellers and saleswomen made him nervous.

Finally he talked with a counselor who helped him discover that *younger* women in authority didn't bother him at all. Only *older* women caused him trouble.

As you might guess, he grew up with a bossy older sister who watched over him while their mother worked. The girl resented her assignment. She did her job well, but she rarely gave the little boy any tenderness or love. In fact, she frequently scolded him and tattled to their mother about his small misbehaviors. The mother backed up the sister when she scolded or punished the little boy. Many years later, older women in authority still stirred up those feelings of resentment from years ago.

Of course, all little boys don't grow up resenting their older sisters. The point of the case is that childhood attitudes—both pleasant and unpleasant—may hang on long after you grow up and part company with sibs.

Many older brothers and sisters forgive their sibs the battles of childhood and grow closer as the years pass. Others may keep a little war going. Some continue to compete with each other in childish ways.

CASE EXAMPLE

Two sisters, both now grandmothers as well as close and loyal friends, recall their early struggles. The younger still accuses the older: "The only time you'd let me play with your

Greg and Sue belong to the "traditional American family" of two parents and two children. In small families, siblings spend a lot of time together. They play, compete with one another, and get into trouble once in a while. This brother and sister are grown and separated today, but they still share a special closeness. You can see how they look as adults on pages 24 and 38.

friends was when I'd be the slave and wait on you!"

The older laughs, but defends herself, "You were a pest. You always butted in and wanted to do what I did." It all happened years ago, but the memories are fresh. Do such squabbles sound familiar to you?

Something to think about. Studies show that in spite of early struggles, sibling bonds often remain strong and close throughout life. Think of the adult sibs you know who still enjoy each other's company and affection. Discuss such relationships in class. Give reasons why you think the older sibs remain good friends.

ATTITUDES AGAIN

What really happens between the parents, between parents and children, and between brothers and sisters does not matter nearly as much as what family members *think* happens. For example, some parents seem able to make each child feel well-loved and secure. If there is a favorite, it's kept a secret. Each child feels special.

In such situations the parents control the kinds of rivalry and hostility that encourage sibs to grow up with long-lasting bad feelings about themselves and each other. All children need their parents' experience and wisdom to limit fights and to keep the family peace. At one time or another everyone thinks that a brother or sister gets better treatment. Sometimes, however, one child really receives special favors. Favoritism of this type causes trouble when it's unfair and almost always works for one child and against the other. Sibling rivalry becomes bitter and intense if one or more children don't receive their share of parent love and attention. Losers in the "parent love contest" get angry at

the winners. Losers look for ways to show their resentment and to get even.

At times everyone needs some correction. Most persons know when they've gone too far. However, it's no treat to be blamed and come out the loser every time.

Brothers and sisters imitate their parents. When parents are not considerate, or fail to protect a weaker child from the threats of a stronger one, siblings may imitate parents and attack each other.

Your attitude counts. Siblings sometimes forget that parents have feelings, too. Your behavior often decides their attitude toward you. For example, one child in the family can be loving and responsive, and another may seem cold and indifferent (as in the case of Sara and Lisa, page 157). It's natural for a parent to turn to the child who gives smiles and hugs in return. If one sib frequently offers to help at home and another usually finds excuses to avoid work, parents may feel gratitude towards the helper and annoyance towards the slacker.

Something to think about. This book includes many reasons for rivalry and disagreement between siblings. However, in some families there is much more agreement, friendship, and love than there is conflict.

Write a paragraph. On a separate sheet of paper select one conflict issue and explain how the situation could be solved or improved.

DO NOT WRITE IN THIS BOOK.

Something to think about. Following are some common conflict issues between siblings.

• Not enough privacy for each.

• Borrowing clothes or other possessions without permission.

• Uneven work load around the house.

• Uneven privileges granted by parents.

- Hogging telephone or TV.

What other areas of conflict can you add to this list?

Which issue causes the most trouble for you?

To learn more. Select one idea or topic from this chapter that applies to you and the way you live your life.

On a separate sheet of paper describe your selection in one sentence.

In no more than three sentences explain why you chose it.

DO NOT WRITE IN THIS BOOK.

RECAP

Feelings of competition and open rivalry are common between siblings. However, friendly competition can be a helpful and healthy rehearsal for the tougher challenges of adult life.

In every family, the sex of the sibs and the months and years that separate them in age help decide how they get along. Children close in age and of the same sex compete the most. As age separates them, competition and rivalry usually drop off.

Parent rules affect the way that sibs get along together. However, plenty of give and take goes on that parents never know about. Brothers and sisters find clever ways to get around the family ground rules and practice power plays and other tactics on each other.

A mother or father's past history as a child affects that parent's attitudes to each child. A normal kind of parent favoritism shifts from one sibling to another as each child earns or deserves special attention. Some parents seem able to make all their children feel special sometimes.

Children notice unfair favoritism quickly. They usually resent it. Sometimes the youngest child in a family gets extra consideration from parents. Or parents may favor one sex over another, especially if a child is a "one of a kind," with several sibs of the other sex.

Although most offspring are quick to sense injustice or favoritism from parents, they often forget that the way the child treats the parent greatly influences parent attitudes towards that child. Co-operation and affection, or lack or either, help decide the way that a parent feels about a child. When parents and children offer each other love and consideration, they are far more likely to get it in return.

Sibling favoritism happens in families, too. Although all brothers and sisters may be loved, one is singled out for special friendship or affection.

Sometimes changes in family life upset the expected patterns. An accident or an illness may bring the focus of attention on one child and away from the others.

Attitudes and feelings toward siblings—both good and bad—tend to linger on through the adult years. So powerfully are these old attitudes built in childhood that they may even influence relationships with other people. Events from years ago continue to affect the persons that adults choose to like or dislike.

TERMS		
Sibling rivalry	Control	Favoritism
Friendly rivals	Teasing	Sexism
Power	Special friends	Sibling favorites

CHAPTER 10

My Place in the Family

It's tough being an orphan. An only child gets lonely. The middle one gets squeezed. It's taxing to be the oldest, and a struggle to be the youngest. It was once suggested that there's no easy way through childhood except to be born an adult.

Are you a firstborn child? An only child? The youngest? Somewhere in the middle? In this chapter you'll read how your position in the family can help determine not only your personality but also your relationships with others.

Birth order. Birth order means which child was born first and in what sequence the others followed. Studies of how birth order affects children in a family are incomplete. The results are often puzzling. Most of the research findings apply only when:

- The age spacing between sibs is from two to four years.
- Firstborn and younger sibs are of the same sex.
- Children come from middle-income families.

The fact that brothers and sisters are alike in some ways doesn't surprise anyone. After all, siblings share the same parents and usually grow up in the same home. Most of the time they go to the same schools and play in the same neighborhoods.

Natalie Leimkuhler
"I take thee, my kid brother . . . "

Sibs often lock alike. They often also tend to have the same level of intelligence. However, even though they share the same parents, sibs never share exactly the same heredity, environment, or learning opportunities. Their places in the family birth order decide some of the important differences. You will read about these differences in the sections to follow.

Different treatment. Parents do not treat each child alike for many reasons. In turn, no child reacts the same way to each parent nor to every brother and sister.

Consider this example: The first baby born to young parents is a boy. The mother and father give him much time and love. Years later the youngest son arrives to the same parents who are now older and busier. There is also a houseful of other brothers and sisters. As you can see, the oldest and the youngest boys will grow up under very different conditions at home, even though they are brothers in the same family.

ONE AND ONLY

Did you ever hear a statement like this: "Only children are spoiled. They are self-centered and lazy"? The facts don't support this popular claim. Children with no brothers or sisters are quite often the opposite of spoiled. In fact, only children seem to use extra parent attention and affection to become successful and happy adults.

Natalie Leimkuhler
There are times when life can be lonely for an only child.

CASE EXAMPLES

Read what two only children say about their position:

A son says, "I never doubted my parents' love. They say 'We may not always love the things you do, but we will always love you.' Yet, at times, my parents expected too much of me. Also, I never had to share anything. I'm often lonely. I wish I had an older brother."

Another only child, now a successful physician, recalls her childhood. "We didn't have much money, but if I needed cash for books or school expenses, I always got it. I knew that my parents would sacrifice to send me to college. I never questioned that I'd go and get good grades. My mother and father expected a lot of me. But they gave me a lot in return. I really wanted their approval, and I worked hard for it."

All about O's. O's (only children) have been studied closely, so a lot is known about them. In most cases O's learn fast, get good grades, and often achieve much in life. When it comes to getting ahead, only children seem to have a built-in booster. Their lives are more often busy and productive, rather than spoiled.

Whether it's good or bad to be an O depends mostly on the adults in the home. As you know, children try hard to please their parents. Mothers and fathers of an O are likely to pin all their hopes on their only child. Often, parents of O's achieve more themselves, so they provide a strong and successful model for the O to imitate. Even when parents have not achieved much themselves, they may still pay plenty of attention to the achievements of their child. Love and approval usually reward an only child's good grades and honors.

Good feelings about self go hand in hand with success and happiness. O's usually think well of themselves. They feel special. They are often cheerful and secure. They take for granted that people will like and help them, just as their parents have always done.

O's tend to feel at ease with people in charge. They usually think for themselves and rely on their own decisions. As children, O's often think up make-believe playmates and exciting adventures. Their ability to dream up new ideas may lead to inventions or other creative achievements during their adult years.

The only child doesn't have a perfect life. O's may find it hard to figure out other children, or be less skillful at getting along with persons their own age. That's because O's spend most of their time with adults and feel more comfortable with grown-ups than with other children. Many of them wish they had brothers, sisters, or other "built-in" playmates.

O's are watched more closely by their parents than are children in larger families. For that reason these same parents may demand constant love and attention from their only child.

Of course, brothers and sisters in the home cannot be sure that any one of them will grow up to be popular, generous, and tough. However, with no siblings there are no rivals. O's get no chance to benefit from the challenges of living with competitive brothers and sisters. As a result, O's may indeed have an easier life, with more privileges and more possessions.

In a nation concerned about too many people and dwindling natural resources, the idea of one child appeals to many married couples. Also, today many women want to combine marriage, career, and motherhood. Having just one child may have special appeal be-cause mother will have more time for her other interests.

FIRST

CASE EXAMPLE

Every F (firstborn) is an only child for a while. Things change when sibs arrive. Read what three F's say:

1. Denise says, "I like being the oldest, but I don't think I get many advantages. I do get to stay out a little later. But then Mom expects more of me. My parents tell me I must set an example for my younger brother. When I was his age, I had to be home by 10:30. Now he comes in at midnight and they hardly say anything. Maybe they are easier on him because he is a boy and they think he can take care of himself and stay out of trouble. As far as my brother is concerned, we like each other. We never fight much. We joke around a lot, but we haven't been in a real argument in a long time."

2. Debra says, "Being the oldest is a challenge which has helped me to mature faster. I try hard to set a good example for my younger sisters, who look to me for guidance and companionship. I offer them advice when they need it or ask for it. Offhand, I can't think of any drawbacks to being the oldest. I've always enjoyed my position."

3. Bart says, "I like being first. I won't say I'm the favorite, but I do feel special. The main drawback is that I always have to persuade my parents to give me more independence. Then my kid brother comes along and gets the same freedom without even know-

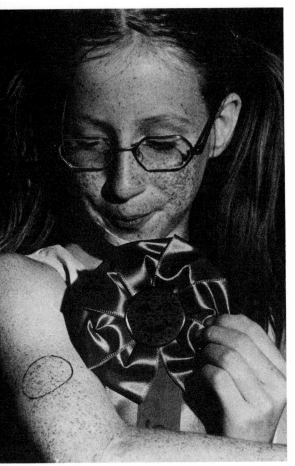

Dick Vellinger, Journal and Courier, Lafayette, Indiana
Firstborn or not, everyone likes to be tops in something. Here Shannon displays her prize ribbon for the most freckles in a two-inch circle.

ing what I've done for him. Also, I think parents make more mistakes with older children. By the time younger ones come along, parents are more relaxed and discover that some of their ideas weren't so great after all."

Throughout much of world history, the oldest son inherited most of the family titles, money, power, and land. This was true even though a younger brother or sister was smarter, stronger, or more capable.

In the United States today, one sibling is as good as another in terms of law and inheritance. However, first arrivals still hold a special place.

Definite differences have been found in the development and behavior of firstborns. F's tend to be smaller and lighter at birth than later children in the same family. But this is not always true. F's are more often premature babies (born sooner than expected). First children also have a more difficult time being born. Such differences seem to even out in time. The general health of firstborn and laterborn sibs is usually quite similar.

Firstborn children are no smarter than later brothers and sisters. As a group, however, F's compete more and achieve more. They strive harder for excellence and do better in school. These are some of the reasons why F's so often achieve higher levels of success in life.

For example, there was a striking number of firstborn sons among astronaut candidates. Spacemen were chosen for mental quality, competitive spirit, leadership, maturity, and proven achievement.

In a group of twenty-three astronauts selected for training at the Manned Spacecraft Center in Houston, psychologists discovered that twenty-one were either an oldest son or an only child. One who did not fit the pattern had but one brother thirteen years older, which made the astronaut an "only child" for all practical purposes.

No one knows exactly why oldest children do so well in life. It may be because the first child is the only child for a while, with the full attention of the parents. Grown-ups may talk more to an F or an O for the simple reasons that they have more interest in them and more time. As a result, the children usually speak sooner and more clearly than later sibs who spend more time talking with each other. Thus, F's of both sexes are often treated better, trained more, and made more responsible. Parents expect more of F's and usually get it.

Remember that no position in the family is all good or all bad. F's may get a lot of attention, but their parents are younger and less experienced. First-time mothers are often nervous. They worry about every sneeze. Parents feel more practiced and relaxed with later children. Like O's, F's also miss out on the company and competition of older siblings.

In terms of personality, some research results suggest that F's pay a price for their favored position. They tend to be more fearful and need more human closeness than later children. Firstborns don't perform as well under pressure as their younger sibs.

F's often like the company of adults. They may be less popular with peers (persons of the same age). Also, F's tend to be more serious, less carefree, and more conservative. They are also more willing to go along with the group.

Male F's, especially, seem to be more influenced by those around them. In contrast, firstborn girls are generally more responsible, aggressive, and competitive than are firstborn boys. Perhaps you can think of some reasons for this sharp contrast.

F's of both sexes continue to need reassurance and guidance. Parents usually help them with tasks like home-work, but in return expect high levels of performance. In later years, F's retain a strong need for achievement.

Older children more often use their power and influence over younger ones than the other way 'round. Younger children (Y's) often imitate F's. While Y's may tease or bother older sibs, they may also admire their strength, good looks, or achievements.

For good or bad, F's are important models for all Y's. Often the older child thinks of having a superior place in the family. Parents often give F's roles of power and strength to enforce family rules.

F's like their privileges, but they often admit strong feelings of jealousy for younger sibs. Usually firstborns learn to conceal such feelings (at least from parents). F's discover that it's danger-ous to let grown-ups know about such resentments for the younger children.

Although F's may act disgusted with Y's, they are well aware of the admira-tion they can receive from younger sibs. Instead of acting on their jealous and hostile feelings, many F's turn their en-ergies to becoming leaders and heroes. F's plan projects, and organize their brothers and sisters. If an F feels lonely or rejected by outside friends, a younger sib is usually handy for company. Also, because Y's are almost always around the house, hurts and disappointments can be taken out on them.

Changes. Of course, many family cir-cumstances can change the way an F or any other child will turn out. For exam-ple, in a poor family the oldest son or daughter may have to quit school to help pay the bills. Sometimes F's stay home longer than usual to act as a parent substitute. Where there's enough money, an F (and every other child) may

Kathy Tuite

The oldest child often serves as a model for all who follow.

have equal chances for a good education.

Conditions in the home can change as sibs get older. A family may start out poor and gain income later on, to the benefit of the younger children. Or things may work just the opposite because of a business failure, a parent's long illness or death, or other misfortune.

Make a list. By sharing classmembers' experiences, or by using examples from families you know, make a list of the ways that older brothers and sisters act as parent substitutes. For example, older sibs are asked sometimes to baby-sit or to discipline the younger children.

Write your list on a separate sheet of paper.

DO NOT WRITE IN THIS BOOK.

MIDDLE GROUND

CASE EXAMPLES

Andy is the second of three boys. He dislikes the squeeze on him in the middle position. "When I was little, my older brother bought me things. He even gave me his toys. My mother and father gave me lots of attention, too. Things sure changed when my kid brother arrived. He got all the attention and I got yelled at more and more."

Mindy is an M (middle child), too. She has two older married brothers and a younger sister. She says, "My spot in the family is a case of 'get a little, give a little.' I've always watched my older brothers and learned from their mistakes. I've already been where my little sister is now. So I try to help her."

If you're not an F or a Y, then you must be an M. First and last children get permanent roles. M's switch around. Every M was once a Y. You can also be a Y for several years and then become an M when a new baby arrives.

A large family has many M's. The more children, the harder it is to know who influences whom and how much. The effect of sibling give-and-take is hard to figure out. For example, a middle child is a Y to a firstborn. But that same M becomes an older brother or sister to one or more younger children.

Family positions change when the older children grow up and leave home. Despite all these possibilities for differences between them, studies show that M's turn out to be quite similar in many ways.

Most younger children get built-in playmates close to their age. At the same time they must find ways to get

Natalie Leimkuhler
Just one year apart in age, brothers Ben and Tom are close friends. Here they dress up for Halloween.

their share of attention and approval. M's can't grab responsible leader roles from F's. Those positions of power are too well guarded. M's look for other ways to get praise. Often they become family diplomats, gaining notice and

183

No one place in the family is best.

reward by being both agreeable and easygoing.

M's learn to get along in groups. They make friends easily and usually feel comfortable when with the other sex. M's may be less possessive (insist on owning everything), less controlling (want their own way), and less impatient than their older sibs. However, both M's and Y's tend to be more aggressive than F's. That may be because the younger sibs rough and tumble so much with each other.

Alfred Adler, a famous psychiatrist, studied power plays among brothers and sisters. He believed that younger children grow up wanting to be leaders and bosses. Throughout life they continue to struggle for a higher place because of their long years as Number Two or lower on the family totem pole.

M's almost always get less attention from parents. Also, middle children don't inherit power positions in the family, even after an F leaves home. Without advantages of size and weight, M's must search for other ways to gain power and status. "Baby" Y's sometimes tease F's so much that the older child often loses control in a home where fighting back is not OK. In such cases, M's may take a beating from F's. Then M's may bully the next child down the line, or take revenge on someone else who is weaker.

OLDER SIS

As you know, boys are usually expected to be stronger and more aggressive than girls, even though things don't always work that way. You live in a world where people try to outdo each other. To be younger brother to a sister can be an unhappy position. If a boy comes second in size and strength, he's sure to suffer for it. If a bigger, older sister can beat him up too, he may be forced to use his wits to hold his own. Even if an F sister is not allowed to use physical force to control younger siblings, she will usually find other ways to hold on to her position of power as the Number One child. Of course, younger children need ways to protect themselves. M's can weaken the power of F's by making their complaints loud and clear.

Difference in size and ability can make some younger children aggressive—especially boys who are born second. Actually, it's hard to tell if younger children imitate the power tactics of the older ones, or whether the young M's and Y's make up their own weapons in order to survive in the very competitive family atmosphere.

F's may use grown-up-type tactics to fight. For example, firstborns may insult and criticize younger children and then make up smart excuses for their own mistakes. A younger child, not yet so clever with words, may know only how to

Natalie Leimkuhler

An older sister teaches a younger brother how to build a tunnel in the sand.

scratch and fight with fists. In time, size and weight differences even out. Even though M's and Y's may eventually grow taller and stronger than their older sibs, it is hard for the younger ones to shake off the habit of feeling smaller and weaker.

Did you know? Children learn to do certain things better when they have a new task explained to them by someone close in age. The "teacher" understands the learner's problems, and can talk at the same level.

Examples of things that children teach each other are:
- Games like checkers, dominoes, cards, and chess.
- Skills such as gymnastics, sewing, weaving, or model building.
- Information about death, divorce, and other unfamiliar subjects.
- Homework and school projects.
- How to act in certain situations.

LAST

CASE EXAMPLES

In every family with two or more children, one child has to arrive last.

185

Pat Hirschl

Because of the years that separate her from her older brothers, this baby will grow up like an only child.

Todd was born five years after his next oldest brother. He says, "I used to hate being the baby. The older kids called me 'runt,' and I was always left behind or out. Yet as I grow older I see some advantages. Mom and Dad never had enough money to give the older kids extras, but now there's always plenty for me.

"Living around older people, I study them. Usually they have good ideas. I think about what my brothers tell me and I often do what they suggest. I've learned to ask for help and then decide for myself what's best."

José says, "I'm the youngest of three. My parents look out for my welfare. They don't let the older ones gang up on me, even when I deserve it. What I don't like is listening to my older brothers complain, 'We never

got things like that,' or 'Why don't you punish him the way you did us?'"

Cass sees no problems at all in being the baby. "I think it's great to be the youngest. My parents were pretty strict with my older sister. They admit their mistakes. What they did wrong by her they want to do right by me."

Like every other child in the family, a Y has both advantages and disadvantages. Much depends on the ages and sex of the older sibs.

The more years that separate a Y from the next older sib, the more the Y will be like an only child. The youngest child may enjoy all the achievement and popularity of the firstborn without the same pressures to succeed. Y's often have mother to themselves after the older children start school or leave home. The more years that separate sibs, the fewer interests and experiences they will have in common. In fact, when a baby is born after the older children are in school or almost grown up, all older siblings—like the F—may become "assistant parents." They act more like an extra mother or father than a competitive sib.

Character. Y's can be complicated persons. Y's often see the bright side of things and are self-assured. At the same time, they may resent the baby treatment. Parents of Y's are usually more experienced and relaxed. Because parents frequently expect less of them, Y's may be left on their own and have more chances to develop initiative or creative talents. On the other hand, if less is expected, a Y may stay childish longer. Y's may cry and complain a lot.

Sometimes Y's struggle to catch up and to achieve like the older children. However, Y's never feel in charge of anyone or anything. For all of these

Natalie Leimkuhler

Alan and Brian are fraternal twins. Although they look somewhat alike, their personalities are different.

reasons, it is understandable why the youngest children try harder to develop their own skills and abilities.

Did you know? Simply because you are an O, F, M, or Y does not mean that you are sure to become a leader or follower. Your position in the family will not be the only thing that decides how well you will succeed in life.

Although such basic influences seem to have some effect on a person's future, your natural talents, interests, and how hard you are willing to work will also play a big part in the kind of person you become as an adult.

TWINS

Every twin is also a brother or a sister. A set of twins is born about once in every 100 births. Triplets (three) come along once in 8,000 births. Quadruplets

(four), quintuplets (five), and sextuplets (six) are far more rare.

Identical twins share the same sex and the same heredity. *Fraternal* twins are like ordinary brothers and sisters except that they share the same position in the family and any special treatment or interest that twinship brings.

Twins are special. Yet they face the same problems of getting along that sometimes trouble other children.

Psychologists like to study identical twins. When two persons share the same heredity, differences in the way the two sibs act are more likely to come from the twins' individual experiences or from how they are treated by other persons. Studies of twins help scientists figure out what roles heredity and environment play in personality differences.

Natalie Leimkuhler

Even though they are identical twins, Leslie and Laura choose to dress differently.

When identical twins are separated right after birth, for example, they still tend to be even more alike in intelligence than ordinary brothers and sisters or fraternal twins. Twins often enter the same work if not exactly the same branch. For example, twins may both become scientists even though one is a chemist and the other a physicist. Or both may become teachers, even though they teach different subjects.

Because every twin is either a brother or a sister, the built-in closeness of twinship becomes a mixed blessing.

Each gets the security of companionship. Twins are often very close friends. Yet twins also complain that people treat them like the same person—two bodies with one mind. Twins think of themselves as individual persons. One twin complained that when her sister got in trouble, their mother complained, "Now look what *they* did."

When twins are treated too much alike, they sometimes feel resentment and strong competition. They may solve such problems by deliberately attempting to look different and by leading separate lives. One set of twins agrees that they get along very well, but that they always try to meet people individually so they won't be compared.

Actually, many twins enjoy the attention they get. They like dressing the same and fooling friends. One girl who was good at languages took French exams for her sister. In turn the sister did math tests for her look-alike.

Twins often describe a way of thinking the same. Says one, "If I ask a question in my morning English class, often my sister asks the same question that afternoon when her group meets. When we see home movies of ourselves as children, we can't tell one from the other."

Twins share the same birth order position in the family. Even so, experts agree that twins should be treated as individuals with both similarities and differences in personality, interests, and abilities.

SOMETHING TO THINK ABOUT

Psychologists study the way people behave. They offer ideas to explain *why* persons act as they do. Such ideas or *theories* can rarely be proved like an answer to a math problem. Nor do the theories of psychologists hold true for every person. However, a theory may give you something to think about and a new understanding of yourself and others.

Walter Toman is a psychologist who studies the effects that brothers and sisters have on each other. Toman has a theory that brothers and sisters help decide the kinds of persons each picks for close friends and marriage partners.

"New relationships imitate old ones," says Toman. He thinks that, to be followers, younger sibs get used to doing what older ones want. In adult life, M's and

Y's choose jobs and friends that permit them to continue to be followers. On the other hand, firstborn children, more used to being leaders, look for friendships and jobs that put them in charge.

Toman goes a step further. He thinks that even husbands and wives may choose each other on the basis of long-ago sibling relationships. In some ways the marriage will copy sibling patterns from childhood. The closer the marriage is to what happened in childhood, the more successful it is likely to be.

Suppose a man, the older brother of a sister, marries a wife who is the younger sister of a brother. In marriage, both get the same position they had before. The husband is used to having a younger female around. The wife knows how to get along with an older male.

You can see how much a child's place in the family can decide future relationships—especially those in marriage.

Write a paragraph. On a separate sheet of paper write a paragraph entitled "My Place in the Family."

Be sure to explain what you like best about your position in the family birth order.

DO NOT WRITE IN THIS BOOK.

To learn more. Select one idea or topic from this chapter that applies to you and the way you live your life.

On a separate sheet of paper describe your selection in one sentence.

In no more than three sentences explain why you chose it.

DO NOT WRITE IN THIS BOOK.

RECAP

No one place in the family is better than any other. You can be a first, F, last, Y, or squeezed-in-the-middle, M, and still be a happy, successful adult. However, your position influences both your experiences and feelings about yourself.

The more years that separate siblings, the less impact each will have on the other. Each will grow up like an only child when the number of years between them is large enough.

However, even closely spaced children of the same sex never share exactly the same life. Each child in a family is an individual. Each reacts to parents and every other sib in a different way.

Sibling positions change when a new child is born or an older one leaves home.

Generally speaking, only children, or O's, get a lot of attention. O's may feel lonesome, but they have no rivals. Often, they grow up to be independent, secure, and creative people.

Firstborns are studied most. Competition and achievement mark their lives. F's get a lot of parent attention until Y's arrive. Then the F's may share parent duties and authority over younger sibs.

F's are often serious people who have more fears and worries than their sibs.

They like peer company, but may favor older people for friendship and guidance.

Younger children look up to F's and imitate them. However, F's often feel jealous or resentful toward Y's. The F's can also show genuine love and concern for the welfare of the younger sibs.

In every family there is only one spot for an F and one for a Y. M's share the middle ground. Middle children must find ways to get attention. Often they are charming, easygoing, agreeable people. M's don't inherit power, so they struggle for it. As a result, M's are usually tougher and more aggressive than F's.

Y's usually like their special place, yet resent being treated like babies. If there's a big gap in years, Y's will miss out on closeness with older sibs who are more like assistant parents.

Twins and other multiple-birth children share the same spot in the family. Identical twins often enjoy their sameness but still need to be treated as individuals.

TERMS

O = Only child	Premature	Triplets
F = Firstborn child	Peers	Quadruplets
M = Middle child or children	Possessive	Quintuplets
	Controlling	Sextuplets
Y = Youngest child	Identical twin	
Birth order	Fraternal twin	

UNIT IV
Peers and Friends

CHAPTER II

Friendship Groups

At age fifteen, Shannon wrote in her diary, "When I try to put my feelings into words, all I can say is, *I want others to like me.*" You may share Shannon's attitude. You want other teens to like you, to make you feel welcome, and to accept you.

Acceptance may be the most comforting word during the adolescent years. It goes by other names, such as *popularity* or *status.* Teens still want to be liked and accepted by their *peers,* or others their age, even when they have understanding parents and siblings.

You've already read about the importance of relationships with parents, brothers, and sisters. In this unit you'll learn about relationships with peers.

Harry Harlow, a world-famous psychologist, raised baby female monkeys all by themselves. The infant monkeys were kept away from parents, brothers, sisters, and playmates.

Later, when the monkeys grew up and became mothers themselves, a terrible thing happened. The new mothers paid no attention to their own babies. Sometimes the monkey mothers hurt or killed their young. Because the motherless monkeys never received any love from their own mothers, they never learned how to love and care for their own offspring.

Natalie Leimkuhler
A friendship group can be just you and one other person sharing a mudbath.

Harlow's work with monkeys includes an important lesson about the way humans behave. *Each person must learn how to become a friendly and loving person through warm and enjoyable contacts with others.* This ability to show concern for others develops in a series of steps:

1. Parents show love for the new baby during the first years of life.
2. The growing child learns about give and take from play with siblings at home and contacts with peers at school and in the neighborhood.
3. The adolescent develops a closeness with a person of the other sex.
4. The married adult completes the cycle by becoming a parent and showing love for the new baby.

Dr. Harlow claims that when a child does not follow these steps of normal development, it will be difficult for that person to become a close friend or a responsible, loving parent.

In this unit you will read about:

• Peer relationships.
• Some of the ways that friends help each other to control hostility and aggression.
• What happens when strong negative emotions take over a person's behavior.
• Other problems in peer relationships.
• How friends can counsel and help each other.

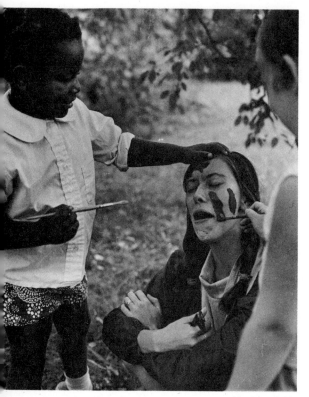

Natalie Leimkuhler

Small groups serve many purposes.

GROUP MEMBERSHIP

Between ages eleven to thirteen, most boys and girls join a friendship group. For girls, belonging to a group becomes very important by age fourteen to fifteen. For boys, the need for group membership peaks about a year later.

Why groups? A friendship group can be just you and one other person. A group can also be a *clique* (clik) of three or four close friends. Or a group can be a larger number of friendly persons who belong to a club. Members may share an interest like stamp collecting or hiking but rarely see each other between meetings or trips. You might be part of many such groups.

Groups are important all through life. The younger you are, the more you are limited to your family group. As you grow older you move away from your home and make friends in the neighborhood. As you advance in school, your social world grows larger. By early adolescence, group membership includes many other friendship groups, large and small.

Unless you decide to be a hermit, you'll spend a lot of time in small groups. At school, in the neighborhood, at church, the "Y", and later at work, you'll belong to groups.

Have you ever wondered why you want to be part of a group? Or why it hurts to be left out? Being part of a larger organization pays off. If it didn't, so many people wouldn't go to so much trouble to spend time with others.

Almost everyone *needs* and *wants* human companionship. In this chapter you'll learn why and how group membership influences your life. You'll also read about the difference between membership in larger groups as compared with smaller ones.

When you think about it, you already know a lot about groups. You know the good feelings of belonging, or being an "insider." You might have suffered some "outsider" feelings of loneliness or rejection, too.

Make a list. On a separate sheet of paper, make a list of all the different school groups that you and your classmates can join.

Then write out the names of the clubs and other organizations in the community that are not connected with school.

Now record the groups that you and members of your family belong to.

DO NOT WRITE IN THIS BOOK.

Groups change. Adolescent groups can be a lot of fun. Members find ready-

This high school band brings together a large number of boys and girls who like music, marching, and football games. Close friendships often grow out of such shared interests and activities.

made companionship. Insiders share gossip and secrets. They visit each other, eat together, plan good times. They share new experiences—first dance, first double date, first trip with someone outside the family. Teen groups often develop into larger and older social groups.

By middle adolescence, members of the other sex become important. Mixed groups form. Crowd membership lingers on into adulthood. Then larger friendship groups gradually break up. Couples pair off and move toward marriage or other arrangements. Friends leave town. The older the group members get, the fewer original members remain. Some tend to build new friendships with church, social, and sports groups.

Rarely is anyone cut off completely from the company of others their age. Of course, not everyone gets the same amount or quality of group contact. If you live on a farm or just outside town, the school bus schedule or responsibilities at home may limit your social life. If you live in the city and your parents

Dick Mroczynski, Journal and Courier, Lafayette, Indiana

The members of this group are trying to live with the bad news: their team lost.

work, time spent with other teens may be much greater.

In Chapter 4 you read about the changes that technology and automation brought to North American family life. As home chores slack off and family members' dependence on each other lessens, friends outside the home become more important.

CONFORMITY

Have you ever heard teens criticized because "they always go along with the crowd" or "they don't think for themselves"? One way to feel that you are accepted in a group is to dress, talk, and act like other members. *Conform* means to go along. Unless you do conform in some ways, you are likely to be treated like an outsider.

Each person is different. But behaving like others is part of human nature. Most everyone conforms, at least a little. It's human to imitate those close to you, especially those persons whose company you want. In a way, conformity is like paying dues. In return for conforming, you expect to receive group acceptance and companionship.

Conformers may give up some personal freedom. However, in return they know how to act in an uncertain world. From your point of view there may be other reasons for following the crowd. For example, your parents may think you are just wonderful, but only your peers can give you the kind of acceptance that counts most.

Individuals. Not everyone feels the same need to go along with the crowd. For example, you may dress like other teens, but prefer classical music to rock or jazz. In fact, conforming among teens isn't always as widespread or demanding as it may seem. Think of all the different groups in your school. Each has a different interest or purpose. Each has members to keep it going.

Group psychology. It's important to remember that there's nothing wrong in conforming with a group's goal. Groups can exert powerful influence for good. When alone a boy may be quiet and shy. In a team situation he may be fired up by the enthusiasm of others to help win a game. Persons who might never act on their own may band together to aid the victims of a flood or tornado.

On the other hand, problems can occur when a person joins in the harmful acts of a destructive group without thinking of the possible consequences. For example, with just one other companion a girl may act kind and considerate. In a large, angry crowd, she may hurt others with words or deeds.

You need only scan a daily newspaper to learn that a group can be more than the sum of its members. Gangs terrorize neighborhoods. Crowds at soccer matches or football games some-

Kathy Tuite
When rain washed out their game, this Little League team started a spitting contest.

times lose control. They may injure some of the fans or destroy parts of the stadium.

Larger crowds can reduce an individual's feelings of responsibility. In a group it is much easier to lose control and to give in to aggressive or explosive emotions.

What about me? Until now you may not have thought much about whether you are a conforming person or not. You may not have considered how you make up your mind to go along with the group and when you decide to act on your own. All during your life you'll be asked to make decisions about whether to conform or not. It is at such times that a clear and solid value system will be very helpful to you.

In the following pages you will read some of the familiar ways adolescents and adults conform. As you read, think where you stand. In which cases would you join the majority? In what circumstances would you stand alone? Do you know why you would make such choices?

You be the judge. It's not always easy to know when to go along with the group and when to back off.

The following happened at a freshman initiation (ih-NISH-ee-AY-shun) of the Sunshine Club, a high school service group that does a lot of good work.

New members were told to report to the ceremony dressed as babies. As part of the hazing, older members decided to feed the newcomers baby food mixed with hot peppers.

Although the freshmen gagged on the menu, things soon got boring. One club officer came up with the bright idea to have the "babies" run to the nearest business section of town. They were instructed to approach strangers and beg for money to buy more baby food.

The Sunshine Club members cheered the new plan. From that point things got out of hand. Not only did the initiates approach strangers, but they insulted them if they refused to donate money. It wasn't too long before someone called the police who took several embarrassed teenagers to the nearby station. The police then notified the parents of the freshmen-beggars.

The next morning angry parents expressed strong protest to the school principal about the initiation ceremony the night before. The principal called in the club officers to get the whole story. Then she made her decision: The Sunshine Club was on suspension for three months. No meetings, no activities, no fund raising.

In cold and angry tones the principal told the officers of her disappointment in them. She reminded the leaders that they used bad judgment, set a poor example for the younger adolescents, and behaved like little children.

Suppose you were the principal? Would you have made the same decision? Give reasons for your answer.

Do you think that all the club members deserved to be punished for one member's suggestion? Explain your reaction.

Have you ever been caught up in a crowd action that you would never have done alone? Can you recall your emotions at the time?

Suppose you had been one of the "babies"? What would you have done when told to beg for money?

FADS AND FASHIONS

Fads are an example of conformity. A fad is a new or different way of doing things. Fads may be around for a few short weeks or turn into a lasting style. Hair styles and skirt lengths are good examples. Sometimes the fad is long, sometimes short.

If you adopt a fad when it's brand new, you are alert. If you pick up an ex-fad after everyone has moved on to something different, you prove that you are out of step.

Fads for youth are special. In fact, when a teen fad catches on with adults—as new clothing or hairstyles often do—teens tend to look for a new fad. Adolescent styles change so fast that heavy-footed adults may be left behind frantically trying to copy last month's look or slang term when both have been dropped by the young crowd.

Many fads become fashions and hold on because they serve a useful purpose. Sneakers, for example, used to be confined to the gym and blue jeans to the ranch or road crew. When first worn as street clothing, jeans were considered a fad. Now sneakers and jeans show up in every adolescent generation, probably because they are comfortable and durable.

Unfortunately, you can feel like an outcast if you don't have the right item of clothing. Even the lowly sneaker can be a status symbol. If you don't own a special brand, that means you can't keep up with the crowd.

CASE EXAMPLE

Consider the case of Swifties and Rejects (made-up names for two types of sneakers). If you don't buy Swifties you have bought a Reject (any brand other than Swifties). No imitations will do. No room for individual style here.

In one school almost all the boys wore sneakers. The lad who wore Rejects got teased with this ditty.

"Rejects.
They make your feet feel fine.
Rejects.
They cost a dollar ninety-nine."

Each boy interviewed declared that he'd prefer a beat-up pair of Swifties to a new pair of Rejects. Shoe sales-clerks in the neighborhood reported open conflict between mothers who wanted to buy sneakers cheaper than Swifties and sons who refused any substitute. One rumor had it that certain boys refused to go to school until their parents gave in and bought the right brand.

The accepted sneaker (or sweater or jeans) may cost twice as much as a sturdy substitute. However, few parents can resist such steady nagging that "only Swifties will do."

Of course, the case of Swifties is an extreme example of conforming to a fad. Do you know other examples of this kind?

In some schools, one kind of sweatshirt may carry more status than another. A twisted friendship ring may show more prestige than a plain one. Keeping up with fads can be a tricky game.

What fads are popular in school this year?

Why will one article of clothing "pass", while another will be laughed at?

Write a paragraph. On a separate sheet of paper give two or three reasons why you have or have not adopted a current fashion.

DO NOT WRITE IN THIS BOOK.

Fad makers. Not everyone can start a fad. When a popular girl wears a man's belt around her waist she may start a fad if many imitate her. A less popular girl may do the same thing first, but no one notices. Worse, the second girl may be teased about wearing her father's belt.

If a star athlete shaves his curly hair to look like an Indian warrior, he may get admiration and imitation. However, if an honor roll student dares to be first to cut his hair that way, someone is sure to ask who scalped him.

If you study fads, you'll learn a lot about people. For example, even in following a clothing fad, there's still room to be yourself. Everyone may wear jeans, but you may decorate yours in a clever way.

Cost. A fad-of-the-moment is not always expensive. Sometimes an old beat-up hat or a tattered military jacket serves as the current status symbol.

What's important is that you know what's favored this month and that you join the fad before it becomes old-fashioned. Even a tiny emblem may separate the "in" group from the "out."

Avoiding fads. Some teens choose not to play the fads and fashions game. In fact, it could be a fad *not* to follow the newest style.

Slang. Slang words start as a special *fad* language. At times the words you use with your friends show a strong kind of conformity. Often adolescent slang

When Jill tied a scarf around her head she started a fad in her school.

means selecting certain words and giving them a different meaning. For example, "junk" has always meant something no longer usable. Some youths switched the meaning and applied the word to drugs.

Most slang words fade away. A few become part of regular language. Words like Jeep® and Coke® began as slang words for the products they represent. Now they are trademarks.

Most teen slang seems to spring from nowhere and change so rapidly that only the insiders know what words are really current. Chicago slang can be different from Montreal's. By using this semi-secret language you can side with other adolescents and shut out adults and children.

It makes little difference what the words are. In one group, the words for insiders and outsiders could be *zeeks* and *zorks*. What's important is that you and the members of your group use the same words to mean the same thing. Your close attention to current slang is a normal and harmless part of conforming.

When adults eavesdrop on adolescents they may hear a chatter so complicated it seems like a secret code. Did you ever notice that teens often express themselves to each other with special words, gestures, tones, and slang? In fact, adolescents often apply a "slang test" to discover who belongs to the group and who is an intruder. Even using a word in a slightly different way can brand someone instantly as an outsider.

It's a mixed world. When people can express a complicated idea with a few familiar words, communication becomes easier. If you speak the current language and understand the gestures, your chances of being understood and accepted improve.

It is risky to include teen slang in a book like this. By the time you read it here, special words may be out of date. However, just to show how old words get new meanings, some samples follow.

After the Vietnam war, the United States Air Force gave returning prisoners of war a list of slang words that had come into use while the airmen were in prison. "Bread" now meant money. "Rip off" meant to steal, cheat, or deceive. "Uptight" meant nervous and tense. All these phrases were new to the returning POW's.

The women's liberation movement gained attention during the early 1970s. "Women's lib" became the slang term. "Ms." refers to any female, Miss or Mrs., just as Mr. means any male.

None of those terms is new anymore. Some have already disappeared.

Swearing. Swearing is called street language. You've probably felt the urge to use daring words. Some people swear or use obscene words to seem strong or tough. Experimenting with swearing is often a stage in maturing for both boys and girls. Some adolescents use street language to be accepted by the group.

Why swear? As oldtime standards for language have been lowered in recent years, swearing has become more common among males and females, young and old. On the surface, swearing can be a way of conforming—saying what everyone else is saying. However, swearing is also a way of *not* conforming—of shocking or upsetting others. However, swearing has deeper meanings that may interest you.

● Swearing, or obscenity, is a way to show off by getting attention. Street lan-

"You're one, too!"

guage is often used to shock some people into noticing a person who might not get attention otherwise.

● Four-letter words are frequently used to express disgust. After dropping a carton of milk or wrecking a fender, even mild persons may let loose with a salty word or two.

● "Really telling someone off" may express helpless revolt against a boring job or a feeling of not being appreciated.

● Using street language can be a way to fight against rules. By swearing, a person may do something that's forbidden—and get away with it.

Swearing is an age-old way of letting off strong negative emotion like frustration or anger. Words can be used in place of an action. If you refer to someone by a bad name that is insulting enough, you may no longer need to attack physically.

Teens—both male and female—sometimes without thinking imitate peers or older people who swear. Also, in movies, TV, and newspapers, language is no longer censored so closely. You live during a time with lots of room for individual behavior.

Still, habitual rude behavior like swearing can cause personal loss. A constant string of cursing may get you known as a clod or an annoying attention-seeker. A bit of swearing may be accepted or even encouraged among close friends. Simple common sense will tell you that it's smarter not to swear in front of most teachers, possible future employers, or the parents of friends.

As a guideline, think of it this way: No matter how customs change, no matter what your group does, consideration for others will always be important. If you accept an invitation to eat, it's an unspoken rule that you not criticize the food—at least while you are still at the table. In the same way, mature people are expected to conform by controlling their language in certain settings, like the classroom or church.

Four-letter words are a poor excuse for vivid language. Street language limits your expression and confines you to the same old tired words and phrases. Even the shock value of such words fades away when others learn that you can't express strong feeling in any other way.

In time, many young persons discover the joy of accurate self-expression with regular everyday words. By learning to use language well, you can say what you really mean in words that anyone can understand.

Did you know? Dr. Reinhold Aman is an expert on insults. He has even written dictionaries to explain the background and meaning of certain curses.

Although he doesn't encourage people to use strong talk, Dr. Aman claims that cussing can be an outlet for built-up emotions.

Dr. Aman points out that only the child-like person would make fun of another's looks. Persons who don't know any better have to depend on insults about a person's skin color.

He also believes that Americans don't try to improve their street language. Those in other countries do much better. Turks, for example, make little poems of their insults. Eskimos sing curses to each other.

Among Dr. Aman's favorite curses is one from the Yiddish that says, "May all your teeth fall out but one, so you can still get a toothache."

SMALLER GROUPS

So far you've read about the importance of feeling welcome in large groups. Smaller groups, often known as cliques, are also important.

A *clique* is a small, exclusive, friendship group. Cliques are often thought of as snobbish because they deliberately shut others out. Clique members are not always close friends, although "best friend" pairs often belong to the same clique.

Many adults join service clubs and civic organizations that are more formal than cliques. Teachers and other adults form cliques by joining bowling or golf teams.

Rules. The rules of clique membership aren't written down. Even so they are quite real. The rules don't need to be spelled out because everyone seems to know them. Rules may change as members set new goals.

Names. Small cliques may go without a name. Others are known by the name

A clique is a small friendship group.

Natalie Leimkuhler

of the leader, like "Sandra's bunch" or "Josh's gang."

Street cliques in large cities split up according to territory, or "turf." They may take their name from the street or section where their members live. Sometimes they use mysterious or scary titles like Purple Raiders or Savage Skulls.

In some schools across the nation the students divide into the Jocks, the Pencilheads, and the Freaks. Although the labels may be different in your school, the Jocks are the athletes. The Pencilheads are the serious students. Freaks often claim to hate school. They avoid schoolwork, at least when anyone might catch them at it. Members of the three

groups may use separate entrances to school and different halls when inside.

Of course, group names make little difference to those involved. What's important is who joins and who does not.

Being accepted. Cliques tend to keep new members out. When the wrong ones slip in, old members may make the newcomers feel unwelcome or inferior. However, membership isn't closed to everyone. A new boy or girl who is very attractive, talented, or has some special appeal can be brought into the clique.

Being accepted into a clique usually depends on similar achievements and interests. Social leadership and athletic abilities rate high. For someone "different" to get into an established clique

When classmembers join together to beg for homework relief, they've got a better chance of getting it than if just one person asked.

takes unusual skill and personality or lots of courage and push. Once in, members still aren't entirely safe. A person who refuses to go along with group decisions or acts stuck up may be dumped.

Many adults carry similar standards into the clubs and societies they form or join. Often a sign reads "For Members Only." A country club, for example, is a big adult clique.

HOW GROUPS HELP

You read earlier in the chapter that there can be many advantages in being a group member. Adolescents help each other depend less on home. With group members you get a chance to act on your own and practice new ways of living.

New roles. At home you may be a second or third child and rarely get a chance to give orders or make plans for others.

In a friendship group, however, others may see leadership qualities in you that have not been noticed at home. When friends turn to you for help, you may discover talents you didn't even know you had.

"Helping" parents make decisions. Parents sometimes back down from their old rules when they hear about other mothers and fathers permitting more freedom.

"Jill can go to out-of-town games. Why can't I?"

"Cherie's mother lets her wear eye makeup to school. Why won't you let me?"

One familiar, if sneaky, approach is to hold back important information. Jim, for example, tells his father that Dave's parents will let Dave go on a two-day camping trip. At the same time, Dave reports to his parents that Jim's folks have given their OK.

Joining forces to turn parents' decisions your way isn't anything new. It's just another advantage of belonging to a friendship group. Friends urge each other on. At the same time they strengthen their own determination to challenge old rules and gain new freedoms.

Group decisions. Group pressure is used for much more than just changing the minds of cautious parents. Groups make other important decisions and then act on them.

Group pressure carries a lot more influence than a single complaint. For

This track team just won a regional meet. The girls rejoice together as they share the triumph of Sandy's new state record for the half mile.

example, if several students band together to protest an unfair assignment, the teacher is more likely to change it than if only one class member complains.

In groups you learn the advantages of sharing both decision making and responsibility for your decisions. You realize that members can help each other to accomplish major goals in life.

Here are some other ways that group membership helps individuals:

• *Encouragement.* Did you ever notice that you feel braver when with others? In a group you need not break new ground all by yourself. The leader may do some scouting in order to make decisions for group action. The leader's directions encourage group members to follow along.

Friends may encourage you to do things you'd never try alone. They may even come along to bolster your confidence. For example, you may approach members of the other sex with a group of friends, something you might not dare if you were alone.

• *Safety.* Among friends you can let off steam and even pretend to be angrier than you are—all in safety. As you know, talking about negative emotions not only releases tension, but often prepares you to discover why you feel so upset.

For example, you can threaten, "I'm going to murder my sister if she doesn't stop wearing my clothes without asking." Everyone knows that you don't intend to kill your sister. But they do realize that she gets on your nerves. In turn, you may discover that you have strong feelings about others using your things.

Sympathetic listeners can ease your feelings of guilt when you complain about your family. You feel less disloyal when a friend echoes the same complaints.

• *Sharing and closeness.* In a group you enjoy the triumphs of some members and help soften disappointments for others. When one friend sets a new track record, all team members enjoy some of the glory. When another member goofs, the group rallies around to offer reassurance or sympathy.

• *Identity.* During adolescence, membership in a group gives you identity. Identity means having a clear idea

More than anything, friendship groups are fun.

of who and what you are. It also refers to how you are separate and distinct from others in your life. If you move on to a larger school, for example, for a time you might feel like just another face. However, at the lunch table, with your group of old friends, you become a person again—someone with a name, a personality, an identity.

- *Learning.* In a group you learn how to get along with others. You experience loyalties and rivalries firsthand. You judge others. You also feel the sting of being judged. You learn about ranking: Who rates most and why? Who doesn't and why?

- *Discovery.* In a group you discover what's important to you by keeping close check on what you care about. You may have questions like these: What do I do best? How do I rate compared to others? Do they consider me attractive? Do they like me? Am I a leader or a follower?

Because of such questions, teens seem to talk to each other a lot—in class, after school, on the phone. You want to find out more about yourself—as fast as possible. All things considered, it's a fair exchange. "You tell me that I'm a nice person, and I'll do the same for you." This discovery process is all part of growing through adolescence into adulthood.

PEER GROUP PRESSURES

Next you'll read some of the helpful ways a group can bring pressure on an individual to act more mature or to change behavior that group members don't like. As you read, think if and how you've been subject to such pressures.

Approve. Usually you can depend on your parents to love you. However, you must earn the respect of your peers. Parents may forgive you your sulky moods. They may excuse rude demands or inconsiderate behavior. However, your peers usually judge you more evenly. They rate you on your real merits instead of promises or excuses.

Labels like "spoiled," "selfish," or "stuckup" fall easily from the lips of group members. The evaluations may be unkind at times. However, they are often accurate. Such pressures of approval and disapproval influence all group members and help keep them in line.

Approval is so important that you may even change old habits in order to be accepted.

CASE EXAMPLE

Ben's mother nagged him regularly about his dirty fingernails. He paid no attention. One day a pretty girl in his English class wrinkled her nose, pointed, and said, "Ugh, gruesome!"

Quick as a flash, Ben became a clean-fingernails guy.

Bernard Crumpton

Sometimes there's just nothing to do.

Group pressure often reaches beyond language, clothing, fads, grooming habits, or planning school events. Most teens are willing to do a lot to impress the peers whose friendship and respect they want. Fear of disapproval can be a powerful force.

Groups vary in what they demand as an entry fee from new members. Some social service clubs require that a candidate do a good turn such as serving as a volunteer in a community project, or collecting money for a good cause.

Other groups encourage pranks like soaping windows or draping toilet paper over trees and shrubbery. Street gangs might even insist that a newcomer commit a dangerous or illegal act. What is expected of the members depends on the group. The pressures to go along are great.

Decisions for joiners. You can see how important the right decision is in selecting a group. A good question to ask yourself is "What can this group do for me?" A street gang's hero may be considered the best thief in town. Nonmembers may see him as a delinquent.

On the other hand, the boy or girl who volunteers to work with handicapped children has a chance to meet others with similar goals of helping and serving. Teachers and parents approve of such unselfish behavior, adding to the good feelings of the volunteer.

How much? Of course, not everyone needs or wants the same amount of group contact. Nor is everyone interested in exactly the same activities.

A few persons are so popular and well liked that they seem welcome in any group. Others want very much to belong to one group or another, but they get overlooked or frozen out by the insiders.

You'll read more about such popularity and rejection in later chapters. For the moment, remember that for many young persons, family life and private interests still come first. Such boys and girls enjoy group companionship, but they don't seem to need it as much as some others.

CASE EXAMPLE

Francis was a recent finalist in a national science contest. He comes from a close family in which both parents and an older brother are scientists. From early childhood Francis showed great promise. In kindergarten he made a magnetic spring. In first grade he built a periscope. A friend gave him a Venus flytrap for his thirteenth birthday. For a ninth grade project he outlined the nitrogen metabolism of the Venus plant.

Francis plays no school sports. Yet he gets up at 7 A.M. each school day to attend sessions of his high school math team. He enjoys competition with others who share his special interests.

Francis seems to need less group companionship and activity than most

boys his age. Already his interests and career preparation are well ahead of average. His parents and brother not only share his talents, but they also praise, encourage, and challenge him to develop his natural gifts. As a result, Francis chooses to be more of an individual at an age when his peers spend a lot of time in friendship groups.

What about me? How much time do you spend on your own special interests or hobbies?

Are there things that you always wanted to try but never found the time for?

Some people would say that if you really wanted to learn a new hobby that you would make the time.

Could that be true of you?

If yes, will you do anything about it?

To learn more. Select one idea or topic from this chapter that applies to you and the way you live your life.

On a separate sheet of paper describe your selection in one sentence.

In no more than three sentences explain why you chose it.

DO NOT WRITE IN THIS BOOK.

RECAP

Every child must learn how to become a loving person through close and loving contacts with parents and other family members. Peers, too, are important in human development. In peer relationships children learn to control hostility and aggression. Peer relationships also open the way to friendships, closeness with the other sex, marriage and parenthood.

The need for group membership is important throughout life, but especially during adolescence. It's a rare teen who doesn't want to be a member of friendship groups. In small clusters adolescents find companionship, shared interests, and good times. People do much good work in groups.

One way to earn group membership is to conform, or go along with the way others act, dress, or talk. Conformity offers the security of belonging. Not everyone conforms 100 percent. There's room for differences. As teens grow older, the tendency to conform may seem to fade. It never disappears. The need to be accepted finds expression in different ways. Adults have clubs and cliques of their own.

Conformity can cause problems when a person goes along with dangerous or harmful group action.

Copying the latest clothing style, imitating new slang, or using the same old street words are familiar ways of conforming. Abusive or obscene language is also a way to get attention in expressing disgust, anger, or rebellion.

Cliques are smaller friendship groups without actual rules, but with a code that holds the members together. Belonging to a small group can bring many advantages to teens. Friends help you grow up and become less dependent on your family. When young persons bunch together they can influence parents and teachers to change old rules and grant new privileges.

Clique membership can teach you how to make and keep friends. You learn to compromise. You also learn to consider the wishes of others besides yourself. You learn how to rate others. As they react to you, you learn more about yourself. You learn more about what's expected of you. The approval or disapproval of the group also helps shape your behavior and form your decisions. In many ways group influence helps decide the kinds of relationships you will have as an adolescent and in your later years as an adult.

TERMS			
Popularity	Acceptance	Semi-secret language	Jocks
Status	Status symbol	Women's lib	Pencilheads
Peers	Fads	Ms.	Freaks
Crowd	Emblem	Clique	Identity
Conformity	Fad language	Territory	
Individuality	Slang	Turf	

CHAPTER 12

Stages of Friendship

Friendship is like a beautiful car. It has much value. However, without regular attention and repair it won't run well. In this chapter you will read how friendships start and how to keep them running smoothly.

You inherit your relatives, but you can choose your friends. In friendship you pick and get picked. You give and you get. Each person benefits.

Actually, friendship doesn't always work so smoothly. You may select a friend who picks someone else.

Friendship is very important to adolescents. Friends help you to become less dependent on parents. A friend is like another self in the serious business of becoming an adult.

Sometimes it happens that a brother, sister, or cousin is your closest friend. More often, teens choose a non-family member of the same sex to be a friend.

Automatically you belong to a large circle of peers at school. However, you also need the closer relationships of friendship.

FACTS ABOUT FRIENDSHIP

Did you ever think about how or why you choose someone to be your friend? Or why someone picks you? Friendship is not a mystery. In fact, one person usually selects another for good and simple reasons. For example:

• Friendships happen most often between neighbors. The farther you live from someone (even a few houses or blocks away) the less likely it is you'll become close friends.

• Friendships happen most often between teens who share similar experiences, such as being in the same class, participating in the same sport, or having the same after-school interests.

• Friendships happen most often between teens who share similar attitudes.

Friends share experiences. Here, a summer shower has given Pat and Brad a place to enjoy themselves.
David Snodgress, Journal and Courier, Lafayette, Indiana

Rohn Engh
These friends always have some news to share.

211

Friends.

Natalie Leimkuhler

Simply, the more a person agrees with your viewpoint about issues important to you, the more likely that a friendship will develop.

• Friendships happen more often between teens who meet each other's needs. For example, if you find a person who is patient and helpful when you need someone to listen to you, and you provide the same acceptance for him or her, friendship is likely to blossom.

Try to remember these points as you read about the growth of close friendships.

BEGINNINGS

You've been practicing friendship ever since you first offered a soggy cookie to another baby. At first, toddlers sit side by side, so absorbed in themselves and their own play that they barely notice each other. Then, suddenly, one grabs the other's sand shovel. Friendship (or disagreement) begins.

Gradually, little children begin to play more with each other. They chatter, make up games, build forts, play house. From shaky new friendships that may collapse with the first squabble grow stronger and more lasting bonds.

Many kinds of friendship draw two people together. Some friendships cross lines of both age and sex. For example, an older person and a younger one may get along especially well.

In the next case example you can follow one girl's growth of friendship from late childhood through mid-teens. In her own words and those of her friends, Amy offers you a history of her friendships that may be much like your own.

CASE EXAMPLE

Amy is both a scribbler and a saver. She kept her earliest jottings in an old shoe box. Later, notes and letters from friends piled up.

Amy and Kim lived on the same street. Because they were the only girls in the neighborhood, they played together. Both girls were bossy and competitive. Usually one or the other ran home in tears. One day when they were about nine years old, Kim invited a mutual friend to visit. Amy felt left out and hurt. She marched home and wrote out her version of what happened. (Note: The misspellings were in Amy's original.)

A Speech about Kim

"Kim had Tina over. She tried to show off to me with Tina. She started talking about me in a mean way. I don't think I will go with Kim too much. Oh, I wish she had never moved here. She ruened my friendship with Tina. She is a lier too. I'm not her tipe and she's not mine. I'm

David Snodgress, Journal and Courier, Lafayette, Indiana

never going to forgive her because she said things that hurt my feelings. She said to Tina 'I do not like Amy.' I'm tierd of her. She promised to play with me but then she tried to make me mad and play with Tina."

Despite the misspelled words, Amy expressed both her hurt and anger very well. Of course the girls made up, only to fight again. Spats or not, they needed each other. Still struggling with her emotions a year later, Amy wrote:

"I thought Kim was a very nice girl but she turned out to be an untrustful person. In my own words I say she is a cheater and a doble crosser because she tries to be on one team and because when the other team is better she goes over to that team and turns us down. She thinks she is so great. I think she is the bully of the naborhood. I personaly am going to say to her: look at my pinky you are

stinky. And here is another one: see my fingers see my thumb see my face and I think youer dumb. I don't like Kim any more. And when ever she doesnt want to play with you she says, 'my mommy does not want any people in the house and she does not want me to go outside,' in a squeaky voice. I just hate Kim's guttes."

Of course, not every friendship is so stormy. Indeed, two years later, in junior high school, the relationship between Amy and Kim changed greatly. The girls went to different classes and each made new friends. More grown-up and independent, each felt free of the forced companionship of neighborhood boundaries. They fell into an easygoing and less-demanding friendship. Today the girls are in high school. Each regards the other as a friend, but not a close one. Often they walk to school together. If they disagree, it's no longer

213

Close since they were much younger, these girls continued their friendship all through junior and senior high school.

a life and death struggle. It's been a long time since Amy has needed to write notes to herself about Kim.

Something to think about. Can you trace one friendship of yours that has developed from childhood into adolescence?

How does the relationship between you and your friend compare to the Amy/Kim match-up?

Write a paragraph. On a separate sheet of paper write out a year-by-year history of your friendship. Use one sentence for each year.

Bring the review of your friendship up to date.

DO NOT WRITE IN THIS BOOK.

EARLY ADOLESCENT FRIENDSHIP

We meet Amy again in junior high school. Now she's no longer writing to herself. She has stacks of notes passed in classes and exchanged in hallways. The correspondence reveals the growing importance of friends and social life in these years. Of course, note-passing has little to do with social studies or English, but it breaks up the long school day. Notes serve as a way for friends to exchange ideas, check out opinions, and pass on the latest gossip.

Judging from Amy's collection, most messages move from girl to girl. Once in a while a boy may scribble a brief yes or no to a girl's repeated question. But most of the signatures are female.

Some of Amy's notes appear later, a good sample of everyday back-and-forth between friends. The messages reveal the plans, pranks, worries, and concerns of young persons. Amy's answers are not available. They probably rest in someone else's secret collection.

CASE EXAMPLE

Plans. Detailed plans, many of which never happen, pepper Amy's notes. Some are brief and to the point.

"I'm grounded tonight, so let's go roller skating Saturday if we can get the money."

One series was filled with details of a proposed trip. Apparently, a friend named Marcy wanted to include Amy on a family trip. Marcy's mother didn't like the idea. Marcy wrote:

"I'll ask my mother again today if you can come to Beachville with us. Here's a list of what I'm bringing. Copy my list." Two pages of detailed items followed, including toothbrush and comb, color of shoes and hair ribbon. Another note urged: "Come home with me after school and we'll crack that crab [Marcy's mother]. She's got to let you come with us!"

Pranks. Dreaming up silly things to do can be fun on a slow-moving day. Amy and her friends planned many more pranks than they ever tried. Her notes reported the details of several plots designed to make someone else look foolish.

One plan to use shaving cream instead of whipped topping on a friend's birthday cake was never put into action. Another plot, however, got the full treatment.

Good friends don't demand much of each other.

Natalie Leimkuhler

"At Polly's party let's really fool around," read one message. "We can make instant pudding and throw it in someone's face."

To her mother's dismay, Amy returned from Polly's party gooey with chocolate pudding. In this case Amy ended up victim of her own scheme. Pudding oozed from her hair, ears, and clothing.

Practical jokes also rate high as pranks. One note made reference to "hot pepper" gum for gum-chewing friends. Another scrap carried a plan to liven up friendly handshakes with a hand buzzer. In this case, the butt of the joke gets an unexpected "shock" when the tight spring in the buzzer lets loose.

Life at school. In the absence of really big news such as who likes whom, casual comments on teachers, assignments, and school life fill the notes. "What page are we on?" said one. Another contained the locker combinations of friends. A third listed the cafeteria menus for the week. Others included comments on the personalities and the peculiarities of certain teachers.

"I hate Mrs. Stone [an English teacher]. Don't you? I'm not going to give my mom the note she sent home, are you? Mine said, 'Particularly needs improvement in behavior.'"

"Who do you like better, Mrs. Taylor or Mr. Arthur? Circle one."

Solving conflict. In exchanging notes the girls try to find ways to work out disagreements and still stay friends. "Are we still best friends?" wrote Jane to Amy. "I like you best, but please don't get so upset when I'm with Maribeth."

Another read, "At lunch when you and Julie whispered and you told her about you and Kevin, that didn't make *me* feel like a best friend."

Later came an apology after a fight: "I felt terrible when I told you off. I'm sorry I said the things I did, but I was jealous that you like Julie better than you like me."

It seems that the friendship cooled between Jane and Amy, for in a later note Jane wrote: "If you don't think we can be best friends I'll always like you as a really close friend."

Please like me. Many notes seek reassurance. "Do you think this top

215

looks like a maternity dress? Dolores said it does."

As mentioned before, early adolescents seem to want to be more like each other than different. Still uncertain about tastes and opinions, they feel more secure when they dress, think, and act like their friends. An ability to accept differences among friends develops later as they grow older.

CASE EXAMPLE

One writer wants reassurance that she is liked.

"Do Lee and Nancy like me? I hope so, because I think that you are all really nice girls.

"Is Cathy mad at me? She's acting funny."

Gossip. Many of Amy's tightly folded scraps are filled with opinions and comments about other people, some unkind. "Diane is trying so hard to get popular. How do you like the way I told her that in social studies? It was mean, but she knows it's true and she won't face it. It's sickening. Like when she goes to a party she acts so fake just to get in good. She won't be herself."

"Kathy was elected snow queen but she didn't deserve it. Ginger should have gotten it."

Secrets. Labeling a note "private" seems a sure way to be certain that the enclosed news gets read and repeated quickly. Another technique to guarantee instant communication is to send the note across the desk of the person for whom the message is *really* intended.

"Don't tell anyone" sometimes means "pass this news on right away." For example, "I won't ever tell anything you tell me not to, but I really want to know. Do you like Joe?"

Secrets aren't kept too well: "I'll admit that I told Tabby that you said you like Andy. It makes me mad that Julie told you I said so. She promised she wouldn't. She can't keep a secret!"

Boy-girl. Who likes whom may be the most interesting news of all. It involves a lot of guessing and some deliberate planting of ideas. Often, a girl may never think seriously about a boy—or the other way 'round—until a friend mentions that one likes the other. Then, suddenly, mutual interest grows.

One note read: "Bruce, do you still like Sally as much as you used to? I won't tell her. Check Yes__ No__."

Poor Bruce checked Yes, and within moments a note sped out in the other direction informing everyone of his deep love for Sally.

Still another message read, "I'm mad at John because he won't tell Janet if he likes me—and she asked him three times!"

The writer of the next one seems somewhat uncertain of her facts, but quite willing to pass on a rumor anyway.

"Dave made out with Joni after school behind the pool. Ask Dave about it. If he asks you who told you just tell him you heard a rumor and you wondered if it is true or not."

What about me? Amy's notes offer a revealing picture of social life during her early adolescence.

How have your emotional reactions been similar to Amy's?

How have your friendships to date been different?

Do boys go through similar stages of friendship?

MIDDLE ADOLESCENCE

At age fifteen, there's a noticeable change in Amy's collection. There's less emphasis on plans and events, less gossip and news, and more thoughtful exchanges.

CASE EXAMPLE

Since eighth grade, Amy has been on a best-friend basis with Marla. They write each other long letters exploring their emotions and explaining themselves. One event, reported with Marla's words, helps you understand how much maturing can take place in a few years.

In junior high school, Marla liked Kurt and he liked her. After a few months, Kurt switched to other girls, but Marla kept liking him. She daydreamed that he would come back to her.

Then, unexpectedly, Kurt invited Amy to a Hi-Y picnic. The girls faced a crisis in their friendship. Amy really wanted to go with Kurt, yet she did not want to hurt her best friend. In a note to Marla, Amy wrote that she'd decided not to go to the picnic.

As you read Marla's answer, compare the concern and the feeling with earlier notes. Obviously, Amy and her friends have matured a lot.

"Amy:

"Let's clear up some things, okay? We have a difficult situation but it doesn't have to be worse than it is. For one thing, you are taking the blame where you didn't do anything. It's really a matter of me facing the truth.

"No boy is worth the friendship of two good girl friends. This little Hi-Y thing isn't going to break that rule. You've got to stop feeling bad. After

Natalie Leimkuhler
The latest boy-girl news travels fast.

all, Kurt's the one who asked you— you didn't ask him!

"I'll admit that the timing on this is bad. Real bad. Because I realize that Kurt and I will never get back together. No one wants to say that something is over when they don't want it to be. I don't think you can honestly say that you think Kurt and I could ever get back together. I'll always like him, maybe because he was my first love. I can't explain it. It's just how I feel about him.

"Anyway, I don't hate you and I'm not mad at you. Please stop thinking that you are taking Kurt away from me. You aren't because he's not mine.

"I'm depressed and it's not all Kurt. Bart [a new boyfriend] and I aren't good friends any more. We're still friends but communication has stopped. Everything happens at once, but none of it is your fault.

217

Girls become close friends between ages four-teen and sixteen. Meg and Jill are right on schedule.

"Please don't let this come be-tween us. I don't want any guy (well, so Kurt's not just *any* guy!) coming between us.

"So go on the picnic and have fun. It doesn't mean that you're going to marry him or anything. I'm going to stop living on the false hope that he'll come back to me. Me and my won-derful imagination."

Love,
Marla"

The growth of friendship in Amy's life may remind you of your own experienc-es. Male or female, as you grow older physically, so grows your ability to offer and accept friendship. Of course you may not seek friends. But if you do, you spend more time with them and share more confidences than when younger. You will learn to work out disagreements and to survive quarrels. You will discov-er that you really care about certain persons. In fact, the beginning of lasting friendship is closely tied to your grow-ing ability to feel loyalty and affection for others. Little children have not yet de-veloped such qualities.

Young adolescents often think that having many friends means automatic popularity. By mid-adolescence they usually discover that the right type of friend is more important than how many. Gradually, as you meet and know more and more persons, the number of close friends in your life grows smaller.

Something to think about. Friend-ships are much like adolescents. As friendships get older they mature in the process.

Sean says, "I used to think my friends had to be just like me—enjoy what I enjoy, be ready for something when I'm ready. Now I'm tired of that. Many of my friends are different from me. It's more fun to have differences and challenge each other once in awhile."

Make a list. On a separate sheet of paper make a list of the ways that your friends are similar to you.

Then make a second list of ways in which they are different.

DO NOT WRITE IN THIS BOOK.

What about me? Sean has given his friends and himself freedom to go their separate ways and to think their own thoughts.

What reaction do you have when a good friend disagrees with you?

Suppose that friend openly challeng-es you in front of others?

GOOD FRIENDS

In spite of much shifting and chang-ing of friends, a surprising number don't ever switch. In one research study of city and country students, the teens inter-viewed chose the same person as best friend 60 to 90 percent of the time. Also,

A best friend is a good friend with something extra.

Natalie Leimkuhler

the eleven to fifteen-year-olds showed more friendship changes than those who were sixteen to eighteen.

Close friendships reach a peak for girls during the years from fourteen to sixteen. As you know, girls are often more advanced than boys in social give and take.

Ages fifteen to seventeen see the most close friendships for males. Then, as boys and girls become more interested in each other, males have less time for friends of the same sex. However, long after they become adults, friends of the same sex remain important.

Childhood playmates sometimes remain close friends for a lifetime, exchanging Christmas cards and family pictures as the years go by. However, most young friends drift apart as new interests and values draw them in different directions. Growing up may sepa-

rate close friends and change the selection of new ones. This means that when you are forty you may have a few friends from childhood, some from school years, and more from adult contacts at work, church, or in the neighborhood.

BEST FRIENDS

Best friends are good friends with something extra. A best friend is someone you like and admire. He or she may be a little bit smarter or more talented than you. However, a best friend is rarely so much better or worse that either of you suffers by comparison.

What makes best friends special is that each fills a particular need. One may share a hobby like bottle collecting or chess. Another may understand you better than anyone else.

Movie plots sometimes tell of the unselfish loyalty of one close friend for

219

another. In war stories, for example, one friend may give his life to save a buddy.

Examples of such devotion do show up from time to time. In most cases, however, friendship is a two-way street. Each friend gives something to the relationship. Each gets something in return. Close friendships don't last very long when one person provides all the loyalty, companionship, understanding, and fun.

As you read the following opinions of some students about best friendship, pick out those qualities that seem to turn a good friend into a best friend.

CASE EXAMPLE

Caren, an uncertain preteen, once said it this way: "I'd like Patti for a best friend. She's about the nicest person I ever met. I considered Cathy for a best friend, but there's something missing from her that Patti has. Cathy and I can like each other only as good friends. Patti knows that best friends must trust each other. She doesn't have to tell me more than once that she won't do something or won't repeat something. I believe her."

Actually, Patti and Caren never became that close. But a few years later Caren found a best friend. Now she seems to know what she wants. She says, "My best friend is in my class. We stay all night at her house or mine at least once a week. We can talk about anything to each other. We talk out our problems until we find a solution. Every teenager needs someone to tell their problems to. I trust her. When I tell her something she keeps it a secret. I can depend on her to be honest with me. We've never had a serious quarrel. We don't talk behind

each other's back. Ours is what I'd call true friendship."

Shana reports, "My best friend is a lot like me in many ways, but we are different, too. We've known each other since second grade. Even our parents like each other. We like the same kind of clothes and we go shopping together. We talk a lot about boys and give each other advice."

Ed, an older adolescent, has his opinion. "To me, real friendship has nothing to do with trading off favors, or how much time you spend together. My best friends are people I may not talk to for weeks. But when I need to share my feelings, they are there. When I'm busy or want to be alone, my best friends understand. They don't get angry or feel neglected. Real friends know each other's moods and respect them."

Peter is a young adult. He says, "Friendship is hard work. It's not always easy or a pleasure to meet a friend's needs. My grandmother died when I was fourteen. My best friend didn't say anything. He just came and sat with me in silence. It was the warmest, most wonderful thing anyone could have done. We will always be buddies."

People need people. If a best friend values you highly, you feel good. With best friendship goes the thought, "If I'm liked that much by such a fine person, I must be a fine person, too." On the other hand if a best friend frowns on something you say or do, you'll probably feel down in the dumps. Your self-esteem balloon gets deflated.

All things considered, best friends help each other grow as persons. They like and respect each other and meet

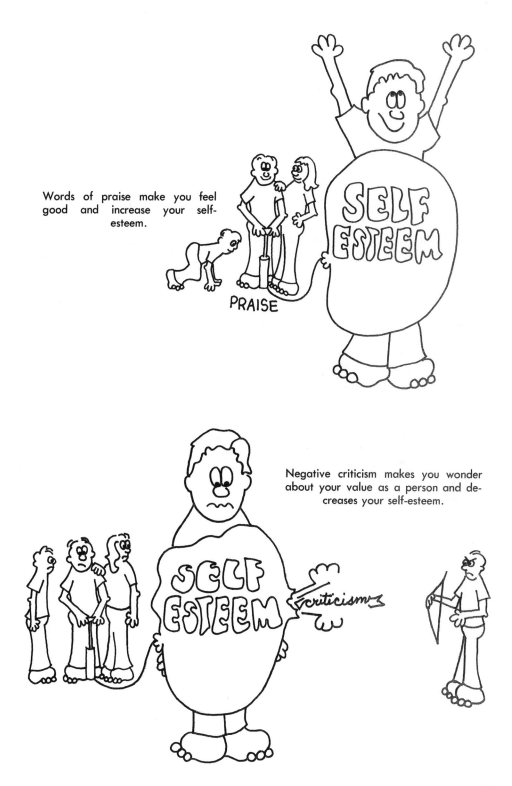

Words of praise make you feel good and increase your self-esteem.

PRAISE

SELF ESTEEM

Negative criticism makes you wonder about your value as a person and decreases your self-esteem.

SELF ESTEEM

criticism

each other's needs, especially in emergencies.

Make a list. The following words are often used to describe best friends.

Loyal	Trustworthy
Generous	Understanding
Humorous	Accepting
Thoughtful	Honest
Kind	Helpful

On a separate sheet of paper select three words that describe your best friend.

Now list three words that describe the qualities that you try to bring to a friendship.

DO NOT WRITE IN THIS BOOK.

BROKEN FRIENDSHIPS

CASE EXAMPLE

As you grow, so grows your ability to be a friend and to offer friendship. Yet you know that not every friendship ripens into a close and lasting one. Joel recalls his experience:

"In grade school we all stayed in the same room. In junior high we began to split up and make new friends. At first I kept looking for kids from my old school. I was afraid that I'd lose my friends to someone else. I wanted to hang on to them but find some new ones, too. It took me a while to learn that two people could still be friends even if they don't do everything together."

Change is part of life. Childhood groups break up. Playmates drift away. Friends part company for many reasons. One may physically outgrow the other. A girl who matures early, for example, may become popular with boys long before her slower-growing girl friends.

Some friendships die a natural death. Sometimes outside circumstances interrupt. One person moves away. Another may switch schools. Still, friends separated by many miles sometimes keep a warm fondness for each other. They meet again and pick up where they left off. They may write or phone. They always enjoy each other.

Friendships often die because interests and values change. After all, you don't continue to wear your sixth-grade clothes, nor like the same kind of music, nor admire the same TV stars.

CASE EXAMPLE

Perhaps you've felt confusion like Anne's, revealed as she tried to explain her feelings to Lorene.

"I want to be best friends with you. When I'm with you, I really like you. But when I'm with Marie, I like her best. I don't understand myself!"

Following you'll read some reasons why close friends break up. As you read, *think about your own experiences.* People of all ages run into problems in getting along. Indeed, sometimes close friends become bitter enemies. Chances are you've lost a friend or two and wonder why.

Betray. Stealing from a friend is to betray that friend. Gary asked to talk to the school counselor. With shame he told his story.

CASE EXAMPLE

Gary and a few friends visited Bert, who was home recovering from an appendix operation. Immediately, Gary noticed a stack of the best sport magazines. He asked to borrow one he hadn't seen. Scowling and in a bad mood from many days of confinement, Bert snapped, "No!"

Gary thought, "Selfish bum— serves you right to be sick." Yet the urge to read the magazines was more than Gary could stand. So when Bert wasn't looking, he sneaked one under his school books.

No sooner had Gary left the house than he felt guilty. He had never taken anything before. Yet he couldn't bring himself to return the magazine for fear of what Bert and his mother would think.

That night Gary couldn't eat supper. Later, without interest, he turned the pages of his stolen prize. He found no pleasure in reading.

On his return to school the next week, Bert was very cool. He shot Gary some dirty looks. Their friendship was all over.

Gary felt sorry. He wanted to make up, but he didn't know how.

Friends sometimes steal from, lie to, gossip about, or otherwise mistreat each other. Such behavior often happens quickly, done before there is time to think of possible results.

Gaining control of such impulses is an important step in growing up. A single theft doesn't make a thief. Most young people make mistakes like Gary's. Later, they usually regret their behavior. Most try not to repeat.

Something to think about. How would you explain Gary's actions? Can he mend his broken friendship? If yes, how? What would you do in his place? What can Gary learn about himself from this experience? In what other ways do friends betray each other?

First impressions. Perhaps you've had the experience of meeting someone for the first time who really impressed you. At the outset, your new friend seems better looking, smarter, funnier, and superior in every way to your old friends. Then things change.

First impressions may wear off to reveal just a nice, ordinary person. Or you may discover you've made a complete mistake. Your new friend may turn out to be a cheat, liar, or someone who always seems to want to pick a fight over little things.

Such discovery is part of learning that one person is not likely to be much different from most people after all.

Expect too much. It's easy to think up good things about people we like—especially from a distance. A football hero seems the perfect man, a TV star the ideal woman.

Closer to home, you may hear it said that another school turns out unbeatable athletes or the prettiest cheerleaders. Yet when you meet them they look and act exactly like the gang in your school.

It is easy to ask too much of friends in much the same way. When a friend doesn't measure up to the ideal picture of a loyal, faithful, and attentive pal, do you get angry? Of course it is unfair to expect that one friend can meet all your needs for attention, affection, and praise. You kid yourself when you expect too much.

Mistreatment. Most people of all ages let each other down once in a while. "Friends" sometimes use each other as stepping-stones to someone better. For example, a boy or girl may deliberately be nice to a fringe member of a desirable clique. Once in the group, however, the new member may drop the less important one for someone with more influence or popularity.

Or a girl friend may pass on the details of another's crush on a boy—adding a few made-up details in the process. Such persons sacrifice their friendship to gain a feeling of importance. They act as an "inside source" by

Charles Riker

Every girl wants to choose her own friends.

repeating a confidence or passing on a juicy bit of information—whether it's true or not.

Competition. Most young friendships can't take too much competition. Tami shares a painful memory.

CASE EXAMPLE

"I used to have a friend I thought I'd like forever. We were so close we were like sisters. After I got a lead in a school play she changed overnight. She was critical and said sarcastic things to me. I was very hurt. I told her it was just a school play. I wasn't going to Hollywood or anything! Even after the play was over we never got together again."

Competition surfaces in other ways, too. One person may get better grades, buy nicer clothes, or become so popular with the other sex that a friend can't stand the constant reminders of being second-best. It's easier to look for another friend whose competition won't cause so much pain.

Status. Status (STAY-tis) means how well known and important a person is. As you move through your teen years you will become more aware of people with status and what they can do for you. Status is very important to adolescents.

Some young people are shut out by former friends for reasons that have nothing to do with how they act in the crowd. They may only lack status. Where you live or your father's type of work may decide the future of a friendship. Listen to Casey as he explains how status changed his life.

CASE EXAMPLE

"My family lives in the housing project. I always got along OK with other kids through sixth grade. I had many friends and we all played together. The year we started junior high school, our gang seemed to break up. None of us were good friends any more. Most of the gang made new friends and joined cliques.

"The poorer kids got left out. Suddenly, we were outsiders, but we didn't know why. I got tagged with the poor clique—I guess because I lived in the project. My old pals stayed away from me. My family had an average income, but it made no difference. To our age group, if you didn't have a neat bunch of new clothes you were an absolute nothing. I was classed as an outcast. Nobody said it, but I knew it anyway."

What about me? What do you think of Casey's reactions? Does he see things as they really are, or does he seem to be kidding himself to invite sympathy? What emotion would you guess Casey felt when he realized what was happening to him? How important is status to your school life?

Parent influence. "My mother doesn't want me to be with Barb."

"My father thinks that Robby is a bad influence on me."

Directly and indirectly, parents influence the friends you pick. Years of growing up in a family can push you toward choosing friends with the same backgrounds and interests. Although you may change as you grow older, your mother and father have taught you ways of living and thinking that make you feel at ease with others like yourself.

During your adolescent years, however, you may begin to test, challenge, and even reject parent opinions. In fact, hearing your mother say, "Liz seems like such a nice girl" or "Why don't you bring Frank home?" may be enough to sour you on two nice people. You want to choose your own friends, even if you make mistakes.

Parents often frown on friends whose life-style seems to go against family values. Parents are concerned and afraid that you might get into trouble. They may be right.

Sometimes, however, adults object to certain friends for other reasons. There is a difference, for example, in parent protests against a drugging or drinking crowd and objections to a friend because of skin color or religion.

Disagreement about your choice of friends may cause open conflict between you and your parents. You'd probably like your folks to respect and approve of the boys and girls you pick. If they criticize and cut down a friend, it's like picking on you and your judgment. As a result, you may defend your friend strongly even when you suspect your parents could be right.

What about me? Using the ideas on pages 121–124, how can parents and adolescents work out differences about friendship choices?

Give an example of parent objections that you wouldn't mind.

What kind of objections to your friends bother you most?

Something to think about. Teens are criticized sometimes for doing what their friends think is best. Perhaps you have been the object of such criticism.

However, at other times adolescents often favor values or standards set at home by their parents.

What about me? On a separate sheet of paper rate each of the following items in terms of who influences your decisions most—your friends or your family.

- Choice of clothing.
- Choice of friends.
- Choice of career.
- Homework standards.
- Personal values.
- Moral choices.
- Weekend recreation plans.

DO NOT WRITE IN THIS BOOK.

Being dropped. Your clique may disapprove of an outsider friend of yours. The less secure you feel as a person and the more you fear possible rejection by your clique, the more likely you'll drop the outsider.

Sometimes it works the other way around. If you join a tough crowd, for example, former friends may drop you.

By now you realize that with adolescence come many more opportunities to pick and choose your friends. You will want your friends to be accepted by others. How your friends act says something about you. After all, you selected them in the first place. So if your friends embarrass or shame you by their ac-

Natalie Leimkuhler
Shopping with a friend makes the job easier.

tions, the easiest way out may be to look for new friends.

"You're known by the company you keep" is an old saying. Friends are not always a good influence on each other. If you start hanging around with a crowd known for drinking or drugs, you'll soon be considered just like them whether you do anything dangerous or not.

CASE EXAMPLES

As one boy explained it, "In this school you get lots of chances to smoke pot or drink booze. It's easy to hang around with the freaky people. If you don't want to try a new life-style, then stay away from them."

Another disagrees: "I hang around with more of the freaky kids. The girls are nicer. They're not so snobbish. It's a better atmosphere. We can talk about anything. I wouldn't take drugs or anything like that, but I'm still friends with them."

What about me? How is it in your school?

Can you be a full member in both groups?

What would your friends say?

How about your family?

Getting out. Easing out of a friendship is usually harder than jumping in. One friend may demand more than the other wants to give.

CASE EXAMPLE

Lynne and Mari were once best friends. Yet when they moved up to new schools, things gradually cooled between them. Lynne became annoyed when Mari followed her everywhere and phoned every night pleading to know whether they were still best friends.

Lynne hinted that she'd like less time together. She cut phone calls short. She also refused invitations to stay overnight at Mari's. The more Lynne tried to free herself, the tighter Mari's stranglehold became. Finally, in desperation, Lynne came straight to the point. She said, "Mari, you are a nice girl, and I like you. But I don't want to be your best friend anymore."

Of course, Mari had gotten the message long before, but she couldn't admit it. Mari felt she was accepted by the other girls in their group only because of her friendship with Lynne. Mari thought that no one would want her if she had to be judged on her own. Mari protested and cried, but Lynne held firm.

Lynne hurt Mari deeply. Yet she did not want to. Only as a last resort did Lynne cut off the friendship.

Worse ways exist to let people know that you don't want them around anymore. Lynne could have snubbed

Mari. She could have ridiculed Mari in front of other girls, or gossiped about her behind her back.

People differ in the kinds of friends who best meet their needs. Lynne didn't like Mari's dependence on her. Another girl might have welcomed a clinging vine type to help her feel more important. Actually, Lynne never told Mari what she didn't like about her behavior.

Another point of view. Sal was direct in handling his troubled friendship.

He reports, "Miguel is my good friend. But he did something I don't like. He lied to his mother. He said that he was coming to my apartment. But he was really going with a gang of guys his parents don't like. His mother called mine. My mother told Miguel's that he had never come to our place. He got into a lot of trouble. The next day he was mad at me.

"I said to him, 'If you want to lie to your parents, that's your business. Just don't drag me into it'."

What about me? What do you think of Sal's attitude? What would you do in his place?

How do you let a friend know that you don't approve of certain behavior?

How do you express praise to a friend?

BUILDING BETTER FRIENDSHIPS

Solving the mystery of friendship. A mysterious element enters each friendship. No one really understands all the bits and pieces of personality that attract one person to another. Pleasure and comfort in each other's company seem much greater among friends, yet this mutual ease is only part of the picture.

Some of the qualities of friendship are mentioned here to start you thinking about what it means to be a friend and to offer friendship. As you read, think about

Kathy Tuite
Good friends share good times together. Here Sue and Julie ham it up for the camera.

your own experiences. Try to discover answers to these questions:

• Why did I choose one friend above all others?

• Why do I feel closer to one friend than another?

• Why did a friendship that started well never bloom?

• How can I improve the quality of the friendships I already have?

• How can I attract someone I'd really like to have as a friend?

Same. During early adolescence, friends want to be like each other in the way they look, sound, act, and dress. The younger you are, the more important it may seem that friends be like you. Sameness provides assurance that you belong and are accepted.

Friends often share the same religion and the same ideas about right and wrong behavior. They even echo each other in special interests like music, science, or sports. The security in sameness makes you feel more comfortable.

As much as you might want to be like your friends, you probably feel equally

Friends often ask each other, "How do I look?"

determined *not* to be like adults. You begin to ask for what *you* want in clothing, food, and recreation.

Self. Talking with friends is a good way to keep in touch with yourself. Relating bad experiences and sharing good ones helps you to sketch a picture of yourself that is both real and approved by others. Indeed, friends help each other find out who they really are just by talking.

Adults sometimes call adolescents too self-centered because they seem interested only in themselves or each other. Yet in the endless exchange of opinion—"Do I look good in blue?" "Do other people like me?"—you perform the important work of moving toward adulthood. Through such exchanges you get a picture of who you are and how others see you. Without such feedback from others, your notion of what you are like would be incomplete.

Share. In Avellion, Italy, Vitorio Petretat recently received a $2,544 telephone bill for 99,000 direct dialing long distance calls made in three months. Either Vitorio had an astounding number of friends, or the phone company made a super mistake.

Friendships seem to thrive on telephone wires. It's not enough to talk during or after school.

Part of friendship is a continual checking out of each other's thoughts and feelings. Each friend wants to learn about the other's tastes, interests, and experiences. Having friends to share the newness of adolescence with you makes the unknown portions of life much more enjoyable.

Needs. Friends meet a human need for closeness at a time when each is seeking a lot more than family ties. Friends help each other survive and enjoy new routines of life away from home. Luci understood this need when her family moved to a new neighborhood.

CASE EXAMPLE

"When I came to this school I was scared to death. You hear stories about how tough it is, how kids get beat up on stairways. Anyone who said one nice word to me—right away she became my friend. That's how badly I needed friendship. At first, I grabbed someone to talk to in each class, someone to wait and walk with me to the next class. I just used people because I needed them, but soon I made real lasting friends."

Loyal. Friends stick up for one another. They don't suddenly quit because some bad news comes along. Stuart knows what loyalty means to him.

CASE EXAMPLE

"The main thing I look for in a friend is someone who is really for me. If he'll stick up for me when I need him, then I'll do something for him when he needs help."

Natalie Leimkuhler
There's always time to talk with a friend.

Matt struggled through a difficult adolescence involving a brush with the police for drug use. He told what he'd learned from his painful experience.

CASE EXAMPLE

"A real friend will stick by you no matter what. When I got into trouble, I discovered that I didn't have any real friends. Later when I thought about it I realized that I hadn't been much of a friend either. I had never been really close to anyone. And I never really accepted anyone else. I'm beginning

229

to realize that I'll have to be the one to make the first move."

Admire. People want to admire their friends. Sometimes you might even think more of your friends than you think of yourself. It is natural for you to want other people to respect and like your friends because your choice says something about your taste. It goes like this, "If I can attract nice people, then I must be special, too."

Since friends help each other to form relationships, it's important that your companions be acceptable to members of the other sex. If the friends you choose are sneered at or looked down on, it's not easy to stick up for them. Nevertheless, the ability to stand by a friend under pressure is still a test of friendship.

Control. Friends also help each other practice inner (self) controls. If you admire someone and want respect, you're likely to act in a way that won't turn that special person against you.

Generous. A friend is generous in many ways. Your friend may not have very much money, but is probably open-handed with time and attention, and usually slow to judge your faults.

Friendship is a two-way exchange. At times each friend gets, and the other gives. One giver puts it simply, "If I like certain people, then I want to make them happy."

Friendship helps you turn from total concern with self to begin to consider the feelings and preferences of others. Often, teen friendships provide the first experience in unselfish giving to another person.

Like. In A.D. 990, in *The Pillow Book of Shonagon,* a young Japanese woman wrote, "There is nothing in the whole world so painful as feeling that one is not liked." In a thousand years, human feelings have not changed.

Friendship really means that someone you like likes you. So rewarding is it to believe that people your own age like you that most adolescents hesitate to exclude anyone who seems to like them. It may seem selfish, but you never know when the others might be needed.

Opposite. Friends choose each other because they are much alike. However, they also choose for qualities that each admires in the other, but doesn't possess. For example, a shy girl may be eager to build a friendship with a more outgoing classmate. In exchange, the bubbly girl enjoys the quiet and thoughtful personality of her friend. Both benefit from the trade.

COUNSELING YOUR FRIENDS

Wise counsel. Earlier you read some of the things that switch a casual acquaintance into a close friend. You thought about what makes you draw closer to one person than all the others. You read that to be loyal, generous, and faithful feeds friendship.

One special ability—wise counsel—is often part of a strong and lasting relationship between two people. Sooner or later almost everyone is expected to listen to a friend's problems. Psychologists and psychiatrists are trained and paid "people helpers." They encourage their clients to talk about their worries in order to understand what is really bothering them and to help them decide what they want to do about it.

Ordinarily teens talk more freely with each other than with adults. Good friends usually counsel each other, too.

Listening to troubled friends gives you a nice feeling. When you help others to figure things out, you feel worthy and useful yourself.

Some people combine a knack for listening with a natural gift for helping others. Sympathetic and understanding, they show a genuine concern for their friends. They also offer a good measure of common sense. Perhaps most important, they seldom give advice like, "If I were you, I'd . . ." or "Why don't you . . ."

Following are some suggestions that may help you to counsel your friends. As you think about these guidelines check yourself:

- Do I use any of these suggestions?
- Could I use these ideas?
- How would I have to change to be a better and more helpful counselor to my friends?

Guidelines for living.
How to Counsel Your Friends

- *Listen.* A friend listens to your worries, understands your moods, and encourages you to talk about both. One girl explained:

"My friends call me Ann Landers. I've learned that friends don't want advice. They want someone to hear them out and understand their feelings. Friends seem to feel better after talking to me. They act as though I did something special for them. All I really do is *listen.*"

When listening to a problem, let your friend get it out. Don't interrupt by changing the subject or talking about similar problems you may have. Save your worries for another time. To butt in with your problems shows that you are more concerned about yourself than your friend.

- *Advice.* Trained counselors rarely tell their clients exactly what to do. Instead of giving advice, encourage your friend to suggest several possible

Natalie Leimkuhler
A good friend always has time to listen.

solutions to a problem. Help your friend to see the different choices that seem open at the time. Then ask, "If you had your choice, what would you like to do?"

- *Action.* Encourage some kind of "take charge" *action* to bring your friend closer to a solution. For example, to someone unjustly suspected of vandalism you might say, "Would you be willing to go to the principal in order to explain your side of the story?"

- *Reflect feeling.* Demonstrate that you understand your friend's emotions. For example, say, "It must have *hurt*

231

when Rae said you looked fat." "I'll bet you felt *mad* when they said you cheated." Even if you're not exactly right, saying how the other person probably feels at the time helps your friend understand the important emotions.

• *Help.* Some things are too big for adolescents to handle alone. If the problem is serious, suggest that your friend talk to someone older and more experienced like a parent, teacher, professional counselor, or church youth leader.

• *Secret.* Keep your mouth shut. Don't blab the secrets that others confide in you. When friends learn that they can open up to you without fear of embarrassment, your reputation as a trusted secret-keeper will grow fast.

Write a paragraph.

On a separate sheet of paper write a paragraph that explains your preferences about the subject of friendship. Select one of the following topics:

• What I Look for in a Friend
• How to Be a Friend
• What I Think a Friend Expects of Me

DO NOT WRITE IN THIS BOOK.

To learn more. Select one idea or topic from this chapter that applies to you and the way you live your life.

On a separate sheet of paper describe your selection in one sentence.

In no more than three sentences explain why you chose it.

DO NOT WRITE IN THIS BOOK.

RECAP

Interest in other children starts early in life. Friendships happen most often between neighbors. Friendships happen most often between teens who share similar experiences and similar attitudes. Friendships happen more often between teens who meet each other's needs.

Early friendships are often filled with squabbles. By junior high school, friendships are still shaky, but growing stronger. Same-sex and same-age ties are most important during these years. Friendships build from shared interests, social life, school events, pranks, and gossip.

Same-sex friendships reach a peak in mid-teens and then taper off as interest in the other sex grows stronger. As boys and girls mature, ability to be a friend and to offer friendship improves.

People need people. Best friends meet special needs for good times, companionship, understanding, and loyalty. When a friend values you, you feel good about yourself.

Friendships change and shift, partly because you change your values and interests as you grow older. Close friends may separate. Sometimes, people expect too much from each other. Or they choose friends hastily, only to discover that they made a mistake. Jealousy and competition also eat away at blossoming friendships.

Social life and status are both important during adolescence. So-called friends are sometimes chosen or sometimes dropped on the basis of who they are and what they own rather than for personal qualities. Parents influence friendship choices. So do members of your larger group or clique.

Good friends attract each other, often for reasons they don't understand. Sameness in personality, intelligence, and interests can draw two persons together. Sometimes special abilities or differences in personality can be the basis for attraction.

In order to grow and last, friendships must offer more than a shared interest. Friends help you to learn more about yourself. They share thoughts and feelings. Friends meet an important need for human closeness. Friends are generous and loyal to each other. They share admiration and respect.

Most persons want to admire their friends. You discover that you are worthy of respect and affection from someone who counts.

Friends often counsel each other. Good counselors know how to listen in order to help their friends see different solutions to problems and choose the best way to act. Good counselors reflect feelings. Good counselors help their friends get outside assistance when it is needed. Good counselors—and good friends—know how to keep secrets.

TERMS

Good friends	Mistreatment	Loyalty	Listening
Best friends	Competition	Inner controls	Advice
Broken friendships	Status	Generous	Action
Betrayal	Parent influence	Counseling	Reflect feeling

CHAPTER 13

Understanding Popularity

Like many adolescents, Katie has a long memory. She is in high school now, but recollections of her earlier efforts for popularity stay fresh. As you read her story you may be reminded of your own struggles to feel wanted and to be part of the group.

CASE EXAMPLE

Katie says, "I always wanted to be popular, but I didn't know how. I tried everything.

"In the sixth grade the most popular girl in our class wore beautiful clothes. She was pretty and smart. Her name was Roslyn. I even admired her nickname, Roz! I did everything to get her to like me: I complimented her. I tried to imitate her.

"She made straight A's, so I tried to be an A student, too. I stayed in at lunchtime and studied, but that soon got to be a bore. Then I skipped lunch and spent my lunch money on candy for everyone. I was popular and very happy, until mother found out and stopped me. After two days, no more free candy. I was an outcast again.

"I felt more alone than ever and my grades started to show it. I couldn't keep up with Roz no matter how I tried. Soon my old B's fell to C's and D's. The word got around and some kids called me 'dum-dum.'

Natalie Leimkuhler
The most popular teens usually have a big smile for everyone.

"I managed to improve the grades, but not what I wanted most—my popularity. Finally that awful year was over. That summer my father decided to move to a farm outside of town.

"At first my brother Richie and I didn't want to go. But after two weeks on the farm, we loved it. We had cats, a calf, a puppy, cows, horses, and pigs. My favorites were three old laying hens that I named Fatface, Feedface, and Goldie. Richie and I did our chores. That summer went by fast.

"I hated the idea of returning to school, and I walked sadly to the bus that first morning. In our town, being a farm girl was even worse than being poor. Any city girl who moved to a farm was considered a real hayseed. I guess I was so afraid of being rejected that I stayed away from the other kids. At recess and noon hour, I went to the library to study. To my surprise my grades improved, and I won a spelling bee. I started to feel good and proud of myself because I proved that I was as smart as Roz, the girl I defeated.

"Gradually other students started to say hello, but not enough to please me. Then one day a friend of Roslyn's asked me to join their 'Society Club.' That was what I really wanted. I sat quietly while several rules were read: everyone had to wear a colored ribbon in her hair, and a different color for each day of the week. Everyone was to meet near the gym each noon

David enjoys a natural popularity. Like some teens, he is always welcome in the group.

hour for a discussion of what to do the following day. Now it all seems silly to me, but to a girl who always felt on the fringe of things, it was wonderful to be accepted."

Some people, like Roz, seem to be naturally popular. Others, like Katie, continually struggle for acceptance. During early adolescence, however, almost all teens are deeply concerned about being well liked and widely accepted.

Look up the word "popularity" in a dictionary.
How do the dictionary definitions match your ideas about popularity?

Something to think about. Some teens are naturally popular.
Think of boys and girls that you know who seem to be popular and well liked.
What do the popular ones do and say to earn them their position?

POPULARITY AND FRIENDSHIP

Popularity is a precious thing. Automatically, it suggests that you know how to get along with people. There's a big difference between being well known and well liked. Popularity is usually measured in numbers. For example, how many people recognize a certain name and face? To some extent popularity calls for politicking: leaders must have followers, get the most votes, and get things done.

Friendship is more concerned with sharing and exchanging on a personal level. Popularity is public. Friendship is private.

Of course, a person can have friends and still be popular. However, to earn and keep a good friend one must *be* a good friend. Popularity isn't necessary for friendship.

THE DESIRE FOR POPULARITY

Not everyone wants to be popular. Some people seem quite content to move quietly through their school years without any special need for praise or awards. Others, even though popular, seem to sense that popularity may disappear as quickly as it comes. They know that a shallow kind of popularity can be bought with a few signs or a batch of votes, so they don't value it too highly. Some students develop special talents or show unusual creativity. They seem satisfied to go their own way whether others notice them or not.

Here's good news for you if you don't feel popular. Studies show that you need not be popular to be liked and accepted. So individual differences and unusual hobbies won't necessarily get you rejected or labeled an oddball.

Popularity is no sure pass to success. It won't always get you better grades, for example. Neither will it produce loyal friends. Popularity doesn't assure achievement in life as a person, worker, spouse, or parent.

CLUES

Popularity sometimes blooms early and fades fast, like the flower called morning glory. The most popular boys and girls in the lower grades may be forgotten in junior high. The rocketlike popularity of early adolescence may fizzle out in high school without real talent and good judgment to back it up. Also, the qualities that are attractive today may not be high on anyone's list next year or even next week.

Popularity is not a mystery. However, studies show that certain values are mentioned again and again. As you read the following, notice that many of the same qualities that make up popularity also contribute to healthy personality and all other assets in life. For example, when adolescents choose others they'd most like to be with, they pick those who take definite stands on issues and insist on fair treatment for everyone. It is important to note that leaders and persons with strong personalities share these same qualities.

In any case, if you want more popularity, this section is for you. The suggestions are not offered as magic formulas. However, if it means a lot to you to be better known and liked, you can begin today.

Not every popular person has all the qualities listed here, but chances are that you already have some and can develop others.

MODELING

One way to be accepted more is to copy the actions of popular boys and girls. This practice is called modeling.

Natalie Leimkuhler
Although he is well liked by others, Brian often goes his own way.

Katie modeled her actions after her ideal, Roz. To some degree Katie was successful.

Everyone learns from imitating other people. You became a North American child rather than European or African not just because you were born in this country. You are American or Canadian because you imitate other North Americans. As you already know, when children imitate their elders, language and customs are passed from generation to generation. This is the modeling process in action.

Seventh graders copy eighth graders. Freshmen imitate sophomores. You've probably studied older teens you admire to learn what to wear, how to dance, what music to like, and how to

Natalie Leimkuhler
The class clown can always get a laugh.

CASE EXAMPLE

Eric, a curly-haired, friendly lad, moved from Boston to a small midwestern town. He won instant popularity. The boys liked him because of his skating skill on country ponds. Soon they were copying his darting moves and daring hockey shots. The girls found him adorable and charming. Within days the teachers noticed the sound of broad New England *A's* mixed in with the traditional prairie speech. The students began to model on the newcomer's "paak" for park and "waak" for walk.

Simply, both sexes admired Eric. Boys and girls paid him the greatest compliment: they tried to be like him.

Models may inspire—as when a youth chooses to be a doctor because of the example set by a wise and unselfish physician.

Sometimes young people imitate the wrong models. A street gang leader, for example, may seem fearless and cool to a younger boy seeking someone to imitate. An older boy or girl who is a clever petty thief may catch the attention of a younger person who wants to be well known in a hurry.

Private and personal. Have you ever followed a poor model and ended up wishing that you hadn't?

If yes, any idea why you *needed* to do so?

MOST POPULAR

Certain roles in school life almost guarantee popularity. Winning a spot as cheerleader or majorette, for example, can make a girl well known and accepted in a hurry. Students often gain instant status by playing in a major sport like football or basketball.

act with members of the other sex. There'd be more straight-A students if everyone studied math or English as closely as they watch the clothes and actions of others.

Modeling often takes place without the imitator being aware of what is happening. Think about it. You've probably copied facial expressions, speech patterns, and even body movements of people you admire. And the class clown can always get a laugh by imitating a teacher.

Often the adolescents who don't model on others have late or poor social development. If you want to be like your friends, it is natural to try to act like them. The types of behavior you decide to imitate will also help decide just how popular you become.

Cheerleaders and athletes are "visible." Many people see them, admire them, and encourage them.

CASE EXAMPLE

Boys and girls who are most popular usually do not step down on their own. Sharon was different. She not only made the cheerleading squad, but she became the first freshman in school history to be elected cheer captain for the following season. Instantly, her popularity soared. She was a golden girl in the center of a golden circle. At first Sharon was dazzled by her new popularity. Then she learned that instant status can be a mixed blessing.

Sharon didn't like it when people pointed her out or made half-joking, half-hurtful remarks. Gradually, she discovered that she wasn't enjoying her new role as much as she had expected. Over the weeks, she talked to her mother about these reactions.

"The kids call me Mary Cheerleader . . . I don't like this jock image . . . I want to be free *not* to do everything on a schedule . . . I'm being forced into a clique I wouldn't join otherwise . . . I don't like all the after-school and weekend practicing . . . My grades are suffering."

Sharon learned that the most popular students also can be targets for envy and gossip. She told her mother, "Either the kids are jealous of you or they think they're better than you. Some people hate me and they don't even know me! They judge me right away as being a certain kind of person just because I'm a cheerleader . . . I want out!"

After several months Sharon made a difficult decision. She announced

Kathy Tuite

Sometimes one person shows other group members how to do things. Ann Marie's friends admire her gentle ways with animals and people.

that she would quit the squad at the end of the school year. At spring tryouts the students elected a new group. An eager replacement promptly asked to buy her uniforms and pom-poms.

Suddenly Sharon regretted her decision. She had complained a lot

Although some roles seem to guarantee instant popularity, they also require a sense of responsibility from the persons involved.

about what was wrong with cheerleading, but she forgot how much she loved the excitement of the games and the joy of sparking enthusiasm for the team.

After watching Sharon brood, her mother offered advice. "You made your decision. It's too late to change. Instead of thinking about what you've lost, remember all the hours you wanted to spend doing other things.

"You said you wanted to try dramatics. Now there's time to try out for a play. You talked about playing tennis.

Get going. You wanted to read more. Go to the library and get a stack of books."

RESPONSIBILITY

Sharon discovered something that most people learn sooner or later. Accepting an honor, becoming an officer, or taking on any kind of leadership role usually carries responsibilities and obligations. A popular leader often becomes less popular when orders must be given. Even for an older, more-experienced leader, it may be hard to

Team sports help all members learn to work together.

Kathy Tuite

know ahead of time what will be expected or how others will react to you in a new role.

At first Sharon was so dazzled by her popularity that she saw no disadvantages at all to the cheerleader role. Gradually, the need to give orders and make decisions (especially to older and more-experienced cheerleaders on the squad) bothered her a lot. Also, she suffered from the criticism and envy of others. The many hours of required practice interfered with other plans.

Sharon had mixed feelings—she felt pulled in two directions. She wanted excitement and popularity, but she didn't want to be gossiped about or take on such great responsibility. It may be a long time before Sharon knows if her decision to quit cheerleading was good or bad.

Something to think about. What other choices did Sharon have?

What would you have done in her place?

Notice that Sharon's mother offered advice only *after* Sharon made her decision. How else might her mother have reacted?

REPUTATION

Reputation means what others think and say about you. The way you act and the things you say decide how you seem to others. You earn your reputation. No one gives it to you. A good reputation is very important to popularity, especially for girls.

"Birds of a feather flock together" is an old saying. The reputation of a friend may rub off on you, especially if it's bad.

Sometimes people inherit a reputation from an older brother or sister. They hear things like, "I hope you'll be as smart as your sister was" or "I hope you'll behave better than your brother did." Some adults may expect you to act like anoth-

241

Natalie Leimkuhler
Jean's friendly personality makes everyone feel good.

er family member so much they treat you the same way before you get a chance to show that you are different.

In most cases people live down mistaken first impressions of them. Eventually all persons earn a reputation from day to day by how they behave.

One foolish or thoughtless act can spoil a good reputation. It can take a long time to repair the damage.

CASE EXAMPLE

Mimi saved baby-sitting money for many months to go on a school ski trip. The first night away, everyone in the girl's dormitory felt giddy and excited. Girls challenged each other to do silly things. Mimi decided to top everyone.

Against the rules, she sneaked into a room in the boys' dorm and hung a "Do Not Disturb" sign on the door. She enjoyed a few moments at the center of a group of admiring, whistling, shouting boys. She encouraged their good-natured kidding before she slipped back to her dorm. Then Mimi made the mistake of bragging to the other girls about her adventure. She even called them "chicken" because no one else dared to do the same.

On Monday morning several girls promptly spread the story around school. They added a few made-up details. Mimi's reputation suffered badly.

You be the counselor. Mimi risked her reputation and lost.
Suppose she came to you for advice?
How would you help her?
How can she live down her bad reputation?

PIECES OF POPULARITY

Of course, a girl needs more than a megaphone to hold on to popularity. A boy needs more than a football uniform to gain lasting leadership.

Next, you'll read what popularity requires. Obviously the items listed aren't the only things necessary. You may think of others. The suggestions are meant to start you thinking and discussing.

Something to think about. The text includes just a few of the items that make up popularity.
From the following list, which ones count most in your school?

Items of Popularity
Member of a prominent group

Good grades.
Good reputation.
Family background.
Athletic ability.

Money to spend.
Nice clothes.
Good looks.
Liked by own sex.
Liked by other sex.
Leader in school activities.
Full of energy.
Self-confident.
Considerate of others.
Likes others.
Uses good judgment.
Has high moral standards.
Friendly to others.

Private and personal. Which of the items do you have?

Which three would you most like to have?

Which could you develop if you tried?

Following is a popularity guide to help you think about the way you act with others. Although the points do not cover every possibility, they can help if you want to be more popular.

ELEVEN-POINT POPULARITY GUIDE

1. *Be friendly.* Being friendly won't make you popular for sure. However, the opposite—acting unfriendly and cold, or cruel and mean—will make you unpopular in a hurry.

Even though it may make you a little nervous, try to say hello first when you see someone you know. Shy people sometimes seem like snobs when they are really just too unsure to speak up.

You can be friendly by offering smiles, waves, and hellos. You can also respond generously when someone asks for help, or when someone seems to need a friend. These are just some of the ways that you can show interest and concern in others. That's what friendliness is all about.

Rough and tough adolescents are not likely to be very popular. As you know, how friendly a boy or girl is with child-hood playmates seems to tell in advance the degree of friendliness during the teen years and later.

2. *Notice emotion.* Empathy means the ability to feel what another person feels, or "to put yourself in another's shoes." Popular people usually are able to set aside their own emotions to be aware of the strong feelings in those around them.

Visitors to the Indianapolis zoo did double takes recently when they saw a creature in a cage marked: "Modern Man, Homo sapiens." The "Modern Man" was a high school student named Nancy who volunteered to get into the cage to study people's reactions. Most adults laughed at her as they passed her cage. Small children stared in wonder. Some ran in fear.

After a few hours in the cage Nancy became tired of the sea of faces passing by. Soon she began to experience and understand the reactions caged animals might have. Nancy was practicing empathy. She was trying to feel with the animals.

Empathy requires that you try to understand the emotion another person feels at a particular moment. Is it uncertainty? Anger? Jealousy? Confidence? Joy? And when you have the same feelings, how would you like to be treated?

3. *Be kind.* It may sound corny, but kindness to other people is basic to lasting popularity.

Kindness goes hand in hand with empathy. It really isn't enough just to understand how others feel. The next step is to try to meet people's needs in a friendly and considerate way.

Kindness means that you are thoughtful and accepting of others even when they don't act the way you think they should.

It is easy *not* to be kind by saying what you think. Here are some examples: "You look awful. Don't you feel well?" "That dress doesn't seem to fit you. Oh, you made it!" "Are you getting bald?"

Some people think that "being yourself" or "being honest" means you can stomp on the feelings of others. Instead of earning popularity, such attitudes usually cause the speaker to be resented or disliked. If you really want to be popular, try to be kind.

4. *Listen.* A bore is someone who talks when it's your turn. Learning to listen can help you become more effective in conversations and more popular. Keep alert for the things that interest others, like topics that either please or worry them. Most people like to talk about themselves and their present concerns—just as you probably do.

You can develop your skills in conversation by listening, by encouraging others to talk, and by showing your interest in the persons you are with at the time. Avoid talking about yourself every chance you get. Try not to talk about others in a critical or unkind way.

You can earn a piece of popularity by becoming a good listener.

5. *Don't destroy.* Almost everyone gossips. News about someone else gets attention fast. However, some people seem to pass on bad news or outright lies about others with great pleasure.

Perhaps you've been a victim of gossip. Even in junior high school ugly rumors seem to fly on wings. One girl wore a smock to school. Another started to gossip, "It looks like Debbie's pregnant." Soon the story became, "Debbie's pregnant!" Rumors grow and often get worse as they move on.

A lot of gossip is about sex and angry feelings. That's why worried and inse-cure people usually gossip more than those who are better adjusted. Gossips get rid of their hostile emotions by shooting them, like poison arrows, into someone else's reputation.

As you know, most everyone has some bad thoughts about others. It's what you do with such feelings that shapes your personality and your life. If you must always act on your anger, you will probably get into trouble and hurt others—even those you love.

Gossips act by talking. They need to feel superior. If the news is juicy enough, for a brief moment the gossip is the center of attention.

If you want to be popular, don't gossip.

6. *Know what's expected.* The more you act your age, the better your chances for popularity. You know that values change in early adolescence. For girls, being attractive to boys becomes more and more important. Boys seek the admiration of other boys. Consider these two extreme examples of *not* acting according to age:

Any girl who plays with dolls into her high school years isn't acting the way she is expected. And any boy who would rather assemble small car models than learn to drive a real car is out of step in much the same way.

Popularity is more likely to go to those who know what to do and when to do it.

7. *Become visible.* If you hope for popularity you must be seen. Sports events, dances, and parties all offer opportunities to be noticed.

However, adolescents find other spur-of-the-moment ways to get together and learn about each other. Recently a large group of boys gathered on an empty lot on a fall Saturday afternoon. A game of touch football started. They had

Natalie Leimkuhler

"Did you hear what Tina said about Lee Ann?"

such a great time that they agreed to meet again a week later.

The news leaked out. The second week an equally large group of girls gathered to watch. At first the girls talked only to each other. The boys ignored the girls but played with more pep. A few of the girls joined the game. Everybody mingled, talked together in small groups. Soon weekly football was forgotten.

All the players and spectators understood that the real purpose of the game, after the first Saturday, was to provide an excuse for the boys and girls to get together. In much the same way, adolescents are seen at swimming pools, in school parking lots, in eating places, and near soft drink machines. They know that *keeping visible* contributes to their popularity.

8. *Participate.* Jump in. Join. Hanging back, waiting, or daydreaming about what you'll do and say will get you nowhere.

Enjoy yourself. Then others will enjoy you. Ever notice that perky, outgoing people seem to attract others?

Look for school clubs with open membership. Hard workers are always wel-

Kathy Tuite

With a skill like swimming you can either compete in a race or just relax and enjoy the fun.

come. Join church groups, attend school games and activities where you'll contact those you'd like to know better. The more you do, the more you are likely to be invited to do. You may never be the center of a chosen circle, but you can find a place.

The wider the circle of boys and girls you know, the more likely you are to meet others through them. The more activities you try, the better your chances to discover new ones you enjoy doing. The more confidence you gain by being accepted into one group, the more willing you'll be to try another.

Persons who keep active are usually more popular.

9. *Develop talents.* Learn to cook, sew, or weave, whatever you do best. Practice swimming, handball, or running. If you like music and play an instrument, try out for the school band.

Pick something you already do fairly well. Keep at it until you are skilled above average. Most likely you'll soon have a chance to display your talents and gain popularity.

Terri was a mediocre student, clumsy in sports and awkward at dances. She never knew what to say at a party. However, she loved to act in school plays. Over the years Terri developed her talent for acting character parts. This added much to her life.

Juan, a quiet and reserved boy, enjoyed track. In time he became a specialist in cross-country and other distance events. Juan liked the idea of running alone but still being part of a team. He won for his school, made friends, and gained admirers.

Notice that Terri and Juan didn't really change themselves very much. Each overcame the tendency to be shy by taking part in and practicing the things they *did best*. Then they worked hard to become even better. As a result, both became more popular.

You can use any special ability to help others. You won't lose anything by sharing. By itself, a talent for needlepoint or engine tinkering won't make you the most popular student in school. By offering to teach others, however, you may gain friends.

Even if you have no special talents, you can still join in fun and games. A good sport who plays along is liked more than someone who refuses to try—even if the awkward person gets kidded about not doing so well. It helps if you can laugh at yourself.

10. *Know how you look.* Physically perfect human beings are rare. Even so, some people seem to do a better job than others in making up for their shortcomings in appearance with good taste and the right clothes.

Look around you. The best-liked people are not necessarily the best looking. Neither do they always own the most expensive or biggest wardrobes. The most popular seem to have a sense of what's in fashion. They make a good

Natalie Leimkuhler
Maureen gets advice from a friend about belt height.

choice of flattering clothes and colors. It all adds up to a popular look.

Television and magazines are guides on what to wear and how to match accessories.

You don't have to be a style setter and undisputed leader if you notice what others wear.

Much of looking good is *feeling* good. Although good health is partly inherited, it is also tied to a nutritious, balanced diet, enough sleep, regular exercise, and good dental care. The most popular students not only look best but also enjoy the best health.

11. *Keep flexible.* Popular teens are not stiff and unbending. They keep flexi-

247

ble by showing a willingness to change. Flexible persons try to adapt to a lot of situations. A flexible person is one who can change even though things don't go exactly as planned. In this sense "flexible" does not mean weak and limp like a soggy sock, but more like a willow tree—firmly rooted but adjusting to the wind.

Of course, not everyone fits in everywhere. Part of being flexible is to know that you may be welcome in one situation but not in another. One boy joked about his "two left feet." He always got picked last in neighborhood sports. Yet when it came to getting together, the crowd always chose his home first.

Flexible people think for themselves. They disagree if they believe something to be wrong. However, they are also willing to change their minds in less important matters if it means peaceful cooperation for the group. The most popular students don't always insist on having their own way.

Private and personal. Read all the first sentences in the popularity guide again.

For each point mentioned, try to think of one change you could make in your own life to accomplish that goal.

To learn more. Select one idea or topic from this chapter that applies to you and the way you live your life.

On a separate sheet of paper describe your selection in one sentence.

In no more than three sentences explain why you chose it.

DO NOT WRITE IN THIS BOOK.

RECAP

Most adolescents go after popularity because it means that one's attitudes and behavior are acceptable to others. Status in the group leads to good feelings about self.

Your parents can't buy popularity for you. You can't bully or bribe others into offering it. Popularity must be freely given and must come from your peers.

Try to remember that popularity alone won't make you successful or even happy. In fact, many people are mistaken about what popularity is. For example, there are differences between just getting attention and gaining popularity; between being talked about and being admired; between being feared and being liked.

For near-beginners in life, it may be hard to understand what makes up popularity. The requirements seem to change. Membership in a particular group may suddenly improve your standing. The same might happen if you receive an unexpected gesture of friendship from another popular person.

Some basic rules of popularity seem to remain the same no matter who you are or where you live. Almost anyone can become better liked and more popular by following these rules:

• Be friendly, reach out, say "hello" first.

• Notice the emotions and reactions of others.

• Be kind to others, including those not your friends.

• Listen carefully when others talk.

• Don't destroy the reputation of others.

• Learn what's expected of someone your age.

• Become visible. Go places where other youth gather.

• Participate in any way you can, even if it means cleaning up.

• Work on your special talents.

• Know how you look.

• Stay flexible and open to the ideas of others.

Lasting popularity seems to go along with the same things that make for a well-adjusted, stable person. However, it's important to notice that those who pursue their own interests, rather than chasing after popularity, are not always rejected or left out. If you choose not to go the way of the crowd you may still find some acceptance and much personal satisfaction.

TERMS

Modeling	Empathy	Participation	Flexibility
Responsibility	Good listener	Developing talents	
Reputation	Becoming visible	Aware of looks	

CHAPTER 14

Left Out and Lonely

Everyone wants to be liked and accepted by others. Such feelings start during infancy and last a lifetime.

Have you ever been shut out of a group because others decided you did not belong? Or because someone whose company you want just didn't want yours? Hurts, doesn't it?

Most people know about rejection from both sides of the fence. Perhaps you've been on the inside and rejected others. Or maybe you've found yourself on the outside, ignored by others.

In this chapter you will be reading about the other side of friendship and closeness—rejection and loneliness. You'll also learn how to understand and deal with such negative emotions.

WHY?

Reasons for one person or group to lock out another seem endless. You may do nothing at all to deserve such treatment. Or you may get dropped because you brag a lot or show off in ways that irritate others.

Sometimes rejection comes from a mistaken impression. A good-looking but shy boy might be considered stuck up because he doesn't talk to girls, even though he'd like to.

Some teens do nothing to earn rejection, but they get shut out anyway. If you come from a family troubled by alcoholism, or if a relative is in prison, others may avoid you as if you had the same problem.

Suppose you go away for a long vacation. Your pals at home may form new ties while you are gone. Another boy or girl may become close with your best friend. Upon your return, you find yourself excluded.

Cliques form for a while and then break up. You may get left out in the switch.

Someone may become jealous of you. Or you may feel that way about them. Popularity and acceptance both come from others. Peers can take your feelings of belonging away as easily as they gave them in the first place.

Perhaps even worse than being rejected is never getting noticed at all. Others act as though you are not important or don't even exist.

Natalie Leimkuhler

David Snodgress, Journal and Courier, Lafayette, Indiana
Almost everyone knows how it feels to be left out.

251

Shelly gets closed out.

CASE EXAMPLE

One Friday evening Shelly went to a basketball game. As usual, she expected to meet her girl friends there. Surprisingly, her closest pals seemed cool. Giggling and talking loudly, several girls formed a tight little group and actually turned their backs to Shelly. To her horror, Shelly suddenly realized that they were talking about her!

Stomach churning, she left the game and ran home. Her mother noticed that something was wrong. Shelly started to cry. Between sobs she explained: "They ganged up on me. I've done that to other kids, so I know what it means. Why are they mad at me? What did I do?"

For many weeks Shelly stayed home at night. She drew closer to her parents again. She helped her mother. She laughed at her father's jokes instead of sighing impatiently.

Shelly never learned what she had done to deserve such bad treatment. She just watched and waited. She welcomed friendly smiles and offered a few of her own. In time she was once again accepted by her clique.

Many of the short "returns to home" during the struggle for independence from parents are the result of experiences like Shelly's. For months she left the house at every excuse, eager to be with her friends. However, when rejected she acted like a little girl. She needed to be comforted. She moved back into the safety and warmth of her family until she felt strong enough to stand on her own again.

Something to think about. Have you ever had an experience like Shelly's? At one time you feel accepted and well liked. Then suddenly one or several friends turn away from you. It's enough to make you feel sick.

Why do friends shut each other out?

What might Shelly have done to earn such rejection?

Later, recalling the incident, Shelly shrugged and said, "I guess it was my turn." What did she mean?

CASE EXAMPLE

Angela also got rejected, and far worse than Shelly. She started as a popular girl but soon fell from favor. As you read her case, look for the ways she handled her rejection. Ask yourself what you would do in her situation.

"In junior high school I got accepted right away. I was put up for several offices. After being elected I really felt good. After being Pep Chairman for awhile I began to notice a difference. A few of my so-called friends didn't like my rising popularity. At first they showed their jealousy by teasing me. They'd talk and act like I wasn't even there. This ugly treatment bothered me greatly. I told myself I'd have to be strong and live with it.

"I thought I could get along without the girls who rejected me, but it didn't work. Then some others decided that I wasn't good enough for them, either. I remember clearly it was at that time that I first felt inferior. Those girls did everything possible to make me feel that I didn't belong.

"When I talked to my mother she insisted that I should try to keep with the crowd to prevent any trouble. Mom told me that in a small town like ours a person is either accepted or rejected by the leading group. If you are rejected by them you are out of everything.

"Of course, I tried to act like it didn't matter. It was difficult to pretend. I'm the type of person who likes responsibility. I like to be around interesting people.

"I decided to look for a new kind of activity in the county 4-H Junior Leaders organization. Joining it helped cover up my feelings of inferiority because my high school classmates didn't belong to 4-H. After giving most of my spare time to 4-H, I felt rewarded by the new jobs I did. I won trips and developed lasting friendships.

"It was fun to attend the county functions. No matter what meeting or game I went to, there was always someone there I knew. I even made friends from other county schools.

"Yet in my own school when I met my former friends I couldn't help feeling like a second-class citizen. I took a back seat, or walked hurriedly by so I wouldn't be noticed."

Angela was still suffering from rejection, even though she had found new friends and fun away from school.

SELF-WORTH

You know that what you think of yourself comes in part from the attitudes and comments of those around you. If

Natalie Leimkuhler

Active teens who join group activities are seldom lonely.

son. People who get left out often believe that it's their fault. They think, "I really must be a nothing."

The fact is, many nice people receive cruel treatment for reasons that have little to do with their personality or actions. A boy or girl may be rejected because someone else feels inferior.

For example, Mary failed to make a leading clique. The other girls felt jealous, afraid that Mary would outshine them. So they voted her down. Of course, the girls gave other reasons. "Mary is too loud. Her clothes aren't right."

Actually, the girls who rejected Mary saw her as a threat to their own popularity. They were afraid that she would steal boys away from them.

One of the reasons that adolescents are often so mean to each other is that they feel so insecure themselves. Criticism of hairstyles, cutting remarks about clothing, and the smallest defects of others—all are tied to worries about personal value. The main worry becomes "just how good am I?"

By pointing out the weak spots in others, the picky, critical person hopes to look better by comparison. During the teen years there's a scramble for acceptance. Because of such intense competition and so much eagerness to feel well liked, few adolescents dare to be too different. So boys and girls who feel insecure may not allow much room for others to be different either.

Acceptance in adolescent groups comes in part from knowing what's expected of you and following those unwritten laws. As you know, few people can afford to be very different in dress or behavior and get away with it. Only a few stars and trend-setters dare to be very different.

enough people say, "Gail has a great personality," or, "Don is a dope," soon Gail and Don begin to believe what they hear said about themselves. Gail and Don may actually begin to behave the way other people say they do. Gail works harder to amuse her friends. Don withdraws into a shell.

When friends want to be with you, ask your advice, or invite you to join them, you feel good. The more acceptance you get, the more you like it.

On the other hand, suppose others avoid you, sneer at your ideas, or ignore your talents. You may begin to wonder just how much you are worth as a per-

NORMAL REJECTION

Most persons get rejected at one time or another for some reason. No mistaking the signals:

- Former friends plan together and make a point of not asking you.
- No place left for you at lunch.
- The phone doesn't ring.

So great is the need to belong, however, that the hurt remains long after the blow has been struck. Repeated attempts to win back acceptance and companionship often follow rejection.

What about me? Do you have old memories of being rejected?

Try to recall the circumstances to share with class members.

How did you regain acceptance?

DEFENSES: WITHDRAW OR ATTACK?

Too many rejections and not enough opportunities to win back acceptance almost force people to use defenses to protect themselves against being hurt even more. Some people just refuse to fight. They *withdraw* and wear an "I don't care mask." Others try to *counterattack* with open aggression or by plotting against the rejectors.

Actually, there are some positive and helpful ways to make up for ordinary rejection. Consider them for your own use.

Guidelines for living.

Ways to Handle Rejection

- *Wait it out.* Storm clouds may blow over quickly. If you think you have fallen from popularity, remember no one holds the spotlight forever. Singers and actors know the painful experience of being everyone's favorite one day and a has-been the next.

Novelty—being the new boy or girl in town, or winning some special award—may suddenly catapult a person to the

Natalie Leimkuhler

When Ruth feels left out she goes window-shopping, or pokes around her favorite store.

top of the heap. However, such newness fades quickly. After the first excitement dies away, your value is measured by what you really are and what you really can do.

- *Try a direct approach.* Sometimes it helps to ask directly if you've done or said anything to earn the rejection you are getting. Such a head-on approach can clear the air. Also, you might learn something important about yourself.

Perhaps you can't find the courage to ask someone else, "What did I do

255

wrong?'' You can always ask yourself: "Am I a gossip? A disloyal friend? A snob? Do I look only for friends who are popular or powerful? Do I overlook or drop others who might accept me as a friend?''

● *Take the hint.* Some efforts are useless, like watering weeds. Suppose you've really tried to win certain friends or to join a group you admire. You've been snubbed and rejected repeatedly. It's time to ask yourself, "Why do I want to be with a crowd that doesn't want me? Status? To please someone in the crowd? To please my parents?''

If you try and try, and fail and fail, maybe you don't belong. To be different or unaccepted by any one group doesn't mean that you are worth any less. There's more than one track to friendship, happiness, and success.

● *Settle for less.* Some people get left out of close friendships but get included in informal group activities. Fringe members participate but don't get full acceptance.

Think back to childhood. Remember the boy invited to join the game only because he owned the ball? Recall the girl who was asked to play only because her doll had the most clothes?

Some fringe members work their way up to a position of influence and power. Others stay on the edges, glad to be included at all. Many are pleased with life on the edge because it doesn't demand too much of them.

Among chickens there's always a pecking order. The strongest and scrappiest take the lead and peck the best feed. Weaker and meeker chickens get what's left.

Every leader needs a follower. Every boss needs a worker. Although you may not develop first-line friendships, you can still enjoy group companionship. The basketball manager doesn't play in the game but is a member of the team group.

● *Catch up later.* Some teens are late bloomers. They develop their personalities and talents a little later in life. Such boys and girls live so quietly and so much in the background that their classmates neither accept nor reject them.

When a journalist wants to write a story about a famous person or someone in the national news, the writer sometimes goes back to old school yearbooks, or interviews former classmates or teachers. What's discovered is that many successful adults started out as so ordinary that their more popular peers recall them as just members of the class. Sometimes they don't remember them at all.

Private and personal. Which of the guidelines on how to manage rejection have you tried?

Which ones could you begin to use to make your life easier and more pleasant?

LONELY

Few persons are so popular that they have never felt the sting of loneliness. The enjoyable company of others is fun while it lasts. However, the good feeling of being part of the crowd can disappear like a puff of smoke.

Loneliness often gets mixed up with rejection. They are not the same thing. Rejection means that others prefer not to be with you. When you try to join them they shut you out. Some lonely adolescents never get rejected because they may not even try to join a group. However, they do feel cut off anyway because they spend so much time by themselves.

Loneliness means *not* being part of a group—large or small. The lonely person feels left out and usually doesn't make friends easily.

Some lucky people rarely feel lonely. Others feel lonely much of the time. Lonely feelings come from inside self. For example, a salesperson could feel lonely during a sales meeting with hundreds of others in the room. Yet someone fishing or hunting might not feel

Sometimes Julie would rather be alone to sort out her thoughts.

lonely even when hundreds of miles from civilization.

Alone on purpose. Being alone by yourself is not the same as feeling lonely. Not everyone wants company all the time. Because persons spend a lot of time alone, it doesn't always mean that they are rejected or lonely.

Many teens like company, but they enjoy time with themselves, too. They are normal, just more quiet and thoughtful.

Even outgoing friendly persons enjoy privacy once in a while. They may spend their quiet time in collecting, sewing, reading, or just thinking. They

257

enjoy these activities without feeling lonely.

CASE EXAMPLE

Scott explains his feelings this way: "There are times when I want to be by myself. I enjoy peace and quiet after being in a crowd of kids all day. Lots of times I just sit and think about what I'll do on the weekend. I like to plan things before starting them. Right now I'm thinking about tearing down an old lawn mower engine in the garage. I can use some of the parts in a racing cart I want to build."

Adolescents like Scott aren't pushed out by others. Early in life they learn to like their own company, even if they spend their time tinkering with gadgets.

Adults sometimes think that teenagers are so full of energy that they never need relaxation. You know that isn't true. Like Scott, everyone needs time alone to take it easy. Everyone needs a chance to sort out thoughts and dreams about the future. Everyone needs time to feel like an individual person rather than a robot steered by a computer.

Silence. During the silent times you can get to know yourself best and to think without being disturbed. Most creative persons like artists and writers prefer to work quietly, undisturbed by visitors. Great ideas are often hatched when a person is alone.

Adolescence is a good time to learn to enjoy your own company. Yet some youth (and adults, too) feel so uncomfortable when by themselves that they rush to fill each waking hour with talk, TV, or music. It's almost as if they can't stand to be without some type of sound.

Temporary. Some loneliness is temporary. Feeling lonely may mean only that you have't yet found a group of people who share your interests. Imagine moving from a farm or a small town to a big city. Just before the change you know everyone. Once in your new home you may feel like a stranger. Until you make some new friends, you will probably feel lonely.

Even in a small town or city neighborhood it may be hard to find someone who shares your special interests. Sometimes a simple change of scenery can help a lot. Boys and girls who attend summer camp, for example, often report finding new friends who share their love of animals, nature, or tennis. Some teens don't find anyone to share similar ideas and goals until they start working or go to college.

Keep searching for the kind of friends *you prefer.* You'll discover that persons with unusual hobbies or interests find each other all over the world. Some raise tropical fish. Others collect paperweights, old bottles, or comic books. Every day ham amateur radio operators talk with pals around the country that they may never meet in person.

Even more important than looking for the right company is discovering the real you, and what you care about. Once you learn your own interests, you can begin to look for others who like what you enjoy. Although it may take a while, chances are good that you'll find the right group.

Try to remember that everyone feels lonely sometimes. Out of such feelings can grow better self-understanding and stronger inner resources.

Inherited. To some degree you get your temperament from your parents. If you have always been a quiet kind of person, you aren't likely to change greatly, even though you can learn to be more friendly and outgoing.

WAYS TO CHASE LONELINESS

If you feel lonely a lot of the time and want to understand why and then do something about it, the next section may be helpful. Ask yourself the following questions. Take time to think about your answers.

• *Do I belong?* Are you lonely because you can't get into the group you want, or because you can't find anyone in a group to be your special friend?

Try to remember that few people are *always* left out. In the same way, few are always picked. Of course, it's important to try to be a friendly person, but that's not the whole story. A person who feels lonely may be struggling to find companionship in the wrong place or with the wrong group. It may be hard to face, but perhaps you feel lonely because you really don't belong in the clique you think you'd like to join.

Sometimes "hangers on" do manage to force their way into a clique. However, they seldom feel accepted. Always struggling, always on the edge, always a bit out of step, they feel like outsiders even when on the inside.

• *Do I make the first move?* Lonely people often think, "Why don't others appreciate me? Why don't they pay more attention to me? I have a lot to offer."

Wishing that others would notice you and seek you out does not solve the problem of loneliness. Lonely people often simmer in a soup of self-pity. They may even feel resentful and blame others for their isolation. A better attitude is

Kathy Tuite

At age fourteen, Brian is already a crack photographer. The more you develop your skills and interests, the better company you are for yourself and others.

to take action and do something positive to chase lonely feelings.

For example, there's always a need for volunteers to work behind the scenes—to decorate for a party or to clean up later. Every school play needs costume makers and scenery builders. When you are genuinely helpful and easy to get along with, you are more likely to earn attention and respect from others.

Some teen groups offer open membership and a form of companionship that grows out of working together on a

Natalie Leimkuhler

Pam uses yoga to relax her body and clear her mind. All forms of thinking by yourself help to fight loneliness.

anyone who isn't just the right age, sex, color, or social class. You could be so exclusive in your demands that you miss chances for friendship that may be close by. For example, older folks may have a lot to offer you, and the other way 'round.

CASE EXAMPLE

One summer Bart spent a few weeks in a northern resort. Older people and children were all around, but not a single boy near his age. At first he felt bored and lonely for his friends. He resented that his parents had dragged him to what seemed like the end of the world.

Then Bart started talking with an older man who walked by each day on his way to fish. One morning Bart asked if he could go along. Pleased with the company, the man generously shared his fishing lures and stories.

Bart quickly learned how to fish and where to look for prized pike. He spent hours with his new friend, sometimes talking, sometimes silent, but never lonely.

community project. In Junior Achievement, for example, teens manufacture a product like aluminum coat hangers and then sell them. With the guidance of local business people, they learn to run a small company. Friendship and satisfaction grow naturally out of shared work and mutual goals.

• *Do I miss opportunities*? Sometimes lonely persons search for friendship with blinders on. They don't seek

• *Do I invest in others*? A well-known cure for loneliness is to offer companionship to others. The idea is easy to understand, and it works: Get involved in a project for someone else's benefit.

Of course, it isn't easy to spend your time and energy for others when you are the lonely one. From your viewpoint, others should show concern for you! Yet when people who feel alone reach out to others who are even more lonely—the aged, shut-ins, children in hospitals—they usually feel very good about it. Sometimes close ties and friendships follow.

• *Do I build resources in myself*? Crafts and hobbies can play an important part in life. Sometimes they open the way to a career or a lifelong interest. Perhaps you can learn a handcraft like knitting or woodwork from an older person who'd be pleased to pass on the skill. Such activities are not limited to either sex nor to any age.

Reading can be a magic carpet to a world of inner enjoyment. Yet many teens flatly state, "I don't like to read." Even if reading is difficult, chances are you can learn to enjoy reading about something you really want to know.

CASE EXAMPLE

Leon, becoming fascinated with the history of firearms, read his way through every book on weapons in the library. Elizabeth bragged that she'd never read a book on her own unless it was assigned. Yet when her mother gave her an Ann Landers book about teens and sex, Elizabeth stayed up until 2:00 A.M. to finish it. Reasons:
- She was greatly interested.
- The writing was simple.
- The examples were familiar.

Other "non-readers" get turned on by history written in comic book style, or by exciting mystery or adventure tales. Read what you enjoy. Don't overlook books written for younger readers. Such stories may be better written and more enjoyable than those for your own age group. Reading is a good way to fight loneliness.

What about me? The text suggests that lonely people may overlook opportunities for friendships or group activities that promise fun.

Have you ever passed up a chance to make a friendship with someone not in your own age group?

A personal checklist. Use a separate sheet of paper to make your list.

DO NOT WRITE IN THIS BOOK.

As a way of rating yourself, in which of the following age groups do you have friends?

Children under twelve
Younger teens
Age-mates (those within one year of your age)
Older teens
Young adults
Middle-aged adults
Old people

What does your final tally tell you about your friendship life?

About yourself?

PERSONALITY PROBLEMS

Sometimes personal problems isolate youth from the company of other teens. For example, certain personality traits, annoying habits, or irritating manners offend others.

If you feel lonely a lot, consider talking with someone who knows you well and cares about you. An older brother or sister, parent, teacher, or counselor may help you to discover something about yourself you've never realized before.

If you decide to ask someone you trust about the way you act, try to consider the answers before getting angry, upset, or defensive. You can usually tell if what you hear squares with the facts. Even if what you hear is false, it never hurts to ask yourself, "Could this be true about me?" Try to remember that selfish and self-centered people are sometimes avoided or not invited to join in. At the same time, they may blame others for leaving them out.

CASE EXAMPLE

Judy hurt enough from loneliness to talk with her school counselor. She said, "It's hard for me to get other kids to want to be with me, let alone make

261

Natalie Leimkuhler

If you feel left out and lonely a lot, it's important to discover the reasons why.

friends. Sometimes I feel so lonesome that I ask a teacher to sit with me in the lunchroom."

Without waiting for a reply, Judy rushed on. She complained about her unkind classmates. She criticized her teachers for not making the others accept her.

"I really know the problem," Judy added without pausing. "It's my glasses. I can't see without them. My eye doctor says my eyeballs are the wrong shape for contact lenses. The kids in my class are just snobs. They won't accept anyone who has a handicap."

Judy did wear heavy "bottle-bottom" lenses. However, she actually blamed a mild physical disability for other personality problems.

So eager was Judy for attention and praise that she often interrupted others. She spoke loudly with an irritating "know-it-all" attitude. Judy was a bright girl with a lot to offer. Still she was a very lonely person.

Actually, Judy suspected that her glasses were not the only problem. She was ready, afraid, almost desperate to hear the truth about herself. Why was she so lonesome?

Gradually, the counselor was able to explain that people with mild physical problems sometimes blame the minor handicaps for feelings of isolation. For once, Judy fell silent. The counselor went on to remind her of a boy they both knew. His glasses were even thicker than Judy's—yet he had many friends and lots of companionship.

Judy hurt enough to want to hear more. She asked to come back. She was listening more and talking less. The counselor explained that many people blame their personal problems on other people or on some events out of their control. The fact is that most personal difficulties are really inside the person. When Judy heard that, she couldn't answer because she was crying. She knew the words were true. To her credit, she was ready to change.

You be the counselor. After earning the label of a know-it-all, how can Judy begin to change? As her counselor, what would you say or do to help her?

Private and personal. Sometimes people earn rejection because of the way they act or treat others. If you often feel lonely and rejected, ask yourself these questions. Am I often

Undependable?
Moody?
Sarcastic?
A show-off?
Demanding of attention?
Critical of others?
A gossip?
Selfish?
Sometimes friendly, sometimes not?

If any of these negative qualities apply to you, do you have any idea why you may *need* to act so?

You be the counselor. Cliff has a problem.

He asks, "How can a guy stay popular without going along with the gang all the time? There are some things like drinking and drugging that really worry me."

How would you help Cliff solve his problem?

Use ideas from this chapter or from your own experience.

On a separate sheet of paper, write your suggestions in no more than four sentences.

DO NOT WRITE IN THIS BOOK.

To learn more. Select one idea or topic from this chapter that applies to you and the way you live your life.

On a separate sheet of paper describe your selection in one sentence.

In no more than three sentences explain why you chose it.

DO NOT WRITE IN THIS BOOK.

RECAP

Everyone likes to be accepted by others. Nevertheless, most persons feel rejected at one time or another. Rejection can go from a temporary chill to a permanent freeze. You can be rejected for something you did, or for what you failed to do. Or someone may decide to reject you for no good reason.

Over time, friendships naturally shift and change. For a while at least certain teens may get left out of a new group that they did not help to form.

Rejection can be both unfair and cruel. In some cases, however, persons who brag and show off may earn the rejection they receive. It's not just getting left out that hurts. Everyone measures self-value from the signals, comments, and treatment of others. If others seem to like you and want you around, you think more of yourself. When others act as though you are stupid or worthless, you think less of yourself.

Some ways to manage rejection include:

• Wait it out. Sometimes things improve by themselves.

• Take the hint and look for persons who *want* to spend time with you.

• Try to find out if you deserve the treatment you have been receiving.

• Settle for less. Every member of the group can't be the best liked.

If all else fails, remember that many teens simply don't get all the acceptance they'd like. However, many build enjoyable companionships and warm friendships a little later in life, when they discover their true interests.

Other people can reject you, but loneliness comes from inside yourself.

Being alone and feeling lonely are not the same thing. Many persons enjoy a balance of some time alone and some time with others.

Everyone needs a chance to be apart from the crowd to think, and to feel free of pressures and schedules. Silence and solitude can help you to understand yourself and others a little better.

Knowing yourself and enjoying your own company can be a great advantage to anyone. However, many persons feel uneasy when alone. Some are even afraid to be by themselves.

Simply growing older helps you to know yourself and your true interests better, helping to avoid loneliness. Also, some teens are more quiet and easygoing, less in need of crowds and companionship.

The loneliness connected with moving to a new town or changing schools is usually temporary. Other loneliness is sometimes caused when teens spend energies trying to find companionship where they don't fit in.

If you feel lonely a lot, ask yourself these questions:

• Do I belong with the group I want to join?

• Do I make the first move toward friendship?

• Do I miss opportunities for fun and companionship?

• Do I invest time and energy in others even when I may not be sure to get anything in return?

• Do I try to enjoy my own company when I can't find other companionship?

More serious problems that cause loneliness can be helped by honest talk with an interested friend, relative, or trained counselor. One of them may help you to understand why you feel lonely and what you can do about it.

TERMS

Rejection	Temperament	Withdraw	Building resources
Loneliness	Self-worth	Counter attack	in self
Solitude	Defenses	Investing in others	

CHAPTER 15

Serious Rejection

Almost everyone feels left out or lonely at times. However, there's a deeper and more long-lasting form of rejection. It is suffered by those who are different from average in their health, intelligence, appearance, or behavior. This type of serious rejection can not be solved by waiting for others to notice you, by trying harder to be friendly, or by correcting a fault in your personality.

In this chapter you'll read about some of the typical physical, mental, and social problems that shut people off from one another to an extreme degree. You'll learn some of the causes for such problems. You'll also be encouraged to think about your own feelings toward those who are quite a bit different from you.

PHYSICAL APPEARANCE

Acceptance and success are tied to physical appearance. For example, persons with average builds are more likely to be accepted into a group. Unless they are outstanding athletes, very big girls or very small boys may be rejected for their size. Much worse, those who are sick a lot or physically handicapped are sometimes left out or simply ignored. Even persons who are mildly crippled or disfigured may not be invited to group activities, even when they have much to offer in terms of ability or personality.

Natalie Leimkuhler
A serious problem may cause a person to withdraw from others for a while.

Nature can be the cause of rejection. However, natural handicaps can be overcome. You know that *attitude* means the way you think and feel about ideas and issues. The attitude of persons with physical handicaps decides the kind of lives they will lead.

Some disabled persons achieve far more than average for their age and education. They seem to want to make up for their handicaps in the very area where they have a physical problem.

Professional football player Tom Dempsey is a good example. He was born with a stub foot. With determination and hard work he became an outstanding placekicker. For booting field goals and points after touchdowns, Tom used the abnormal foot that set him apart from most others. You probably know people with physical problems who accomplish plenty in life and make friends at the same time.

CASE EXAMPLE

Recently, newspapers carried a story of a California boy nicknamed the "Kidney Kid." Not everyone with a serious physical problem does as well as Martin. His story is included here to remind you that some teens turn what others might call a handicap into a spur for accomplishment or service to others.

At age thirteen, Martin lost his energy. Once he had caught hard football passes on the run. Then he began to miss easy tosses. A checkup showed

Natalie Leimkuhler

Sometimes handicaps don't show. A physically healthy person who looks OK can suffer from emotional problems.

that the boy's kidneys no longer worked normally.

At first the doctors tried cleaning his blood through the filter of an artificial kidney machine before returning it to the body. However, Martin's condition grew worse. He had to have both kidneys removed. His mother offered one of her healthy kidneys. Martin and his mother lived through the dangerous transplant operations. So far, so good.

Then, instead of being satisfied with the life of a weak invalid, Martin began to look for ways to make money for himself and the group that had helped save his life. By watching his mother cook he learned enough to run small parties for the neighbors. He talked his class into helping with

the sale of candy for the Kidney Foundation's "trick-or-treat" program. With his brother's help, Martin sold 400 cases of sweets. He made a documentary movie on kidney machines. Costing just $7 for the film, his movie ran for ten minutes. He even became a public speaker. All profits from his efforts went to the Kidney Foundation to buy machines to help keep other patients alive until kidney donors could be found.

Martin not only overcame his serious handicap, but he did far more than the average teen. He wouldn't let people reject him. He is a good example of a handicapped person who produced a lot more than was expected of a normal person his age. Martin's attitude made the difference.

Of course, you need not have a disease or a disability to feel handicapped. Indeed, people with the most serious emotional or mental problems may be good-looking and healthy on the outside.

Something to think about. Did you ever wonder how it feels to be handicapped? Actually, if you are a normal, healthy, and active adolescent it's very difficult to put yourself in the place of a disabled person. It doesn't make any difference if the handicap is mental or physical, if you've never had a similar experience.

A psychologist designed an experiment so a group of young volunteers at a community agency could get a better idea of how life seems to those who are mentally and physically handicapped.

The psychologist displayed the following items on a table:
• Two clean cotton balls.
• A thin, gauzy scarf.
• A small, clean rubber ball (the kind used for playing jacks).

- A brick.
- A piece of rope about two feet long tied securely around the brick.

A volunteer named Josie offered to place one cotton ball in each of her ears. Then she draped the scarf lightly over her head so she could still see a little. She tied the brick to her left wrist.

Josie wore her equipment for the remainder of the session. Despite these artificial handicaps, Josie was expected to take notes, to read writing on the chalkboard, and to hear everything that went on in the classroom.

Everytime Josie wanted to speak she had to pop the tiny ball into her mouth.

By the end of the training session both Josie and her fellow volunteers had a shocking new understanding of the burdens carried by persons who are handicapped.

SUPER-SMART

A small number of children—perhaps 1 in 200—is born with super intelligence. Each is able to work far above school grade level in certain subjects. Some of these very bright students are content to go along with regular classwork, even though they are bored most of the time. Some of these extrasmart boys and girls make friends, join activities, but play down their brainpower. Others feel miserable and out of place. At times brilliant adolescents may seem maladjusted, disinterested, or worse.

A few years ago Johns Hopkins University in Baltimore admitted a thirteen-year-old genius to its freshman class. Gifted in both math and science, the boy was ready for college after he finished eighth grade. He did so well that the university hunted for more like him. A recent count at Johns Hopkins showed sixty students of junior high school age enrolled in advanced math and science. Some have already earned college credits.

Natalie Leimkuhler

Although busy with her own talents, a gifted teenager may feel left out of close friendships and day-to-day adolescent life.

Sometimes an "oddball" doesn't fit into the typical adolescent world because there's no one to appreciate or share similar talents or interests. Imagine trying to talk about computers, stereo components, shortwave radios, or poetry when no one else is interested. A very bright person's problem may disappear by finding an outlet for the unusual knowledge.

CASE EXAMPLE

Nick was unhappy to the point of misery in junior high school. He was unpopular with fellow students. A few teachers regarded him as an uncooperative wise guy because sometimes he would correct what the adults said

Donald P. Vascimini

How do you react to persons with mental and physical handicaps?

in class. Then at age thirteen he was accepted as a junior in college, where he made excellent grades.

Nick said, "In eighth grade I really dropped off. I'm pretty sure I would have lost all interest and turned to other things. I don't know what."

His unhappiness in junior high school was normal. In college he found a greater challenge and new friends who appreciated and understood his talents. Nick's so-called problem disappeared. He almost became a serious reject because of his superior ability.

Of course, not all gifted students can jump ahead in school. However, many teachers encourage speeded-up classwork for those who can handle extra

assignments. They believe that the risk of serious problems is far greater when the student is held back.

Finish this case in another way. Suppose Nick stayed in junior high school instead of jumping ahead to college. What would his next few years as a student be like?

Actually, each case must be considered in terms of the person involved. Also, there is another side to this situation.

Sometimes the person who is *not* as smart as most classmates misses out on the give-and-take that makes a student feel welcome and part of the class. Consider this case at the other extreme.

CASE EXAMPLE

Jamie is a handsome boy. At first glance you'd be impressed with his fine build and clean-cut good looks. However, Jamie doesn't learn as fast as his classmates. They call him "Retard," "Weirdo," and worse.

So eager was Jamie to be accepted by the gang that he grabbed for any chance to get attention. A group of boys used him in a shameful way. They prodded him to do things that would amuse them, but hurt Jamie. They enrolled him in a phony club, sent him on goofy errands, and made up stories about popular girls who wanted to meet him. For laughs they told him about make-believe dates so he'd feel bad when the girl (who had no knowledge of the scheme) didn't show up.

Of course, Jamie's efforts earned him neither respect nor acceptance. More and more he became the class fool. In his yearbook a cruel unsigned greeting read, "Jamie, you'll be forty by the time you get out of school. Ha Ha."

LEARNING DISABILITIES

Jamie's lack of brainpower made him different from the group. He is an extreme example, but studies suggest that at least 10 percent of school age boys and girls have some type of learning disability. They may have above-average intelligence. However, some problem with vision, speech, hearing, reading ability, or memory makes learning more difficult for them. A quirk of nature—the learning disability—makes them different enough to be rejected by their peers. Emotional problems and behavior disorders can also draw unkind treatment and rejection.

Fortunately Jamie and others like him can get help. After ninth grade he entered a work-study program geared to slower learners. In his first year he joined the school maintenance crew. He did so well in the care of shrubs and flowers that his counselor found him a job with a landscape gardener. Jamie still has that job. His employer likes his work, and Jamie has earned the respect of his co-workers. He is also learning to respect himself.

Something to think about. **How are very bright and slower-learning teens treated in your school? What are your attitudes toward highly intelligent teens and those with learning disabilities? Boys and girls who would never be unkind to a handicapped person rarely extend friendship either. Why do you think this happens?**

WHAT'S BEHIND REJECTION?

You've read some examples of more serious rejection. Following you'll learn about some of the emotions that cause unfair or cruel treatment to one person by another. Such attitudes can cause deeply harmful and long-lasting problems in human relationships.

PREJUDICE

"I've already made up my mind. Don't confuse me with the facts." These two sentences demonstrate a joking example of prejudice. The prejudiced person forms an opinion—good or bad—on the basis of looks, skin color, religion, family background, or almost anything else. So prejudice becomes a case of instant acceptance or rejection because made-up attitudes of this type can be either for or against another person or group.

There are two sides to prejudice— positive and negative. *Positive prejudice* happens when someone plays favorites. For example, most people favor family members over outsiders. You would expect parents to prefer their own children to others. You would probably have a similar attitude if you had to select between a friend or classmate who was competing with someone from another school. You might prefer a member of your church to someone of a different religion.

Positive prejudice causes harm when someone is chosen on the basis of previous contact rather than talent, training, or experience. However, in most cases the word *prejudice* refers to a negative attitude. That's the way it is used in this chapter. Negatively prejudiced persons are sometimes called bigots.

Prejudice touches every kind of human experience. Earlier in the chapter you read that both fast and slow learners can suffer from negative prejudice. Both the best and worst students

might be rejected because they are a little too different from average. You may feel prejudice against students from another school district without ever meeting them. Such attitudes often spring up when schools are locked in an intense sports rivalry.

The feelings that go along with prejudice may be:

• Simple unconcern ("I don't care about them").

• Outspoken dislike ("I'm glad they're not in our group").

• Outright hate ("I hope they get into trouble").

Of course there are good reasons for some negative prejudices. Attitudes against locker thieves or drug pushers make sense. However, many prejudices do not come from either first-hand experience or solid fact. Following are reasons for prejudice, plus some examples and explanations of unfair negative prejudices.

Private and personal. Most of us are not good judges of our own positive and negative prejudices.

Following is a list to help you know yourself better. The words in the table are often used as labels to describe certain persons.

On a separate sheet of paper, complete the sentence for each one. Try to write the first thing you think of. What you write will probably indicate your real attitude.

Remember that prejudice can be either *for* or *against* members of a group.

DO NOT WRITE IN THIS BOOK.

• Blacks are

• Bookworms are

• Catholics are

- Cheerleaders are
- Chicanos are
- Cripples are
- Drinkers are
- Druggers are
- Jews are
- Men are
- Persons with mental illness are
- Musicians are
- Old people are
- Police are
- Protestants are
- Retarded persons are
- Sport stars are
- Teachers are
- Very smart persons are
- Whites are
- Women are

What about me? The incomplete sentences were selected to spark basic attitudes.

Did you discover some prejudices of your own that you didn't know you had?

If yes, what will you probably do about them?

Prejudice is learned. Children learn negative prejudices the same way they catch a common cold. By age five, boys and girls notice differences in skin color. They learn that certain families come from other countries around the world and from different parts of town. They also learn the cruel nicknames that go with each national group. From ages twelve to sixteen the prejudices grow even stronger.

Some parents use phrases like, "He's a good person" or "She always helps out." In other homes, however, children are more likely to hear, "I don't like their looks" or "Don't trust them." At first, most sons and daughters tend to think of other people the same way their parents do.

Even without words, parents can teach attitudes of openness and trust to those who are different. Mothers and fathers can also teach their children to be afraid of, or mean to, "outsiders."

Dick Mroczynski, Journal and Courier, Lafayette, Indiana
Rooting for the school team draws boys and girls together for a common purpose. Group experiences like this help reduce suspicion, prejudice, and other negative emotions.

Most youngsters pick up such negative opinions long before they learn the words that describe them.

Damage. Both those who reject others and their victims suffer some personality damage. The damage to prejudiced persons may not be obvious. Often they don't grow up emotionally. They can become rigid and narrow-minded. Although they may be self-satisfied, they cut themselves off from chances to learn about others. They may spend a lot of energy hating or distrusting others. They don't have time for kind words or decent acts. As you might guess, prejudiced people aren't much fun to be with.

Unfairly rejected people, on the other hand, may feel ashamed and worthless. Sadly, these victims may even learn to dislike themselves. After being turned down by so many persons they may begin to think, "If everyone treats me this way, I must be really worthless."

Some targets of prejudice, if they grow strong enough, may turn their anger into cruel acts. Strong negative emotions can lead to group fights, property destruction, and harm to innocent bystanders.

Prejudice also makes it difficult for those who have been rejected to show much interest in forgiving and forgetting. Old suspicions, distrust, and fear make it less easy for rejected persons to let down their guard, even when offered sincere signs of fair treatment.

Look up the word "bigotry" in a dictionary.

On a separate sheet of paper list examples of bigotry that have happened to you during the past month.

Then list bigoted actions you have seen used against your peers.

Were there times when you acted like a bigot?

If yes, do you have any idea why you *needed* to do so?

Racial prejudice. It would be difficult for anyone to reach your age without picking up special attitudes toward skin color. Most persons feel more comfortable with those who look, sound, and act like themselves. Anyone who is different may seem strange or not as welcome. Sometimes qualities similar to yours are not obvious. They must be discovered.

CASE EXAMPLE

Keith talked about conditions he met in an integrated school.

"When I came to this place it was the first time I'd been to a school with white kids. In a lot of my classes they are in the majority. At first I didn't know how to talk to them. If anybody said something to me, I'd find some-

thing to say back. That's about it. After awhile I started finding out more about the white kids. I discovered that we thought the same on some things and not on others. We had some of the same problems and some different ones. I found that I liked some of the white kids and didn't like others, just like my own people."

Keith is beginning to look at his prejudices. He is beginning to think for himself and test out his own set of personal values. He has reason to distrust white people. He still sees a great division between black and white, but he is checking out his white classmates as individuals. Some are worthy of his friendship and respect. Others are not. He wouldn't reject or accept all blacks, either, as he said. He's learning to think for himself.

Prejudices hang on when there's not much give-and-take. However, close contact may change a prejudice toward or against a person. When experiences are good, like Keith's, tensions ease away. Bad experiences, like racial fights, make things worse.

Did you know? Many individuals and groups work hard to lessen the amount of prejudice among all people.

One such organization trains teenage volunteers to help fight racial and religious bigotry. In small groups—usually a black, a Chicano, a Protestant, a Catholic, and a Jew—the adolescents visit school classrooms and meetings of teachers, parents, and community leaders.

The volunteers share their own experiences as objects of bigotry. They also describe times when they have acted with bigotry.

The teens then invite those in the audience to express their own prejudices.

What about me? If you were invited to describe a personal prejudice at a public meeting, what emotion would you expect to feel? Would you admit that you have treated someone badly because of skin color or religion?

Stereotyping is another close relative of prejudice. Stereotype comes from a Greek word for "solid" or "fixed." Printers use a metal or fiber plate called a stereotype to duplicate words or pictures. Because the solid plate always prints the same thing, the results are fixed in advance. You can look at the plate and know exactly what it will produce.

Stereotype also describes how some persons judge others. You know that prejudiced people ignore the facts because they have already formed an opinion. Prejudiced persons often favor stereotyped labels. They just look at someone and believe they know in advance what that person is like— hardworking or lazy, honest or not.

Stereotypes are usually extreme statements, either unfair or untrue. They often begin with the word *all* or say that members of a certain group always think and act in the same fixed way. For example, have you ever heard statements like these: "All women drivers are bad drivers." "Everyone from that street (school, town, neighborhood) is a snob." "People who read the Bible don't think for themselves."

Why similarities? You may wonder about this: If stereotypes are not true for all members of a group, why is it that so many persons of a similar race, religion, or education *seem* to react to certain situations in the same way?

Of course no two persons are exactly alike. However, when boys and girls share many similar experiences, live in

David Snodgress, Herald-Telephone, Bloomington, Indiana
Known as migrant workers, members of this family travel the country picking crops in season. Perhaps you have heard stereotyped attitudes expressed about these hardworking people.

the same neighborhood, and are taught the same values, they may *seem* to be the same. However, such similarities are not inherited nor even present in everyone. Always, if you take a close enough look, you will find an individual person behind the stereotype.

Stereotyping is for lazy people because it doesn't require a person to think. So if you really want to understand someone, you will steer clear of judging on the basis of looks or membership in a certain group. A good attitude is to accept each new person you meet as pleasant and honest until you have reason not to.

Did you know? Psychiatrist Robert Coles exploded a lot of stereotypes. He has lived with the poor of many colors and types—including migrant workers, sharecroppers, and mountain people. Coles found men and women in all groups who were healthy of mind and courageous of spirit. He met strong and determined men, women, and children who were bright, shrewd, and sensitive even though they lacked education and money.

Dr. Coles reminds us that individuals are all one-of-a-kind. Each is quite complicated. Goodness and generosity can exist in all types of persons. So can evil and selfishness. He proved that all poor people are not lazy. He also found that all children raised in poor sections of big cities don't grow up to be delinquents. By gathering evidence to disprove stereotypes, Dr. Coles performed a great service.

Scapegoating is a first cousin to unfair prejudice. A scapegoat is a person who gets blamed for something whether guilty or not. Anyone who is different physically, emotionally, or socially may be the last choice as a friend and first choice as a scapegoat. Group members often blame scapegoats for the wrongdoings of everyone else.

CASE EXAMPLE

With a touch of shame, a grown man recalls that all through grade school whenever anything went wrong a class member was sure to call out, "Johnson did it." If an eraser was missing, Johnson took it. If there was a fight on the playground, Johnson started it. Actually, Johnson often managed to get into trouble without help from anyone. So he was a natural choice when others were looking for someone to blame.

People who use others as scapegoats are rarely aware of why they need to be cruel. First they load their negative emotions or imperfect acts onto someone else. Then they blame the scapegoat for acting badly or for losing the game. This makes the aggressive persons feel better for seeming so good when compared with the scapegoat.

Persons who are weak or handicapped in some way are often selected as scapegoats. It's safer to pick on a person who is obviously different. Johnson was often alone and poorly dressed. He didn't have a gang of pals to help him fight back.

Being ignored, rejected, or made a scapegoat is bad enough. However, sometimes aggression gets even worse. Victims may be hounded with words or attacked physically. Such events take place much more often than many adults realize.

AGGRESSION

Aggression often goes hand-in-hand with prejudice. Although aggression often violates the rights of others with force, it can also serve a positive and healthy purpose. If you are running a race, or competing fairly for a special award, aggressive drive can give you the extra push needed to win.

Following you'll read about the kind of aggression that means to attack others unfairly with fighting words (like Honky, Nigger, Fatso, Skinny) or with fists—or both.

Aggressive emotions are part of human nature. All persons have them to some degree. Try to remember that it's not the negative emotions that cause trouble. What's important is how persons *act* on such feelings, what they say and do because of aggressive urges. Part of maturing and learning to live peacefully with others is acquiring the ability to channel aggressive feelings into useful and enjoyable activities like work, sports, dancing, and hobbies.

Aggression receives mention here because it is so often tied to prejudice. Aggressive feelings often get turned loose when someone decides to take action on the basis of prejudice, strong dislike, or even a misunderstanding. Word battles can lead to fistfights or locker room brawls.

Like other drives, aggression speeds up during adolescence. In fact, teens sometimes become so aggressive (as in school vandalism or street fights) that adults must stop the violence. Girls can be just as aggressive as boys.

The way any teen uses aggression depends a lot on what has been learned at home. Some parents teach children to hold back the desire to lash out and hurt others. Others teach, "Hit 'em hard, before they get you."

Some aggressive teens have been raised in rough-and-tumble homes. Now big and strong enough, these adolescents look for someone else to push around.

OUTLETS FOR AGGRESSION

Everyone has nasty feelings at some time. However, people handle their negative emotions in many different ways. For example:

• *Talk.* A lot of aggression is expressed in words. Gossip, insults, rumors, and threats of what you'd like to do (but won't) all offer an outlet for negative emotions. For example, you may have made remarks such as, "I'd really like to

David Snodgress, Herald-Telephone, *Bloomington, Indiana*
Motorbike competition can be a healthy outlet for aggressive emotions. Martha's been racing her bike since she was ten. She trains like an athlete, rides almost every day, and races every chance she gets.

tell Wendy off" or "I heard that Jeb will get left back."

• *Destructive activity.* Beating up a weaker person or threatening injury is aggressive. Bullies often enjoy their power and the fear they cause. They may even invent reasons for their ugly behavior: "He deserved that." "Serves her right."

• *Spectator.* Watching others be aggressive can be a good substitute for some acting-out that you might like to try. Sports fans enjoy seeing participants belt each other. A fight on the field, court, or ice provides an extra bonus. Spectators at a wrestling match or a roller derby can be a better show than the contestants.

TV shows, movies of adventure and spying, and even comic strips where

Kathy Tuite
Regular workouts provide a release for stored-up energies.

you can take sides with the "good guys" all help drain off negative emotions.

• *Constructive activity.* Much aggression gets worked off without anyone getting hurt. That's one reason why communities build playgrounds and organize sports. Jogging, dancing, and less physical activities like reading, writing, and crafts all help to burn up energies that might otherwise get detoured into aggressive and possibly harmful acts.

CASE EXAMPLE

Eddie became a victim of aggression when a group of his classmates decided to gang up on him. Eddie was a quiet boy and a good student. He got along well with his peers and his teachers.

Then suddenly, a small group of bullies decided to take out their anger and aggression on him. Eddie became both a scapegoat and a victim.

It all started when someone stole $5 from a teacher's desk. Eddie saw the theft and urged the thief to return the money before the teacher noticed that it was gone. The boy who took the money not only refused to put it back, but he and his friends started to taunt Eddie for being such a goody-goody.

Soon events went beyond the teasing stage. Eddie's tormentors began to enjoy picking on him. Making Eddie squirm became a form of fun for the group. It also served to unite the bullies. Each day they made more elaborate plans to scare or worry Eddie. The boys tried to outdo each other by thinking up more exciting forms of torture: whispered phone calls, unsigned threats slipped into his locker, shoves and bumps on the stairs and in the halls. With great skill the boys avoided teachers who might discover the plot.

Eddie became more and more afraid. He pleaded to stay home. He skipped classes and pretended to be sick—anything to avoid his misery at school. He even thought about killing

Natalie Leimkuhler
Eddie's face reflects the results of the cruel treatment directed at him.

himself. Unless you have been such a victim, it is hard to imagine just how desperate Eddie felt.

Complete this case. To encourage you to think about it, the ending to Eddie's story is not given here. What could Eddie have done?

What would you do?

How much would you blame the boys who gave him such a bad time?

Do girls behave like Eddie's tormentors?

If you were able, how would you help Eddie?

What would you do to the bullies who made his life so unhappy?
really hurt someone?

Did you know? Crime and violence have increased in schools all over the United States, especially in the large cities.

Attacks on teachers and students (by

other students or outsiders) include armed robbery and even murder.

Extortion (ik-STOR-shin) and vandalism are not uncommon. Extortion is when one person demands payments of money or something else of value from another. Vandalism means destruction of property for no useful purpose.

Some students carry weapons ranging from knives and chains to razor blades, brass knuckles, and guns.

WHAT ABOUT ME?

Adolescents can be just as unkind, cruel, and aggressive as adults. Checking your own emotions and behavior can change attitudes and do away with prejudices. Understanding *why* you are for or against a certain person or group can help curb the urges of strong negative emotions.

Psychologists agree that mistreatment or intense dislike of another person or group is tied up with feelings about self. If you dislike someone or some group without any real reason, the following comments are meant for you.

The best-adjusted, happiest persons are those who think well of themselves and others. The more you value yourself, the less need you'll have to hurt others. The more capable you feel to deal with different people and different experiences, the less suspicious and prejudiced you will need to be. The more you can understand "how the other persons feel," the less need you will have to dislike or fear them.

Many prejudices and aggressive acts come from the need to feel superior. "I'm stronger, smarter, better." If you respect yourself you don't need to brag or show off in order to feel worthwhile.

Unlearning. As you have read, prejudice is a learned attitude. Because it is, prejudice can also be unlearned or

changed. Now is a good time to begin treating others in terms of what they are as individuals rather than how they look, where they live or go to church. You can use your curiosity and good sense to decide what new persons in your life are really like *after* you meet them, rather than before.

TESTING VALUES

The family teaches young children how they should treat others. So it's natural for you to judge others the same way your family does. Such influences stay with you as long as you live.

Even if you were raised by parents without prejudice, you will probably test the values that you learned at home. Most students your age begin this evaluating process by comparing the standards of their family with ideas they pick up from friends or hear in class. These experiences away from home usually do one of two things. They strengthen your present set of personal values, or they raise questions about what you learned at home. In time you may develop a value system almost exactly the same as that of your parents. However, these standards do not really become your own until you test them out and understand them in terms of your own thoughts and words. When your parents were much younger they had to do this same sorting process for themselves.

A set of values cannot become yours if it is accepted without any question. If it holds up after being questioned and tried, then you know that you can depend on what you believe to be the right and best way to live. Persons who have a clear and dependable value system usually enjoy good relationships with others.

To learn more. Select one idea or topic from this chapter that applies to you and the way you live your life.

On a separate sheet of paper describe your selection in one sentence.

In no more than three sentences explain why you chose it.

DO NOT WRITE IN THIS BOOK.

RECAP

Physical, mental, and social differences sometimes cause one person or a group of persons to dislike, reject, or mistreat another. Although a physical illness or handicap can be a serious problem, some persons simply refuse to let a personal disability get in the way of enjoying life and the company of others.

Sometimes a person is left out or rejected because there's no one else to share special talents or interests. In a different setting where special abilities are appreciated or shared by others, such persons feel happier and more comfortable.

For every gifted person there's someone else with a learning problem. Those who learn more slowly, or with more difficulty, also need opportunities to accomplish, achieve, and feel good about themselves.

For whatever reason, rejection of one person by another always damages human relationships. Prejudice is a form of rejection that means to decide about someone before really knowing them. Prejudices are usually learned early in life. They can be both positive and negative. Negative prejudice is usually a sign of one person's need to feel superior to someone else.

During adolescence, prejudices can harden like cement. They may not change for a lifetime. However, persons who are fair and flexible can change their attitudes when they learn the facts and learn to think for themselves. Negative prejudices hurt both the prejudiced person and the victim.

Rejected persons can learn to dislike themselves and to believe they are worthless. Sometimes they become angry and strike back.

Prejudice can also cause people to be aggressive. Aggressive attitudes may develop during adolescence. Open fighting or non-physical attacks may result. In extreme cases, victims of aggression may be hurt physically or emotionally.

Aggression can be controlled best by accepting responsibility for your own behavior, by finding constructive action outlets, or by watching controlled aggression like organized sports. Harming another person in any way is the most damaging outlet for aggressive feelings.

Stereotypes are unfair labels automatically given to strangers. When members of a certain group share the same skin color or a particular way of speaking or acting, stereotypers may decide that the group members are exactly alike in all other ways. Of course, all persons are individuals no matter how much they resemble others.

Scapegoats are those who usually get blamed for things that go wrong, even if not their fault. Scapegoating also means to blame someone else, often a weaker person, for your own guilt or other negative emotions.

Adolescents can be just as prejudiced as adults. Although it's natural to feel most at ease with those who look or act in a familiar way, it is harmful to both the aggressor and the victim to mistreat those who seem different.

Prejudices are learned. As a result, they can be changed if you are willing to question your present standards for judging others. The more you like and respect yourself, the more comfortable you feel as a person. The more you try to understand the feelings of others, the less prejudiced you are likely to be.

TERMS

Handicap	Genius	Aggression
Disability	Positive prejudice	Stereotype
Learning disability	Negative prejudice	Scapegoat

UNIT V
Boys and Girls

CHAPTER 16

First Signs of Pairing

The long, sweeping approach to the Lincoln Memorial in Washington, D.C., includes many steps. Sightseers climb at different speeds. Some trudge up the grade, one step at a time. Others race ahead.

Living through the years of adolescence is much like the ascent to the Lincoln Memorial. All boys and girls will move at their own pace.

Much of life is spent getting ready for the next step. Right now you would probably like to be more comfortable when you are with members of the other sex. You might already notice a growing awareness and a deeper interest that announce your gradual movement to the next level of boy-girl give-and-take. Some of your classmates may be racing ahead. Perhaps they already date, or go with someone on a regular basis. Or you may be the leader in your group.

Pairing takes place when a boy and a girl get together to enjoy each other's company.

This chapter focuses on the steps that lead to such pairing. You'll read about early stages in these relationships. You'll review the ways a boy shows interest for a girl (or the other way 'round).

For most adolescents in your age group the real problem is not how to propose marriage, but rather how to work up enough nerve to say "hello" to someone the first time. Instead of declaring your love, you're more likely to wonder what love is, or if you could ever be in love.

Boys can be uneasy phoning a girl just to arrange for a time to be together. At parties teens know the squirming discomfort of waiting and hoping that someone—anyone—will show some interest. Such issues are the normal concerns of young adolescents. After awhile almost everyone learns to be more at ease with the other sex.

The stories of Amy and the other teens in this chapter help illustrate different steps in both age and personal growth.

Girls and boys usually discover natural and unplanned chances to enjoy each other's company.

David Snodgress, Journal and Courier, Lafayette, Indiana

Natalie Leimkuhler
Interest in the other sex can show up almost any time.

285

Natalie Leimkuhler

First it's the boys against the girls.

Whether you are male or female, their stories will probably sound familiar to you. Even in childhood, when boys play with boys and girls with girls, each "team" is quite aware of the other.

CASE EXAMPLE

You first met Amy in Chapter 12. At the bottom of Amy's shoe box lay a booklet made of folded papers. Boldly printed in the large round scrawl of an eight-year-old, the cover read: OUR JOHN BOOK, WOW! It was decorated with a huge lopsided heart pierced by a paper arrow.

Amy recalls that many years ago she and two friends spent one rainy afternoon writing their "book." The text was short and right to the point. It read:

"We promise to always love John and adore him every day and to invite him over any time we can.

"John is so cute.

"John is Ramona's, Amy's, and Meg's boy friend.

"He is the most lover boy in the United States.

"He is loved by 34 girls."

Amy's book is a reminder that long before any serious attraction develops, one sex is clearly interested in the other.

Little girls, like Amy and her friends at age eight, are often quite open about their interest in boys. Occasionally they even predict their marriage to a special one.

Boys are quite different. They tend to be more secretive and to deny any romantic interest. Or they declare their everlasting disgust for girls.

Private and personal. Can you recall any of your childhood crushes?

How long did your infatuation last?

What ever happened to the boy or girl you admired so much?

CASE EXAMPLE

Jeremy, age ten, insisted that he hated girls and would always despise them. Suzy, the family's teenage babysitter, was greatly amused by his attitude. So sure was she that he would change his mind someday that she encouraged him to write his anti-girl position and to sign the following statement. He wrote:

"I, Jeremy, will never be interested in girls. Never! Not even 7 years from now. If by some strange chance I should get interested in girls, I owe Suzy $1.00."

Needless to say, Suzy expects to collect.

FIRST CONTACT

You may be worried about your ability to attract others or concerned about what to say at first. Friends can be a big help. They can speak for you. Or they can show you different ways to mention your interest. From the safety of a group of friends you can joke or tease with a smile. You can pretend to be angry or hurt in order to mask your growing attraction. The group provides protection.

Gradually the walls of separation crumble. Both boys and girls leave the safety of their same-sex friends. At one extreme, some rush up the steps, eager to overcome their shyness and to prove their devotion. At the other extreme, a few try to deny or hide their interest in the other sex long after others have declared theirs. They refuse to climb the steps right now. However, the greatest number of adolescents welcome the opportunity to approach boys (or girls) directly and begin the exciting process of pairing off.

CASE EXAMPLE

Karie is fourteen. She's never had a date, neither has she paired off with any particular boy. Yet she and her girl friends talk about boys, openly admire them, and mix with them in groups. Karie and her friends are very interested. They are waiting for some sign that boys care as much as the girls do.

One summer evening, she and two friends climbed out on a low roof of her home. They decided the lofty spot would be a great place to watch boys go by and shout half-friendly, half-teasing greetings. Later, while climbing back through an upstairs window, one girl pretended to slam the window on Karie's fingers. Giggling, then screaming in protest, Karie lost her grip, fell a full story, and broke her arm.

Later, in the hospital, Karie swung back and forth between acting brave and trying to squeeze back the tears that were staining her pillow.

"What's the matter?" her mother asked. "Does it hurt?"

"No, it's not the arm," Karie sobbed. "I miss my cats . . . I miss my brothers . . . But most of all, I miss boys!"

Even in her pain, Karie admitted what was most on her mind.

Many adolescents pass through a time when they have serious doubts about their attractiveness and appeal to the other sex. They wonder if anyone could ever like someone so ugly, so clumsy, and so dumb. Ted, a shy young man, said it this way.

CASE EXAMPLE

"Most of the time I don't care much about girls. But there are times when I wish I had a girl I was completely at ease with. When I go to a movie and see other guys with girls I get a feeling that there must be something wrong with me. I stay awake at night and dream up what would be the perfect girl. But there's no perfect girl. Not for me anyway. My parents kid me about girls. I laugh with them but inside I feel empty. As long as I can fish and hunt, I'll do OK."

Ted honestly believed that no girl could ever like him. Already, he was

Natalie Leimkuhler

Boys and girls always find ways to be together.

getting ready for a future of hunting and fishing to fill his empty life without females. Actually, he was a normal and attractive boy. Many girls noticed Ted and would have been delighted with a smile from him. In time, of course, he did find a girl friend. Before long he overcame much of his shyness and discovered that he was not the hopeless case he once imagined.

Did you know? In one research study of teens, the boys who were interviewed said they liked girls who

- Are not too aggressive.
- Talk and listen.
- Have some social skills.
- Don't show off.
- Have nice manners.
- Dress well.
- Look good.

In that same study, girls who were interviewed said that they liked boys who

- Are nice looking.
- Are clean and neat.
- Act friendly.
- Are cooperative.
- Don't brag about themselves a lot.

GETTING TOGETHER

Parties and other pairing occasions are important steps during adoles-

Natalie Leimkuhler

Unplanned boy-girl games can be the first steps to pairing.

cence. One way or another, sooner or later, young people find the places and the reasons to be together. In your grandparents' day couples met at church socials or the local "Danceland." Your parents may have attended sock hops or gone to skating rinks.

The more formal, dress-up dating of the past has changed a lot. Mixed groups and more casual pairing serve much the same purpose. But no matter what you call it, grouping continues to happen. Boys and girls want to be together to talk, flirt, get acquainted, and simply to enjoy each other's company.

They often pick a special spot to gather. Meeting there becomes a tradition. A certain ritual develops. They pass gossip, down food and soft drinks,

Natalie Leimkuhler

Vince and Kurt put on a great show for the girls.

show off a little, and set times for more meetings.

A traveling reporter for the New York *Times* observed the nightly summer ritual in one small Minnesota town. Earl's, a drive-in on Main Street, serves as the regular hangout.

Around 7:00 P.M. a few kids ride their bikes for some of Earl's ice cream. By 8:00 P.M. the quiet bicyclists give way to the husky roar of motorbikes and fancy cars of the local boys. The autos sport jacked-up rear ends, oversized tires, and open windows. Sounds of radios or tape decks fill the night air. Mufflers seem not to exist. The restless drivers go up and down the shady streets, back and forth, around and around, looking for excitement.

Meanwhile the girls drift onto the scene dressed in cutoff jeans with halter tops or pants with bright pullovers. In pairs they walk up and down the sidewalks, acting surprised and giggling when boys honk their car horns or peel their tires as the traffic lights change. A friendly wave of "see you guys" promises an encounter later on.

By 9:00 P.M., as if by coincidence, the teens all finally gather at Earl's. The jukebox pounds out current hits while the pinball machine clangs its own off-key tune. Soft drinks flow. The joking, mixing, and talking begin in earnest. Couples drift off. By 11:00 P.M. the crowd dwindles to a hardy few.

Change the scenery, substitute a new cast, wardrobe, and local hangout and you could probably describe your own neighborhood. You may be more familiar with city streets where boys stand on street corners to pitch coins, laugh loudly at whispered jokes, or puff away on forbidden cigarettes. On another corner, girls flutter together, twittering like birds about boys, and about all the emotions they can't quite sort out yet.

Whether on city streets or in a Minnesota town, the scenery doesn't matter much. Although the players change, the play remains the same.

Casual groupings often occur at planned events like dances and parties. Sometimes a particular social event seems to speed up the pairing process. The first dance of the year, for example, may be the one best remembered. Usually, girls take the initiative. For weeks ahead they plan decorations, decide on refreshments, arrange for chaperones. At home, they discuss hairstyles and choose outfits.

Boys are just as interested. However, they may pretend a careful indifference, or protest dress decisions, or threaten not to come at all. "I'll play basketball instead," said one.

Girls are also a little anxious. One grumbled, "I might as well stay home. The boys will stay on one side of the gym, the girls on the other!"

Yet comes the big night and most everyone shows up. There's rushing back and forth, excitement, awkwardness.

Mary Lavin, an Irish writer, wrote a story about four young girls who attend a dance wearing their first long dresses. Exhilarated, gawky, scared to death, they stand together, hanging back from the swirl of the party.

One girl, Emily, invited to dance, smiles happily at her partner. Then she soon realizes it was a mistake to smile, because she can't stop! Panic-stricken, Emily wonders what she will do if she can't stop smiling—ever.

Natalie Leimkuhler
Just good friends.

JUST FRIENDS

One nice thing about moving through the years of adolescence is that you can begin to make friends with the other sex without being forced to say that you hate all girls (or boys)—which you probably don't mean. In fact, teens make many more casual, cross-over friendships these days. The sexes mix more and earlier. Crowd activities often replace the earlier pairing off of your parents' generation that was known as steady dating.

When a boy and girl claim to be "just friends," they could mean several things. For one, there may be no romance intended—at least for the moment. Friendship means that you can enjoy the fun of being with others and just talking to them with none of the demands or pressures of pairing.

Casual friendships of this type offer a good way to learn what boys (or girls) like and dislike. If you are a girl without brothers, or a boy without sisters, friendships with the other sex help you to become less shy. Friends also help you get closer to boys and girls you really want to know better. Sometimes a friend of the other sex states your case for you in a way you'd never dare.

CASE EXAMPLE

One winter Becky received many phone calls from Dave. He had a serious problem. The girl Dave really liked, Kathy, was almost a head taller than he. Dave didn't worry about the height difference, but he feared that Kathy might.

As you know, in early adolescence many girls are taller than boys of the same age. Even though most heights even out later, the differences can make boys feel uncomfortable at school dances and other social events.

Becky was Kathy's close friend. Dave enjoyed Becky's cheerful encouragement. He also hoped that she would say a good word to Kathy for him.

Dave knew that he was faced with forgetting about Kathy or running the risk that she might turn him down if he asked for a date. He took small consolation in the fact that the distance between the top of Kathy's head and his would never be greater. He was really happy with Becky's sympathy and her promise to speak well of him.

Actually, Kathy never showed any interest in Dave, even after his own growth spurt put them eyeball to eyeball. Kathy, like many early maturing girls, was busy competing for the few boys who were taller than she. Also, she was interested in older, smoother boys.

However, Dave and Becky became fast friends. Throughout high school they had a lot of fun together. Without ever saying so, they decided to remain "just friends."

Becky and Dave illustrate a special kind of pairing between boys and girls. Each likes the other, but not enough to act on the physical attraction. There's a mutual understanding that neither is seriously interested in the other—at least right now. Often the boy and girl remain good friends, enjoying each other's company whenever they happen to be together. Of course, some such friendships later blossom into love.

Finish this case with another ending. As this case closed, Becky and Dave were just good friends.

How else might their story end?

On a separate sheet of paper write a short paragraph to illustrate a different conclusion to their story.

If you like what you have written, volunteer to share it with the class.

Compare your paragraph with those of others who did this activity.

In almost any boy-girl friendship there's always the possibility for something more exciting. Meanwhile, friendship itself is enjoyable. As you know, any good relationship is based on honesty, trust, respect, and real concern for the other person. Such qualities also apply to friendships between males and females.

One kind of boy-girl pairing seldom works out. The bad results develop when romance ends and the couple decides to try being good friends anyway. Because one person is usually more upset than the other about the breakup, the offer to remain friends seems like a real letdown. In most cases such couples usually avoid future romantic contact.

To learn more. Select one idea or topic from this chapter that applies to you and the way you live your life.

On a separate sheet of paper describe your selection in one sentence.

In no more than three sentences explain why you chose it.

DO NOT WRITE IN THIS BOOK.

RECAP

No single formula or secret advice can make everything in boy-girl relationships run perfectly. Your individual timetable may not be rushing you toward the other sex. Even though your friends are moving faster, you may not feel quite ready to leap. If so, you are not alone. Many teens continue to prefer the company of their own sex. For them, close boy-girl pairings are still in the future. They seem to understand that there's no hurry, that things will work out when the time is right.

The best way to become less tense with the other sex is usually through group activities in which a lot of boys and girls get together. Try to stay active. Join different kinds of mixed activities.

Of course, no one can be sure of winning the friendship or affection of any particular person. In time, most boys and girls find someone special to care about, a person who also cares about them. You will probably do just fine in the process of pairing off as you take the steps of adolescence one at a time.

TERMS

Pairing   Rituals   Casual groups

CHAPTER 17

Boys and Girls Together

One day, a special member of the other sex walks into your life. With a thud you suddenly realize that someone *notices* you. Someone *likes* you. So exciting is the idea that for a short time you may feel a surge of interest in return. You might even get caught up and rushed along when you don't feel ready for romance. Or, as sometimes happens, you feel attracted first before the other person even notices you. Unless a spark of mutual interest catches fire, you will give up hope and look elsewhere.

In this chapter you'll read about early attractions between adolescents and what can happen when romance enters teen life.

CASE EXAMPLE

Valerie had a great crush on Kent. She first noticed him as a fast, flashy basketball guard. Thereafter she attended all school games to watch him. Carefully, she arranged to enter the same school door he used. She often "happened" to pass by just as his classes let out. In fact, Val knew Kent's class schedule better than her own. As for Kent, he was casual and friendly. However, he never showed any special interest in her.

For seven months Val studied Kent and daydreamed about him. When his name or picture appeared in a

Natalie Leimkuhler
"Could this be the one for me?"

basketball news story, she cut it out for her scrapbook. She knew his vital statistics by heart: five feet, eight inches tall. Weight 140 pounds. Black curly hair, brown eyes. Mole on left cheek. Mentally she catalogued every shirt and pair of pants in his wardrobe. She knew where he lived and the names of his friends.

Valerie enjoyed liking Kent. Although she yearned for him to return some sign that he liked her, too, her fascination was fun in itself. Yet first attractions, like Val's, may never move beyond the daydream stage if the second person never shows any interest.

However, one day Kent left a group of boys and headed in her direction. Val's heart pounded with both fear and delight. When he reached her he said, "Hi, Val, want to go to a movie Friday night?"

She thought she'd faint. In a quavering voice, she replied, "Sure, I'd like that."

Heart pounding, she waited until he was out of sight. Then, with a leap in the air, she raced two blocks to catch up with a friend who had tactfully walked ahead. Giddy with joy, she screamed the news. Then, setting another sprint record, she raced home. She shouted the marvelous news to her mother.

Much later, after Valerie and Kent got to know each other, she tried to sort her reactions in order to explain

So far, David doesn't realize that Mary Beth (center) has plans for him. (P.S. He soon found out.)

the great attraction. "I thought he was perfect. . . . He's really not. But he's very nice. He has that nice mole near his nose. He's trying to grow a moustache. . . . He has nice friends. . . . He has a great sense of humor."

Valerie's reasons for liking Kent are the stuff of first attraction, the flickers that keep interest glowing. She was fascinated with Kent long before she got to know him. If her current feeling for Kent lasts and later grows into a warm affection based on his character, in time, Val may develop real love for him.

Actually, Kent proved to be a nice, enjoyable person, even though not the super-hero of Valerie's daydreams. She had little trouble lowering her expectations.

RELATIONSHIPS THAT FIZZLE

Sometimes the difference between the ideal of one's daydreams and the real person is just too great. The attraction evaporates like a drop of water in the sunshine. You wonder how you could have been so wrong. Real people seldom fit the roles given them in daydreams.

Sometimes boys and girls who had been seeking someone to like them soon wish even more to be free again. When a boy and girl begin to spend a lot of time together, new problems may arise. A possessive feeling may grow, along with disagreements, uncertainties, and jealousy.

Perhaps you have felt the mixed emotions that emerge at times like these. You want someone to like you, but you also want to have time for yourself or time to play the field.

On one hand there's a nice feeling of security in knowing that someone really cares about you. On the other you may start to feel like a prisoner. A little devotion is usually welcome. Too much can be a pain. The case of Robin and Jim illustrates such a situation.

CASE EXAMPLE

Jim was Robin's first real boyfriend. She'd known him for years. Then one day after school he phoned her. Robin was so pleased that she thought him more attractive than ever. That's when her troubles began. He wasn't the person he seemed to be.

Gradually, Jim started to run Robin's life. He expected to meet her at all school games. He wanted to sit with her in the cafeteria, walk home with her after school every day, talk to her for an hour on the phone each night.

Robin began to think, "I wish he'd drop me, so I won't have to drop him." Yet she lacked the experience to say, "I quit!" In fact, she didn't even know how to cut short the long phone calls that were ruining her evenings.

Robin yearned to spend more time with other friends. Yet she felt like a helpless fly, unable to wiggle out of Jim's web.

Jim became more critical and demanding. "You pay too much attention to your girl friends and not enough to me," he complained. Worse, he didn't like Robin's best friend, Janet. One day he said, "If you really like me, you'll choose between me and Janet!"

Robin wondered more and more if having a devoted boyfriend was worth the price. When she started thinking about Jim's demands, she realized that she no longer had much fun with him at all. Indeed, when together they usually argued. Each seemed unable to understand the other's feelings.

Jim made his demands directly and openly. Robin's resentment showed itself in less obvious ways. At home she was moody. She often felt depressed without understanding why. She even worried that someday, against her will, she'd have to marry Jim.

Robin wanted to break off, but she couldn't find the courage. No words sounded right. Also, she had many "off again, on again" feelings. One moment she'd think, "I wish I didn't have any boyfriend for a while." Then she would wonder, "What would I do at the mixers?" Robin lacked confidence in her own ability to attract another boy. The safe thing to do was to stick with Jim.

Not until she was faced with losing her best friend, Janet, did Robin act. As kindly as possible, Robin told Jim she could no longer go with him. He pleaded, promised to change. He even cried. So did Robin, because she didn't want to hurt him. However, she stuck with her decision.

Robin's romance came to a painful end. Jim was angry and bitter. He even told untrue stories about her. So, after that, Robin was more cautious. She made no hasty promises she'd regret later.

Robin learned something very important about herself. Although she hated being told what to do, she had found it difficult to express her resentment. She knew that in the future she must stay clear of the bossy type and not drift into another situation that would make her unhappy.

Gradually Robin felt more confident. She was also more willing to risk being without a boyfriend. Even if she had no partner for parties or mixers, she could go with the girls and still have fun.

ENDINGS

Robin's story may be familiar to you. She dropped Jim because she disliked losing control of her own decisions and accepting so many orders from someone else.

Changing your mind about a person you think you like is not bad. It is natural. Most teens fall in love many times. Most also fall out of love. Few boys or girls marry their first love.

Therefore if you go with someone and later change your mind, that's normal. However, kindness and consideration of the other person's feelings rate high. Sometimes a boy suddenly stops calling. Or a girl just snubs the boy. No explanations follow. The rejected person often feels betrayed and confused: "What did I do wrong?"

Many people do not know how to end a romance in a kind way. It's not an easy thing to do. Therefore, like Robin and Jim, many breakups end in bitterness and tears.

Of course, it takes courage to tell someone that your feelings have changed. There's no easy way to say, "I'm tired of you" or "I'm bored being tied down."

How to quit a romance. Once you decide an attraction is over, don't change your mind. Sometimes the one who wants to break up feels sorry for the second person and agrees to try again. Almost always, such good-hearted softness only prolongs the torture on both sides.

In part, Robin delayed the breakup because she feared that she couldn't get another boyfriend. That wasn't fair to Jim.

If one person feels sure that the romance is over, a sharp, clean-cut break is usually best. Forcing a break by saying unkind things that will "get back" to the other person is for bullies and cowards. Equally unfair are uses of invented excuses like, "I'm busy tonight." The same is true of techniques like deliberately starting a fight so you have something to be angry about.

If you've been honest with yourself and the other person, you need not make excuses nor defend a change of heart. It may be better to say something like, "I'm sorry. My feelings have changed." That way you can leave the other person's pride intact. For example, Robin might have said, "Jim, you're a nice guy, and I like you a lot. I should have told you sooner, but I'm not ready to be tied down."

You be the counselor. How would you advise a teen who wants to break off a relationship without hurting the other person?

Jealous. Of course, Jim had no right to boss Robin's life by ordering her activities, by monitoring her time, or by dictating her friendships. His side of the story is not available. He did seem to be jealous and selfish. Jealousy is not proof of real love. Instead the jealous person may demand a monopoly on another's time and attention because of personal feelings of insecurity. Jealousy is a fiery emotion. Sometimes one person deliberately tries to make another jealous by flirting, teasing, or pretending to care more about someone else.

Look up the word "jealousy" *in a dictionary.*

Although jealousy turns out to be part of many boy-girl relationships, it also helps to destroy many other human ties.

Something to think about. Can jealousy play a role in friendships between persons of the same sex?

If your answer is yes, explain how.

You be the counselor. From Robin's point of view, Jim sounds like a bossy, jealous boy. Put yourself in his shoes. Build a case to defend him. Why did he make such demands? What were his real feelings for Robin? If he liked her so much, why did he say untrue things about her after they broke up? How would you explain his attitude toward Janet?

Easier. Some boys and girls, you may notice, seem to ease into smooth and enjoyable friendships with the other sex. Each likes the other. Neither demands too much. Neither is jealous of attention shown to others. Each allows the other to lead a separate life. Neither asks for binding promises. Both talk freely about everything. They share ideas. They know that they will probably find another special person someday. So they enjoy each other while they have no other bonds. When they part—often by mutual agreement—no bitterness remains. Some remain friends. Others fall in love for good.

Unhappily, as with Robin and Jim, some romances hurt both persons. One reason why such breakups are stormy is that neither knows beforehand what is expected. For example, couples sometimes think that because they like each other, all attractions for others will just fade away. Of course, that's not the way human nature works. It's a rare teenager who doesn't keep one eye open for new romance possibilities.

CASE EXAMPLE

Arnie felt disloyal and sneaky about his attraction to other girls until he realized that his girlfriend, Rita, had the same reaction to other boys.

He said, "Finally I changed my attitude from jealousy to thinking it was only normal. I found that I watched girls, noticed what they were wearing, and even wanted to get to know them better. I realized that Rita and I were expecting too much of each other. We were too young to spend all our time with each other."

BUT IS IT LOVE?

Strong feelings of affection for someone of the other sex go by many names. If you are very young, people may call your emotions a crush, puppy love, or infatuation. If you are a bit older you may

Natalie Leimkuhler
Taking a break at a school dance, Luanne seems more enthusiastic than Dirk.

feel charmed, attracted, or captivated. However, the older you get, the more likely you can claim to be really in love.

Perhaps you've had an experience like Valerie's. Boy or girl, you become enchanted with someone of the other sex. In his or her presence you feel self-conscious. If you try to say something clever, the words clog your throat like peanut butter. You may perspire or feel your legs trembling.

A good friendship getting better.

You become aware of a pure affection and a fierce devotion. Anything your ideal says takes on new importance. If he (or she) mentions liking a brand of breakfast cereal, it becomes your favorite, too.

Surely one of the shortest love affairs of all time was recorded in the diary of a 13-year old boy named Greg. "I gave my class key to Tammy this morning. She gave it back this afternoon."

Many curious, active teens fall in love often, sometimes twice in the same day. Adolescence is a time to discover both what you are like and the kind of persons you like to be with. Usually it takes years to learn to trust your decisions without worrying whether you picked right or not.

You can fall in love very fast. If the growing fondness is noticed and returned, that speeds the process. If it is fed with shared interests and a genuine liking for each other, the mutual attraction can last, perhaps for a lifetime.

Adults spend a lot of time trying to convince young persons that their adolescent attractions are not real. Perhaps it would be more accurate to say that if you think you are in love, you probably are, at least for the time. Certainly the feelings you experience are part of love.

HOW TO TELL THE DIFFERENCE

Have you ever wondered how to tell infatuation from real love? The on-again, off-again quality of young love can be puzzling. "Why do I love her one day and hate her the next?" wondered one boy.

Some attractions last for months or years, even if they are not returned. Others live but a few hours. Before they fade, a new one takes over.

Crushes are like helium-filled balloons. They may rise high and fly far. However, eventually much of the air escapes. Or they spring a leak and plunk down to earth.

Crushes are also like sightseeing trips around a strange city where you plan to live. They help you get used to unfamiliar places a little bit at a time. When you settle down, the city's strangeness doesn't put you off so much. Crushes help you get used to regular closeness with one person, which is what love is all about.

Infatuation is not limited to your own age group nor even to people you know. Perhaps you've felt great affection at a distance for someone you've never met, like an actor or a singer. You may even join a fan club, write admiring letters, and ask for a signed picture.

In much the same way, boys sometimes fall in love with older women— even teachers. Girls sigh over older men. In time such day-dream romances fade away. The real thing is much more interesting.

Something to think about. Following are some comments of older adoles-cents who are long past their first love, but they still remember it well. Their descriptions may be similar to your own current feelings.

"First love is a powerful emotion. It's somewhere between friendship and romance."

"When I fell in love for the first time, I believed that I was the only one who had ever felt that way."

"First love is bittersweet. It is a blend of both joy and misery."

"Love for the first time seems like it will last forever."

REAL LOVE

Infatuation sometimes grows into lasting love. More often it does not. However, infatuation and love are part of the same process. The main difference is that love lasts and infatuation fades away. Time is a big help in knowing which is which.

You started to learn about love when you were a baby. Someone held you close and showed love for you. You felt safe and comforted. Loving and learning to love begin that early.

Love is like a circle. If you are loved, you learn to love in return. Then by giving love, you earn love and hope to receive it. Even though all expressions of love are not returned in kind, love still works in a roundabout way.

Part of learning how to love others (not in just a romantic way) is knowing about yourself—your strengths and weaknesses, your virtues and your faults. The ability to care about others also requires that you have a good opinion of yourself—not in a puffed-up way, but just by recognizing your value as a person.

It is normal to keep searching for a person of the other sex you can trust, enjoy, and get to know better. Because you mature physically before you do

Real love is both learned and earned.

emotionally, interest in showing and getting affection usually develops long before true love. In most cases it takes years to blend feelings of lasting affection with the physical attractions that happen in early adolescence. So you are not strange nor selfish if you notice a physical tug toward a person that you don't really like very much.

Romances based mostly on physical interest happen a lot during adolescence. Such boy and girl pairings may not include any tenderness or consideration. That's why a boy may turn a goodnight kiss into a wrestling match. That's why a girl may seem to like a certain boy and then suddenly drop him.

However, respect and affection for another person don't just happen. Love must be learned and earned. When physical closeness and love blend together, chances improve for a good and lasting relationship between mature persons. In fact, adolescence is the part of your journey through life that helps you discover what sort of person you really are. You learn what it means to be a male or a female. You understand how it feels to be physically attracted to a member of the other sex.

The difficult side of love. Most persons understand and seek the getting, or receiving, part of love. That's the easier half. To enjoy a full and happy friendship a true lover must also learn the more difficult half: *giving.* The giving part of love isn't new to you. It's made of the same concern, trust, and understanding that you already feel for friends and family.

When lovers care about someone, they try to make that person feel happy, confident, and secure. Lovers try to avoid anything that would make the other person feel embarrassed, hurt, or alone. Real love adds joy to life. It doesn't make life miserable and sad.

Sometimes people deceive themselves and each other about love. They mistreat or use the other person in selfish ways for selfish purposes. For reasons of their own they refer to this cruel treatment as love. Obviously it is not.

GAMES

Romance is like a game. Cautious people make their moves slowly. At least they wait for some sign that the chosen person is interested, too.

Often, the game is played this way:

Pursuer: The first move is to let the other person know you are interested. You stare. You ask questions. However, you must move in such a way that you can always pretend that you don't really care. The idea is to protect your sensitive feelings from the sting of possible rejection. Yet, you must also play the game well enough to make your interest known. That's necessary to get the other person's attention.

Hardy souls are not bothered by rejection. They merely shrug and hunt elsewhere. Most persons have thinner skin. For them rejection hurts.

One pursued: Often the news that you have an admirer (pursuer) is delivered by a friend. Or it races along the gossip grapevine. You catch the admirer looking at you. Or your pursuer simply comes forth, talks to you, arranges to see you, invites you someplace.

Pat Hirschl
Can wrestling lead to romance?

If you like someone, you send out inviting signals. Depending on your personality and self-confidence, you may move carefully until you see a sign of returned interest. Or you may act more boldly, with the confidence of previous success.

Feelings of affection can show up most anytime.

Natalie Leimkuhler

303

Rules. Everyone plays some games. They add spice and fun to life. Flirtation is a game with many variations. There are fair games and cruel games. Some keep the rules of fair play. Some don't.

At times romantic games are not light-hearted fun at all. They are played without any genuine interest in the other person. Instead, these games seem designed to hurt, tease, or "win" by use of dishonest tricks.

You may know couples who claim they like each other. Yet they criticize, quarrel, lie, and deceive. Some persons consider the other sex as "the enemy," to be conquered or won rather than appreciated and enjoyed. Others seem to be more interested in taking out their resentment on the other sex, instead of trying for mutual affection and an open exchange of ideas.

CASE EXAMPLE

Games may deeply wound another person. Barry is a shy and sensitive person. He still winces at an experience he had many months ago.

"I met a girl named Joy. I thought I could really like her. It took me a long time to get the nerve to ask her out. Finally I did. She accepted. I was so happy I walked in the clouds. That was on Tuesday. I couldn't wait for Saturday evening.

"On Wednesday Joy walked up to me with a note. When I opened it a fire began to build in my gut. There were only a few words on that piece of paper: 'I wouldn't go anyplace with you. Drop dead.'

"The hate I felt for her was more than I can say. I couldn't understand why she would do such a thing. I cried myself to sleep that night. Since that day I haven't asked another girl to go out. I'm not ready for another let-down like that."

You be the counselor. What explanation could you give for the treatment Barry got?

Why might a girl (or boy) accept an invitation and turn it down the next day?

If you were Barry's friend, how would you try to help him get over his anger and his hurt?

MORE GAMES

Perhaps you'll recognize some of these games. They may go under other names in your school, but what happens to the persons involved is much the same.

• *Scalp hunter.* The scalp hunter shows interest in someone. When the "kill" is made, the hunter hangs up another scalp and moves on to new hunting grounds. Broken hearts and hurt feelings remain behind. Variations of this game include persons who show interest only in someone who already likes a third party. Once these heart-breakers win, the game is over. With the excitement of the chase behind them, the conquest means little.

• *Break up and make up.* In this game, one or both persons repeatedly set up situations that give an excuse for one to accuse the other of disloyalty, lying, or cheating. It's the making up after the fights that provides the payoff for this game.

• *No boy (or girl) is any good.* This type falls in love with one person after another. Each new love proves disappointing in some way. Each new conquest is to be criticized, talked about, or discarded as a fake or a phony. The real problem usually lies in the pursuer, who always arranges things to guarantee disappointment.

WHAT ABOUT ME?

Like most teens, you'll probably experiment with romantic games. Sometimes you'll follow the rules, and sometimes you may cheat. Sometimes you win. Sometimes you lose. You may put your own needs for popularity and acceptance first. All others come second.

Such experimenting, it is to be hoped, leads to maturity based on concern about the needs of others. There's a big difference between picking on other people with no intention to change and gradually growing more aware of, and sensitive to, others while making a few mistakes along the way.

When romance games repeatedly involve pretended feelings and dishonest words, it's time to take a look at yourself. Such games can also hurt the player. These make-believe attempts at love hold back the development of real affection. They cut down possibilities of closeness, sharing, and caring.

If you find yourself repeatedly playing games that hurt others, try to look at your behavior to discover why you need to act that way at all.

Reasons. As you know, there are often hidden reasons why people use their attractiveness in selfish and mean ways. Some persons need to feel superior to others. Some boys and girls may pretend affection to receive affection in return. Persons like that may also use each other to climb up a social success ladder.

Adolescents may hold wrong ideas about what the other sex is really like and believe that "all girls want to be dominated" or "all boys are pushovers for a good-looking girl."

Children who are badly neglected by their parents may grow up wanting revenge on the other sex. Without ever knowing why they act as they do, they might try to get even and hurt others as they have been hurt themselves.

Some boys and girls need constant reassurance that they are attractive and likable because they grew up believing they have no value. "Boycrazy" or "girlcrazy" teens need plenty of attention from the other sex. They may never get enough to feel really attractive or confident.

Of course, it takes two people to play a game. Often (as in the case of Robin and Jim) one person is bossy and the other just goes along. Some people enjoy stepping on others. Others may even enjoy being the doormat.

To learn more. Select one idea or topic from this chapter that applies to you and the way you live your life.

On a separate sheet of paper describe your selection in one sentence.

In no more than three sentences explain why you chose it.

DO NOT WRITE IN THIS BOOK.

RECAP

Sooner or later boys and girls begin to spend time together. The relationship may follow an easy schedule, developing slowly in ways pleasing to both. Or it may happen that the attraction you feel is neither noticed nor returned.

Sometimes young adolescents get rushed ahead on a fast track they aren't ready for. Like Robin, they let things get out of control and headed for a life-style they don't really want. If you feel like Robin, you can study your reasons for hanging on when you'd rather let go. It is not always easy to stop a situation that is steaming ahead faster than you want it to go. However, it can be done.

Even during early adolescence there are great pressures for two persons to pair off. Sometimes young people worry so much about their attractiveness to the other sex that they push too hard, afraid that they'll miss out. Or sometimes they feel fine about their progress, but friends urge them to a faster pace. Few persons your age are ready for lifetime promises of an exclusive relationship with just one person.

Up and down mood swings are often caused by the newness and uncertainty of learning about the other sex. One day you may feel warm and happy with your special person. The next, you wonder what you ever saw in such a gross slob.

Early adolescence is not a time for courtship or marriage. Instead, your job is to learn to know about yourself and the other sex. Getting to know what a person is really like can be a great pleasure

In adolescence you may fall in love and then right out on the same day. Both boys and girls usually notice a physical attraction long before they learn to love another. Experiments with physical affection are a normal part of maturing. Usually it takes a lot of growing up before love and tenderness blend with the desires to express physical affection.

Close friendship with someone of the other sex without games or trickery can be a great treat. It is a pleasure to be yourself, to express your thoughts, feelings, weaknesses, and quirks without fear of being hurt or used.

Most teens try some romantic games. Most versions are enjoyable and harmless. Other games are serious and selfish. Some persons use their personal attraction to get close to others. They find neither love nor joy because there is no real concern for the second person.

Only you can give yourself the freedom to use your teen years well.

Only you can decide to get to know lots of boys and girls better.

Only you can allow enough time to mature at your own pace.

Only you can develop your ability to become a lover and a giver.

Only you, by your actions towards boys and girls your age, can show how you like to be treated.

TERMS

Romance	Jealousy	Quitting a romance	Charmed
Crush	Monopoly	Devotion	Romantic games
Attraction	Love	Rejection	Physical affection
Expectations	Affection	Infatuation	

UNIT VI
Special Problems

CHAPTER 18

Death, Divorce and Other Life Crises

A crisis is a serious life problem. Recently, a lost teenager named Bill survived a crisis for five nights in the wild desert country near Flagstaff, Arizona. He ate berries and cactus pulp, an idea he got from cowboy shows on TV. For water, he licked the morning frost from leaves and logs. When found, he was in such good shape that there was no need for a trip to the hospital.

Without warning, Bill was hit by a serious threat to his life. He discovered within himself survival talents he never knew he had.

Not everyone reacts to the challenge of a major crisis in the same way. In fact, how you handle a serious problem can be more important than the event itself. Bill came through with perfect grades when he was lost in the desert. He survived where another person might have died. He used his wits. He made the right decisions. He didn't panic.

You'll never forget a real crisis. However, a serious setback doesn't have to be bad or dangerous. Sometimes, what seems to be a crushing blow turns out to your advantage. Also, not everyone views a crisis in exactly the same way. One person may see the emergency as an overwhelming mess. Another may welcome the very same situation as a great opportunity to make a needed change.

For example, a family moves to another state. To the father the move means a promotion and a big raise in pay. He's pleased and eager to get going. To the mother the move means the loss of familiar faces, doctors, and shopping centers. She's depressed and feels lonely before the trip starts. Brother welcomes the move as a chance to get a fresh start in a new neighborhood. Sister feels scared at the idea of trying to find friends in a strange school.

TYPES OF CRISES

Human crises come in all sizes and shapes.

Little crises are upsetting. Examples of little crises include:

- Lose something important, like keys, or tickets to a game.
- Wake up with a headache the day of the big test.
- Fight with your best friend.
- Make your first speech in class.

Middle-sized crises are not a matter of life and death, but they may be important turning points. For example:

- Win (or lose) an important competition.
- Fail a course that has to be repeated.

Metropolitan Life

Because drug abuse can destroy a young life, it is considered a big crisis. However, even serious problems can be beaten.

• Suffer a temporary injury from an accident.

Big crises cause great hardship or a tremendous challenge and leave a deep, lasting impression. For example:

• Natural disasters like earthquakes, tornadoes, or floods uproot families and destroy property.

• Death takes a relative or a close friend.

• Serious accidents or illnesses leave permanent psychological or physical scars.

• Drug abuse destroys a young life.

Throughout this book you've read about breakdowns in human relationships such as loss of friendship or conflicts between parents and children. The focus in this chapter and the next is on special problems in family relationships.

First you'll read about some serious crises faced by many families.

Then you'll find out how such events can influence the lives of persons your age.

In Chapter 19 you'll learn methods teens can use to get through different types of crises.

Bill was forced to survive in the Arizona desert. Some teens must learn to live in an emotional desert. They may find themselves without love and guidance because a parent has moved out or died.

As you will discover, even big problems can be overcome. You can grow stronger and learn to take care of the ups and downs in life.

Suppose you live in a close and happy family. Your parents get along fine. There's enough money and no serious illness. If so, the ideas in these chapters are also meant for you. You don't have to be unhappy about yourself or live in a disrupted family in order to benefit. Sooner or later, everyone meets crises. Everyone needs to make decisions in order to survive these unexpected problems of life.

DEATH AND OTHER SEPARATIONS

New arrivals to a family, such as a stepparent, can cause a crisis in family relationships. Departures and separations can also bring problems. Families do not stay the same when children grow up, leave home, and marry.

Life is full of comings and goings that can cause crises. Some separations, like going away to college, getting work out of town, or joining a military service, may cause a person to feel homesick.

However, living away from home can speed up personal maturity.

Other separations are like broken bones. They bring pain and hurt. Sometimes, like Humpty Dumpty, the pieces won't fit back together again.

Death is the worst separation of all. The loss of a close family member or a good friend at any time in life is always a serious crisis.

Death. A century ago, sick persons usually died at home, surrounded by the family. Death from disease was common. So, even to the young, death could be a familiar part of family life. Many children lost brothers and sisters to diseases like diphtheria or smallpox. Today, preventive shots and antibiotics (AN-ty-by-OTT-iks) protect children from these killers. Grandparents live longer. Most sick persons die in hospitals.

However, about one child in twenty still suffers the loss of a parent before age five. Wasting diseases and serious illnesses still disrupt families.

By age nine or ten, most children know what death means. They realize that death claims everyone and will happen to them—sometime. You probably see a great stretch of time separating you from old age and death.

Dr. Elizabeth Kubler-Ross studied sick and dying people and their families. She discovered that both the persons dying and their survivors go through certain stages. As you read, look for reactions already familiar to you. You may have used similar responses when meeting some crises in your life.

Steps for coping with death.

Step 1. *Denial.* "Not me!" The mind pushes away both the truth and the shock until the person can get used to both.

Kathy Tuite

Michael has already survived several major crises in his life. As he overcame each one, he grew stronger and more mature.

Step 2. *Anger.* "Why me?" "Why *my* mother or father?" There may be anger with God or others for causing the survivor to suffer.

Step 3. *Bargain.* "Make this go away, and I'll be a better person." Victims promise themselves or God to do something good in exchange if the crisis turns out all right.

Step 4. *Depression.* At this point the truth hits home. Grief over the expected loss of life, or health, or independence sinks in.

Step 5. *Acceptance.* Acceptance of the upsetting facts brings a degree of

311

Most teens have been through the temporary life crises that come with sad and unhappy feelings.

peace when the survivor realizes that the dead person cannot be brought back to life.

Of course, these steps do not always happen so neatly. Sometimes people remain frozen at one stage for a long time. Or some may never reach the point of acceptance. They just remain unhappy and/or angry.

How to help the dying. Healthy people often feel uneasy when they are with persons who are very sick. The hale and hearty may also feel helpless and at a loss for words because they don't know what to do or say.

It's hard to know exactly how dying persons feel. Often they know about their own fate and accept it. The dying face the truth, even though others around them try to act as if they are not aware. Even little children often handle the subject of death better than adult mourners.

Persons about to die need a chance to talk about their anger, fear, or depression without someone telling them, "You shouldn't feel that way." Many dying persons express concern and desire to discuss spiritual matters such as life after death. Members of the clergy spend a portion of their workweek visiting with the dying.

Talk is emotional medicine. Dying people need someone to listen. When doctors, nurses, and family members avoid the subject of death, they slow down the acceptance of it by all concerned.

Still, dying persons hate it when everyone gives up on them. Those who will live a while longer and are not too weak or sick usually want to make the most of the weeks or months that remain.

Some may even want to teach others. One young man headed for death at an early age from blood disease gave guitar lessons to other patients in his hospital. He was pleased to do something that would provide pleasure for others after he died.

Perhaps the loneliest situation possible is to die without any relatives or friends present. Simply having loved ones close is a great comfort to very sick persons.

Survivors. The death of a parent or other relative usually comes as a shock. As a result, the survivors must also go through a series of stages to get used to the great loss. *Mourning,* or crying and talking about sad feelings, helps persons of any age come to grips with the death of someone close.

Denial. Denial is a defense against emotional pain. Sometimes adolescents deny the importance of their loss. They become very active and involved in other things, as if to keep too busy to think about their unhappiness.

Widowed parents, or those who lose a child, often can't help but suffer deeply. In one study of widows (wives of dead husbands) and widowers (husbands of dead wives), the remaining partner spent most of the first month crying and feeling lost. The survivors in the study were restless, edgy, couldn't sleep, had trouble concentrating, and couldn't remember. They often felt guilty about little things they had done or failed to do when the marriage partner was alive. Sometimes the survivors reported that they thought they were going crazy.

A wife who has just lost her husband may suddenly act overconcerned about her children, as though to prevent another serious loss. Parents who are forced to stay busy with work outside the home seem to recover better from the death of a husband or wife.

It usually takes from three months to a year or more for a widowed person to recover from the shock of a partner's death. Helpful family members, considerate and patient children, and counseling can all aid the surviving adult to make a quicker and easier recovery.

The right to die? In this age of wonder drugs, organ transplants, and life-support machines, other serious questions about life and death must also be decided. Some 30,000 babies are born each year with physical defects. Their problems are so severe that even if they live they may never learn to talk, walk,

laugh, and play. You can see that the birth of such handicapped children always represents a crisis for their families.

For an old person, the right to die presents another type of crisis that also demands important decisions. When a person is too old or too sick to have a chance of recovery, someone must decide whether the patient should be kept alive with machines or allowed to die without them.

From the sick person's point of view, a longer life may mean just more suffering. From the family's point of view, hospital and doctor bills may pile up with no prospects for saving the life of the relative. Money may not be the major concern in such circumstances. However, it cannot be overlooked as a real concern in the final decision. A very sick person in the family can also mean many trips to the hospital and many hours waiting to spend just a few minutes at the bedside. Whether or not to let very aged or sick persons die naturally is a difficult choice for doctors, patients, and their families.

Time out. Suppose you had to make such a decision. You suddenly become the one who must say yes or no about the continued life for a very sick, close relative. What emotion would you expect to feel? Any idea why you would feel so? Would your emotions be likely to influence your final decision? *Time in.*

SERIOUS ILLNESS AND ACCIDENTS

The death of someone close may be difficult to bear. However, it is final. Death doesn't linger to cause more worry and care.

Sometimes very sick and injured people do not die. However, they don't get

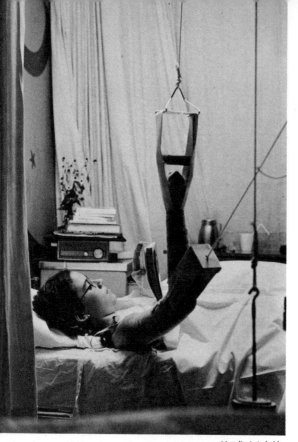

An accident can happen to anyone. Karie's story is on page 287.

Natalie Leimkuhler

Severe illness can upset healthy family members in other ways. The idea that all relatives suddenly treat the sick person with increased devotion and unselfish service isn't always true. Resentment and anger are more normal reactions. Younger family members may feel jealous of the time a parent spends with the sick person. Or, the healthy children may keep to themselves. Schoolwork may suffer. Adolescents sometimes try to shut out the changed home situation by turning to delinquency, or by taking drugs.

Adults suffer, too. They may lose chances for a better job. Parents can feel torn between giving help to a sick child (or husband or wife) or giving enough attention to the healthy family members. Someone must get less.

Feelings of resentment get bitter toward the killing disease itself. Family members may take out their anger and upset on each other. The sick person suffers pain while the others suffer strain.

better, either. A bad illness or an accident can leave a parent alive, but unable to live a full life. Children may feel let down and angry toward a sick parent. Some youngsters may worry that they caused the parent's illness in the first place. Such situations are difficult for both parents and children.

A severe, long-lasting disease like cancer can shatter family life. Even with insurance, medical bills can climb to thousands of dollars. To pay these costs, some middle-income families have been forced to sell their homes, spend their savings, and cut back on food, clothing, and family health care. A sick father may mean no one gets any teeth fixed for years.

You be the judge. Recently a baby girl named Janine was born with many physical problems. She had deformed legs and feet. There was a hole in the base of her spine. She had water on the brain.

In the opinion of several doctors little Janine was so damaged physically and so retarded mentally that even a series of operations could not correct her problems.

Her parents then made a painful choice. They decided to let their baby die rather than let her suffer through the necessary surgery. Janine was put into a state hospital where she would receive good bodily care until she died from natural causes.

However, things changed when she arrived at the state hospital. Another team of doctors decided that Janine had a chance for life if she had an operation. The State Mental Retardation Administration stepped in to act in behalf of the infant. At that time it seemed like the case would be decided in court.

As it turned out, Janine died when she was eight weeks old, even before a court ruling could decide whether the parents or the state are to make the final judgment in such circumstances.

Suppose this case came to your court.

You are the judge.

In whose favor would you decide?

Would you decide for the parents, and let Janine die naturally?

Would you decide for the state, and require operations for Janine?

Now imagine that Janine is your little sister. Would your decision be any different from the one you made as judge?

DIVORCE

Divorce is the death of a relationship between a husband and a wife. Although divorce happens to parents, the lives of children are always affected. Relationships, once close and loving, tear and shatter.

When a child or an adolescent loses a parent because of any kind of split—divorce, separation, or desertion—their reaction is similar to their reaction to the death of a loved one. Children may refuse to accept their parents' decision. The youngsters may feel deep anger and dark depression. They may try to make bargains to keep their parents together. In time, however, most sons and daughters learn to live with what they cannot change.

In the United States at least one family in three is torn by divorce. The parents of millions of American children of school age have been divorced. Some parents separate without bothering to get a divorce. One parent may just walk out without an explanation (desertion).

Natalie Leimkuhler

A single parent shows love and concern by keeping the family unit strong, healthy, and together.

Even a peaceful split can be very distressing. If you have gone through a divorce or separation of your parents, you will understand the emotional pain that parent breakup causes all family members.

The long-range effects of divorce on children depend greatly on the circumstances. If there's enough money, for example, things may not be so bad. However, a cut in income can lead to bitterness, complaints, and real suffering. The parent with custody of the children—usually the mother—may not receive financial support without legal battles. The father may remarry and refuse to support two families.

Upsets in familiar household routines can add to the confusion. Reactions of the children will be influenced by their ages, how long the parents have been unhappy with their marriage, and how the parents feel about breaking up.

An unhappy home full of anger and blame is often more damaging than if the parents divorce each other. Scary silences and the sounds of slammed doors, shouted insults, and terrifying fights leave emotional scars.

Fear and loneliness can make a child of divorce feel angry and rebellious. Or, as a way of preventing further hurt, a child may act uncaring about one or both parents.

CASE EXAMPLE

A wise person once said, "How can I know what I think until I hear what I say?" As you read Kit's story think how you would feel if you were in her place.

Kit was feeling moody and depressed after her parents broke up. She blamed her mother when she pressured Kit to turn against her father. Things were so bad that Kit and her mother hardly talked to each other. Kit was aware of her own unhappiness. However, she didn't understand *why* until she talked to her best friend's mother about the recent split-up between her folks. Kit described the situation.

"I love Dad so much. Mother hates him. Grandmom (Mother's mother) and all the relatives on that side of the family always tell me what a horrible man my father is. They say he was just terrible to my mother.

"I'd rather live with Dad. But mother cries and says she would die if I left. I'm beginning to hate her."

At first the warm and understanding woman just listened. She let Kit spill out all the anger that she had held back for so long. She didn't scold Kit for making such strong, one-sided statements against her mother. She didn't tell Kit that she "shouldn't feel that way."

Gradually, with her anger finally out, Kit began to discover that she really loved both her parents. For that reason she felt pulled in both directions. She was relieved when she heard the woman say, "You are unhappy and disappointed with your mother. I can tell you that your mother is disappointed *with herself.* Notice how touchy she is. She loves you and cares very much about you. Don't close her out. She needs to know that you love her in spite of her faults."

By talking and listening, Kit gradually discovered that she could protect herself from being badly hurt by her mother's verbal attacks. She refused to take sides or enter into arguments with her accusing relatives who spent so much time insulting her father. She also came to understand that both her parents needed her love and acceptance. Years later Kit still remembered what her friend's mother had told her.

You be the counselor. Like Kit, many other teens get caught in battles between their parents. Sometimes the children are asked to split their loyalties and favor one parent over the other.

CASE EXAMPLE

Carl is in a bind just like that. He must decide whether to stay with his mother or move in with his father. Carl explains it this way.

"I know my mom cares about me. But she's wrapped up in her work and is always on the go. She just doesn't have time for me. Besides, she doesn't know how tough life can be for a guy without a father.

"My parents separated because of Dad's drinking. I'll admit he was a different man when he had too much alcohol in him. After he moved out we didn't even know where he was living for almost four years. He never wrote or called.

"Now he's back in town for a visit. He wants me to go to Florida to live with him.

"My mother reminds me of all the rotten things that Dad did. And it is true that we are much better off now in terms of money.

"Still he is my father," explained Carl. "We always understood each other. And Dad claims that he's changed."

You be the counselor. Suppose Carl came to you for advice. What would you tell him?

What other information could Carl use to help him make the best decision for everyone concerned.

In Carl's place, what would you do?

MENTAL ILLNESS

In the United States today, 1 out of every 1,000 families has one parent in a hospital with mental illness. Many other disturbed adults continue to live at home. However, the home-based sick cannot do everything that was expected of them when they were healthy. Naturally a mentally ill family member causes others some worry. In many cases family relationships are damaged seriously.

Mental illness goes by many names, like "nervous breakdown" or "emotional disturbance." Mental illness really means problems in living. Throughout life everyone has emotional upsets.

Usually, the person recovers. Life goes on. Sometimes, however, emotional problems grow so severe that no answer seems possible. Pressure grows. Everyone involved feels the strain.

Types of mental disorders differ from person to person. They range from mild to severe. Some illnesses go on for days, weeks, months, or even years. Most victims recover and stay better. Others struggle with emotional problems for a lifetime.

Why? At one time people believed that evil spirits possessed a person to cause strange and unusual behavior. Today it's known that many different causes can make a person mentally ill.

Although mental illness can happen any time in life, the basic causes often reach back to childhood and adolescence. Longstanding family or social problems like bad housing or lack of employment also trigger mental illness. Misuse of drugs and alcohol can also play a part. Some mental disorders are inherited from one generation by the next. Even so, much debate continues about what mental illness is and how best to treat it.

As mentioned, mental illness becomes noticeable when a person's usual behavior changes. Special kinds of complaints by the victim also indicate trouble. Following are general explanations of some common types of mental disorders.

Out of contact. Some mentally ill persons lose touch with what is real. They no longer understand what is going on around them. They may think they see visions or hear voices. They may imagine that innocent persons are plotting against them. They can't act like normal persons or feel the same emotions that others experience. Thoughts may get so fuzzy that those who are sick don't know who they are, where they are, or what day it is.

Depressed. Extreme mood swings are a form of mental illness. Everyone knows what it's like to feel low or blue for a day or two. Depressed persons can feel bad for months at a time. From their viewpoint they can't imagine ever feeling good again.

Depressed people lose energy. They can't keep their minds on one thing for very long. They see no hope that things will get better. They have trouble making decisions.

Severely depressed people often feel terribly guilty about little mistakes. They may feel so worthless and the future can look so bad that life just doesn't seem worth living anymore. That's why some depressed persons try to kill themselves. Adolescents as well as older persons can suffer from serious depression.

All the causes for depression are not fully understood. However, depression may come from changes in the way the body works. Depression can also set in after a great loss—such as of good health or a job. Even a drop in self-worth can make a person feel and act gloomy. A change like this could happen after failing a test or losing a friend.

For the time, all the causes of depression remain one of nature's secrets. Perhaps some day you will be the researcher who pins down the exact causes of this serious form of mental illness.

Did you know? Until recently it was believed that only adults suffered from problems of depression. It is now known that adolescents, younger children, and even babies can become depressed.

During the teen years almost anything that the adolescent considers serious can trigger depression. You name it: a romance gone sour, rejection by a team or clique, a fight with a friend, a family move, or tensions between parents. Any of these can throw a young person into the dumps.

The important difference between a temporary case of the blues and a serious depression is *how long* the down mood lasts and *how intense* it becomes.

When in an extreme depression the person may act listless, withdrawn, and uncaring about self or others. School work suffers, sleep is disturbed, appetite disappears. When a person's depression is serious and long-lasting, special medical attention becomes necessary.

Guidelines for living. If you suffer from mild depression or want to help a friend with the blues, try these suggestions.

How to Beat the Blues

1. Forget advice or self-encouragement like "Cheer up" or "Snap out of it." Pep talks don't help at all. They may make things worse.

2. Admit to yourself that you feel terrible. Be as honest as you can about your emotions-of-the-moment. Then when you know what you are feeling, you are ready to try to seek causes for *why* you feel low.

3. Look for someone who will just listen. Unburden yourself to a parent, a close relative, a friend, or a favorite teacher. Just by expressing your emotions and admitting what is bothering, you can bring a feeling of relief, especially if the listener doesn't pile on a lot of unwanted advice.

4. Do something. Activity is a proven way to chase the blues. Take a long walk. Try a good workout or dig up your old hobby. Read an exciting book. Anything that brings distraction and new ideas into your life can help you feel better.

5. Seek success. Try something that you know you are good at to restore feelings of self-worth. Use a proven talent or skill. It may be nothing more than washing the family dishes or

When exam time causes a minor crisis, adolescents may become nervous and anxious. Sometimes they seek relief with nicotine (smoking), alcohol (drinking), or other drugs. Extra study time would be a healthier way for Jean to reduce her tensions about the upcoming tests.

cleaning your room. Do something nice for someone else.

Warning: Don't take on a project that is big or likely to last a long time. Look for something that you can do well and finish fast. Even a small "victory" can help boost your self-concept.

Excited. Great excitement and too much activity indicate a form of mental illness just the opposite of depression. Extremely depressed people can do hardly anything. Just getting out of bed in the morning may seem like something to brag about. Overexcited persons can't slow down. They may be touchy and impatient. It's as if their motors never stop running. Minds race so fast with impossible schemes that thinking becomes mixed-up.

Nervous/fearful. Many emotionally upset persons manage to hold jobs and keep in touch with reality. However, they also feel anxious most of the time, even when things go well for them. They worry that something terrible is about to hap-

pen. They may be bothered by a racing heart beat or sensations of choking, even when there's nothing wrong.

Others have a great fear of ordinary things like high places, enclosed spaces, or harmless animals. Such fears can grow strong enough to prevent these people from living a normal life.

A point of view. One way to try to understand mental illness is to think of it as a blown-up version of what is natural and familiar. The victim is pushed to do too much, or held back from doing enough. When a normal mood goes too far in one direction or another, mental illness may result.

For example, everyone feels blue once in a while. However, the depressed person is dragged down emotionally for weeks or months at a time.

Everyone knows how it feels to get a spurt of energy or a big idea. The overexcited person can't slow down or plan sensibly.

Everyone knows what it's like to be afraid or to feel nervous. The anxious person magnifies the normal challenges of life into terrible threats that don't really exist.

Treatment. Most sick persons get well. The mentally ill can recover, too. Some common forms of treatment for mental illness include:

• *Hospital stay.* Years ago many mentally ill persons were locked up in hospitals, away from family and friends. Today it's known that long periods away from home often make mental illness worse, rather than better.

Confinement in a hospital or treatment center is still needed for those who may do serious harm to themselves or others. The same is true for those who cannot get the right kind of treatment at home. However, new medicines allow many sick persons to return home quickly or to live at home and get treatment.

• *Counseling* is a treatment in which the sick person talks with a trained counselor or therapist. The patient learns the causes of problems and discovers better ways to cope with them. You'll read more about counseling on pages 330-331.

• *Drugs* have provided a major breakthrough in the treatment of mental illness. Many special chemicals can help the mentally ill recover faster and live a more normal life. Some drugs calm overactive and very nervous persons. Other forms of medicine lift depressed persons out of low moods and help the confused ones to think more clearly.

Something to think about. You don't hear many jokes about persons with cancer or heart disease. Even so, some people make fun of mental illness and those suffering from it. Words like "cra-zy" and "cuckoo" are often used to describe persons who are mentally disturbed.

In your opinion, why do some joke about mental illness?

What is your emotional reaction to mental illness?

Have you ever made fun of disturbed persons?

If yes, any idea why you acted that way? Some persons treat the sick as scapegoats because of their own discomfort in the presence of someone who is not normal.

Did you know? You can get information about the subject of mental illness from:

The National Institute of Mental Health
Office of Information
5600 Fishers Lane
Rockville, Maryland 20852

Write for a free copy of one or both of these pamphlets. Be sure to include your name and address.

What is Mental Illness?

Mental Illness and Its Treatment.

To learn more. Select one idea or topic from this chapter that applies to you and the way you live your life.

On a separate sheet of paper describe your selection in one sentence.

In no more than three sentences explain why you chose it.

DO NOT WRITE IN THIS BOOK.

RECAP

A crisis is a serious life problem, or a major turning point. Crises like accidents or natural disasters usually happen suddenly. Some crises involve loss of friends or good opportunities. More serious challenges arise when family members become very ill, or die, or parents separate.

Death is final. The stages for learning to live with death and other serious crises are similar for the victim, for family, and for friends.

Many people deny the truth of approaching death. Denial helps keep hope alive and temporarily protects those who must face such trying problems.

Both survivors and the dying person often feel angry when death gets close. They may try to bargain in order to avoid death. Finally the truth registers. Feelings of depression and grief set in. However, for most survivors the final acceptance of the facts makes a normal life possible again.

Both the very sick and close survivors need help. The dying need a chance to express their emotions. Survivors need a chance to cry and to go through a necessary time of adjustment.

More and more, doctors and relatives must decide whether to keep a person alive with machines or drugs when the very sick person would surely die without them.

Serious illness makes demands on family members by taking the victim off a normal schedule. Those still healthy must make some changes in their own daily routines. Chances for new clothes, general health care, and job opportunities may have to be set aside for awhile.

Divorce and other family separations cause major crises, too. When parents split up, children are always affected. The effects of parent separations depend a lot on the circumstances. However, temporary feelings of anger and abandonment or other emotional upsets are common to all those involved.

Mental illness is another life crisis that can strike any family. When people can no longer cope with the problems of everyday life, they are usually considered mentally ill or emotionally disturbed.

Mental illness can be improved, controlled, and cured. However, it always makes life more difficult for the victims and for those who must live with them.

Depression, guilt, and feelings of hopelessness often affect the mentally ill. Depressed persons lose energy and interest in life.

Sometimes, mentally ill persons become very excited and overactive. They use poor judgment in their plans and ideas.

Some mentally disturbed people feel nervous and upset even when things go right. They may even fear harmless situations.

Many mildly disturbed persons manage to go on doing their work and earn a living. However, a person who can no longer tell the difference between what's real and not real, or who is a danger to self or others, needs special medical care.

Some mentally ill persons get better without treatment. Others improve rapidly with good care. New treatments and new drugs often shorten hospital stays and help victims return to family and work.

TERMS

Crisis	Acceptance	Nervous breakdown	Fearful
Survival	Divorce	Emotional disturbance	Counseling
Mourning	Separation	Depression	
Antibiotics	Desertion	Overexcited	
Denial	Mental illness	Nervous	

CHAPTER 19

Finding Help

You wouldn't climb a high mountain without sturdy shoes and strong rope. You also would not go into a desert without a supply of food and fresh water.

Yet many persons try to live their lives without the psychological equipment necessary for survival in today's world. They blunder on, repeating the same mistakes year after year. They muddle into one mess after another, whether with relatives, classmates, or friends.

All through this book you have read that cooperation, compromise, and honest talk can prevent or solve problems between people. However, you can't always avoid or settle difficulties, no matter how much you try. You can't make others change what they do, even if they hurt themselves or you in the process.

Suppose, for example, your parents decide to divorce each other. Probably you could not stop them, no matter how much you might like to. When parents make such a decision, children can't avoid the fallout. During such family upsets schoolwork suffers and life may seem like one unhappy situation after another.

However, there are ways to survive even the worst crises. Long before little problems develop into larger ones, you can try to change the direction of your life. You can grow stronger. You can take action to help yourself, instead of letting unexpected disappointments drag you down. You can learn to make decisions that will make your life easier and better.

Have you ever noticed that some persons seem to harm themselves? You've probably heard, "It's his own fault." "She got herself into that mess." "I tried to warn him." Such comments usually refer to people who seem to invite trouble. Such victims often blame rotten luck or claim they got bad advice. They rarely consider that they might be the cause of their own misfortunes.

SOURCES OF PROBLEMS

Some adolescents don't think much of themselves. They may have a weak self-concept because they lack understanding of why they act as they do. Few know how they might improve their own lives.

Such troubles can be caused by a lack of closeness with parents, by an inability to resist peer pressures, or by the absence of a clear-cut set of personal values.

In this chapter you'll read some general suggestions on how to manage your life. You'll learn:

1. How to discover your own strengths and resources.

2. How to make decisions that will help you avoid crises.

3. How to cope with crises and survive them.

4. How to find the right kind of help for serious problems.

Allied Van Lines
Sooner or later, almost everyone must cope with a life crisis.

323

Natalie Leimkuhler

Which way to go? Taking time to think through a tough decision is the smart way to solve a life crisis.

Life can be tough. All sorts of difficulties can slow you down. Although the examples in this chapter may not match your present circumstances exactly, the recommended methods can be applied to almost any part of life.

DECISION-MAKING

Instead of sitting back and reacting to events as they happen, it is possible to influence your future. You can make things happen. Each major decision can affect your life for months and even years.

Of course, everyone makes a poor decision once in a while. However, if you usually jump before you look, or speak before you think, the suggestions that follow are meant for you. You can learn to slow down and consider the best course of action. You don't have to react quickly without careful thought. You can learn to plan ahead to sidestep situations that promise trouble. Few people make the right decision every time.

Guidelines for living.

How to Make Better Decisions

• *Slow down.* If you tend to decide quickly without thought, check your methods. For example, if you often miss easy questions on exams, don't decide anything until you are sure you understand the question. Don't submit your paper until you review your answers. Don't volunteer to do anything until you know what will be expected of you. Try to slow down for better decisions.

• *Pause before you act.* If you get into trouble making promises you regret later, memorize a few "pause" phrases like, "I want to think it over," or, "I'll tell you first thing tomorrow." A chance to consider a new idea usually helps and seldom hurts. Try to pause for better decisions.

• *List pros and cons.* Write out the advantages and disadvantages of the decisions you need to make. Listing the pros and cons will give you a clearer picture of the choice you must make. Try to see both sides for better decisions.

• *Consider another approach.* Did you ever notice how often people learn one set way to react and never change? Always check other possibilities, even if they don't seem attractive at first. Try to discover alternate ways of doing things for better decisions.

• *Measure.* Compare the decision you plan to make against the standards of some person you respect. Ask yourself, "Would my mother (or father, or teacher, or minister) approve of this decision? Is this choice really fair to myself and to others? Try to test your choice for better decisions.

• *Try out.* Pretend you've already made the decision. Ask yourself, "What happens next?" "Where does this choice lead me?" Imagine the results of your choice for better decisions.

• *Criticize.* Evaluate your decisions after you've made them, whether good or bad. Examine the results. Try to discover *why* a good decision was to your benefit. If you made a bad decision, try to figure out *why* you made the mistake and how you can avoid the same error next time. Evaluate your present results for better decisions.

• *Reward.* Each time you make a good decision, praise yourself. For example, if you learn to pause and think instead of blurting out a quick answer, say to yourself, "Nice work! You really kept your mouth shut that time!" Reward successful efforts for better decisions.

What about me? Which of the suggestions for better decision making could help you improve your study habits?

Which could help you improve your grades?

Which could help you join in class discussions more often?

Write a paragraph. In just a few sentences, describe the kind of student that

Kathy Tuite

Even when things go badly for children they can still grow up to be strong, stable, and healthy adults.

you would really like to be. Use a separate sheet of paper for your work.

DO NOT WRITE IN THIS BOOK.

You be the counselor. Go back to Carl's case on page 316. He needs to make an important decision about whether to live with his mother or his dad.

Put yourself in Carl's place. Then consider the Decision-Making Guidelines.

What suggestions would you make to Carl?

GROWING UP STRONG

In the course of a lifetime you might meet hundreds of different crises. To handle such problems you will need special emotional strengths for the difficult times.

What do you need? Psychologists once thought that all boys and girls should grow up in secure, comfortable homes, with soft and trouble-free childhoods. However, when researchers studied children from such settings they found these surprises:

1. Children who have life too easy may not mature emotionally. They seldom are able to handle normal pressures of living, let alone serious problems.

2. Children with too much protection, or from a home atmosphere that is always the same, often turn out to be dull and boring adults.

3. Children grew up to be stronger when their early lives included some emotional tension and genuine crises. They seemed to develop extra toughness.

The stronger children learned how to handle minor problems early in life. They put forth extra effort. They didn't quit easily. They developed ways to grow in spite of difficulties. The conclusion seems to be that a few hard knocks during childhood can prepare you for the years ahead.

Of course, some problems can be too much to handle, even for those in good mental health. A serious illness, for example, can put the strongest person out of action for a while. At the same time, even the worst reverses need not ruin someone who knows what to do when faced with a temporary setback.

Did you know? A psychiatrist is like a detective who tries to find out what goes on in a person's mind. Psychiatrist E. James Anthony studied seriously disturbed families that had one parent who suffered from mental illness. He wanted

Natalie Leimkuhler

Every fall Jerry sells programs at the university home games. This work, plus his regular responsibilities at home, helps him to mature on his way to becoming a man.

to discover ways to prevent the same kind of sickness in the next generation.

Dr. Anthony's results show that when one parent has serious mental illness, about 40 to 50 percent of the children in that family develop behavior that is delinquent or antisocial. About 15 percent of the children from these homes become mentally ill themselves.

The amazing part of Dr. Anthony's discovery is that about 40 percent of the children *grew up almost totally free from mental and emotional problems.* Many children of mentally disturbed parents not only show no behavior out of the ordinary, but the youngsters develop their share of creativity and imagination.

Young people who manage to escape serious family problems are clear-headed and very realistic. They are not superstitious. They are efficient and self-organized. Even children not so fortunate can help themselves by using the methods of the successful survivors.

HOW TO SURVIVE CRISES

Following are some simple and practical ways to meet problems. Think about how these suggestions might be useful in your everyday relationships with others.

Organize. You can't save a family that is falling apart all by yourself. No one would expect that of you. However, you can put order into your daily schedule. You can decide how to invest your energies in order to live with the pressures in your life.

CASE EXAMPLE

Steve was a "high risk" boy, headed for trouble. He lived in a neighborhood full of crime and decay. His father was in prison. Although his mother cared about him, she was undependable and immature. No one could predict what she might do next. Yet Steve changed himself into a stronger person because of something that happened when he was eight. It wasn't his idea. It just happened.

Steve developed diabetes. To keep himself alive and well he had to give himself shots of a special medicine called insulin. He also had to learn

Brian Ottinger, Trident, West Lafayette, Indiana, High School
Being part of a group that requires cooperation and teamwork—like the band—can bring both order and enjoyment to an upset life.

other tricky medical procedures to maintain his health. Steve discovered talents he never knew he had. He worked out a regular, organized, and sensible daily routine that helped to keep him healthy and strong. Simply, Steve learned to act in his own behalf, even though he lived in a family with serious problems.

Keep active. You don't have to get a serious illness like Steve's in order to take charge of your own life. An after-school job, a challenging hobby, an interest in reading, music, or science, or time spent in sports or dramatics all can help to organize and stabilize a person under heavy pressure.

CASE EXAMPLE

Marita comes from a happy home. She has no special problems. In fact, she could live a soft and easy life and no one would complain. However, Marita loves to swim. Swimming helps her make good use of her time. Her many hours in the pool make her feel satisfied, strong, and independent.

Twice each day, Marita trains faithfully. First she swims laps the width of the pool, then the length. Later she joins with friends for relay races. Marita always emerges dripping, exhausted, but feeling great. "Just slipping through the water fast, I feel really happy," she says.

Swimming splashes over into all parts of Marita's life. Because she applies the same close attention to her homework, her grades are good. She meets everyday problems head on. Then she looks for quick and satisfactory solutions to them.

Concentrating on a sport she loves has helped Marita to know herself. She says, "I want to be good in the things I like, concentrate on them, and do them well. I didn't like piano lessons. I quit. Dancing didn't turn me on either. Swimming I really enjoy."

By keeping herself involved in a healthy and rewarding activity, Marita cuts down chances for minor crises in her life. If a major one comes along she knows that she can take it in her stride.

What about me? Steve and Marita organized their lives. They both became healthier and more productive.

In what *one* way could you put order into your life?

Compare your answer with that of a classmate.

Avoid conflict. Sidestep a fight whenever you can. Keep clear even when others try to drag you in. It's easy to join a fight. It's easy to shout something cruel in return for an insult. It makes little sense to fight with a friend, parent, or an older sib who has lost control. There's no way that you can win or make your point.

Avoiding conflict is a mature way to act. You can start taking charge of your life by refusing to be part of violent exchanges.

When conflict between parents is the problem at home, try to avoid being drawn into the arguments. Don't act as a go-between or a referee. Don't take one parent's side against the other. Don't do what's asked of you if it means telling lies or spying. Children who get pulled into parents' battles usually end up feeling guilty and used, no matter which side they choose.

Some adolescents become cold and unforgiving. They blame their folks and judge their parents' weaknesses.

Other teens try a different route. They accept the fact that parents are individual persons. They realize parents aren't perfect. They see that all people have some flaws and failings.

In Chapter 7 you read about ways to settle conflicts and work for compromises. However, sometimes it is not possible to solve problems that started long before you were born. When living in a family with serious problems, you must become responsible for your own survival and your future life. You can't escape family conflict by not facing it or by claiming that it doesn't exist.

Think. It is important that you learn to protect yourself. If someone calls you worthless, that doesn't mean it's true. If

that same person said you had two heads, you wouldn't believe it.

Always try to think for yourself. Ask, "Is this story really true, or is it made up?" Try to remember that two persons can view the same set of facts differently. Usually it is best to judge for yourself what is real and what is not.

In fact, "think for yourself" is sound advice for handling any situation that upsets you. For example, if you hear insulting put-downs about someone you know, by thinking for yourself you can be both fair and considerate by not repeating what you hear.

Put anger to work. Everyone gets angry at times. Those who say they don't either can't recognize their negative emotions or they bend the truth. Anger is a natural response when things don't work out right.

Anger can be a useful emotion. Anger can help you state your side of a contested issue. The important thing is not to *act on* the anger in ways that will hurt yourself or others.

Usually it's best to let out strong negative emotions by expressing them in a nonviolent way. If you can't state your complaints directly to the person who angers you, you can talk to a friend, or even to yourself. If no one is near to listen to your story, you can get it out of you by writing down the situation as you see it. Pent-up negative emotions need to be released in a way that will not hurt anyone.

TYPES OF HELP AVAILABLE

Suppose you break a leg. You can't ignore it. Both the pain and the fact that you can't walk force you to seek medical attention. No one thinks you strange, weak, or foolish because you need help

You know how good it feels to open up to someone who really cares and is willing to listen.

and can't set the broken limb by yourself.

Yet persons who suffer emotional pain, or who face crises too big to manage alone, often try to limp along without doing anything about their problem. They may not even know about the many kinds of services available to them.

Counseling and Psychotherapy. *Counseling* means to give advice to someone with a problem. However, good counselors usually listen closely to the troubled person's story before asking questions or making suggestions. Then they help the troubled person to consider several possible ways to solve the problem and to select that approach which would be most likely to

work. Counselors may also offer information and encouragement.

Psychotherapy (SY-ko-THER-up-pee) is a "talking treatment" for persons with the most serious problems. Psychotherapists may work with their patients one at a time or in a group. Psychotherapy helps disturbed persons to understand the causes of their emotional upset and to learn how to lessen their fears and anxieties.

TYPES OF COUNSELORS

Friends and relatives. One of the best treatments for disturbed emotions is straight talk. When an upset person can speak freely with a trusted friend, neighbor, or relative, much of the pressure felt may disappear.

Part-time counselors. Clergymen and women, nurses, and teachers often do counseling as part of their regular job. These specialists may be trained to recognize the early signs of mental distress and to deal with mild problems. Sometimes these professionals receive supervision from a more experienced counselor. Part-time counselors may send persons in serious trouble to psychotherapists.

Psychotherapists. Psychiatrists, psychologists, and social workers with special education and experience are usually referred to as psychotherapists (or just therapists). More fully trained than part-time counselors, therapists know how to assist persons who suffer from severe emotional upset. Using a variety of methods, therapists help their patients to live in a better and more satisfying way.

TYPES OF SERVICES

Where to find help is often the first and most important question for a person who can no longer cope with the problems of everyday life.

Medical help. Physicians (medical doctors) sometimes prescribe tranquilizers or other drugs to help their patients get through unexpected emotional shocks or long-lasting problems like depression. These medicines are helpful at the time of a family death or during sudden and unexpected setbacks like a serious accident. In fact, the same drugs that are misused at other times can be lifesavers for those who have been victims of serious emotional ·crises. Physicians don't always prescribe drugs for persons with life problems. Sometimes they counsel or advise patients without giving any medical treatment.

Private counseling. The Yellow Pages of the telephone book list professional therapists who offer counseling assistance for a fee. Such professional services are usually expensive. Thus, the poor are seldom able to use them.

Community mental health centers. Community mental health centers offer "walk-in" aid to those who seek it. Fees are based on the person's ability to pay. These centers provide a valuable service, because help is available as soon as the person in trouble asks for it.

Crisis centers. A crisis center that offers a telephone "hot line" is like an emergency room for the emotions. Many people need to share their upset with an understanding person. As a result, more and more communities provide telephone lines and walk-in centers that offer free and confidential counseling to the troubled. These centers are often operated by trained volunteers from high school and college. In some communities, homemakers, business persons, and retirees help out.

Callers to crisis centers include those suffering from overuse of alcohol and other drugs. Loneliness, depression, and fear of committing suicide are frequent complaints. Volunteers don't give advice. They listen in a helpful way— with patience and close attention. The volunteers may direct the callers to part- or full-time counselors or to another local agency.

GROUP COUNSELING

When a group meets for counseling, members find that their different ways of looking at the same problem can help everyone present. Adolescents with troubles can get both aid and encouragement by meeting regularly with a trained group leader. Young people often feel more at ease talking about their problems with others their own age.

Adolescent group members soon learn that their peers often share similar problems.

They learn what they can change at home and what they can't.

They learn not to blame themselves so much for family problems.

They meet new and understanding friends in a group.

They learn that by putting their fears into words they can relieve much of the tension and hurt.

Some examples of group counseling follow.

• *Alcoholics Anonymous.* Also called AA, Alcoholics Anonymous is a national organization for those who cannot control their drinking. Although most alcoholics are adults, alcoholism is a growing problem among teens. In fact, it is the leading cause of drug· abuse among young Americans. Each year the number of teenage alcoholics grows.

Natalie Leimkuhler

Alcoholism is a growing problem among teens.

Alateen is an organized group for teen children of alcoholic parents. The adolescents meet regularly to talk about how to live with a mother or father who drinks too much. The group members share methods that have helped them out of such tight spots as being locked in a bathroom with a drunk and shouting parent outside.

Parents Without Partners. Also called PWP, Parents Without Partners is another national organization with local groups. PWPs are divorced, widowed, or separated adults who have children. Single adults who have adopted children may also join PWP. Members seek ideas, support, and friendship from other single parents during their talk sessions.

Teenaged children of single parents may face special problems. Without a fulltime father or mother, some school events must be skipped. Youth with single parents may be worried about the parent going out on dates. Other concerns include what might happen in the event of a re-marriage and the appearance of a stepparent, brothers, or sisters.

Parents Without Partners sponsor teen groups for adolescents of single parent families. Group members talk about their feelings and help each other. Here's how two members described their situations.

CASE EXAMPLES

Gus said it this way: "Now I know better. I used to think that I was to blame for the divorce. At night I'd hear my parents screaming at each other. I pulled the pillow over my ears to shut out the ugly sounds. When my father tried to get me on his side, I felt like a traitor to my mother."

Carmela reported that, "The hardest thing for me was learning to say, 'My mother is coming.' The other kids would always say that both their parents would be at the next meeting, play, or game."

Did you know? The members of Alcoholics Anonymous and Parents Without Partners give each other support and encouragement when the going is most difficult.

Similar "help-each-other" groups provide aid for drug addicts, former mental patients, smokers who want to quit, overweight persons who want to lose pounds, and former prisoners who want to stay out of jail.

Do you know of any such groups near your community?

If yes, share your information with the class.

Family counseling. Sometimes things get so mixed-up that everyone in the family needs help. Mental health centers and Family Service agencies offer counseling services for families with problems. Family counselors understand that if one member of a family has a problem it usually spreads to all the other members, just like a common cold. Any family can be hit with a serious problem. The best action is to seek help as soon as possible.

CASE EXAMPLE

At age fifteen, Nelson had earned the title "terror of the neighborhood." He screamed at his parents. Nelson scared his little brother so much that the younger boy began hiding in closets to escape the threat of his sib. As you might guess, Nelson hung out with the toughest gang. Despite his superbrain, (he was a near genius), Nelson was failing in school.

Nelson's parents decided to act. They took the entire family to a professional counselor.

Surprisingly, the counselor pointed out that Nelson was probably the healthiest member of the group. At least he fought for some attention. With his unusual behavior he insisted that others notice him. His brother and sister settled for silent fear as a reaction to their discomfort.

The counselor also discovered that Nelson's parents fought a lot because the father had failed in business for the third time. His most recent setback had forced the mother to go to work, which she didn't want to do. With his wife earning most of the income, Nelson's father felt that he was a failure. The mother resented working.

The counselor used modern equipment in her office. She put the opening conference with the family on videotape. At the next meeting they all watched the results of their first visit. The angry and hostile faces that showed up during the replay got the attention of all family members. It shocked each of them to learn that such feelings even existed. To their credit, they faced up to the evidence they saw on the TV screen.

The family members learned that problems like theirs are often caused by great changes in the routine at home. In this case, mother went out to work when father couldn't. They began to admit their real feelings about each other. It may sound like the happy ending of a soap opera, but today Nelson is a good student and a cooperative, friendly son and brother. He doesn't need to fight himself and others anymore.

Family counseling services also help young persons in trouble, like runaways and school dropouts. In a typical day one counselor worked with the following:

- A boy who quit smoking marijuana. (He still had trouble saying no to his friends).
- A stepmother who worried because her new husband's children hadn't made her feel at home in the house.
- A family concerned about a sick and very old grandfather who had been living with them and refused to go to the hospital.

All these issues are family problems. Families can be helped by a trained counselor.

Did you know? The cost of counseling services can scare away those who **need professional help most.** Mental health centers and other community agencies supported by public funds often provide counseling services for adolescents and their parents for a small fee. In some cases there is no charge.

Many agencies charge on a sliding scale. That means the person pays according to ability. Low income families may be asked to pay as little as twenty-five or fifty cents a session.

You might know someone who needs counseling but is worried about the cost. Encourage the person to call a community agency and ask about the counseling fees over the phone. Better yet, offer to make the call yourself.

Legal aid. Sometimes a personal crisis must be taken care of right away. For example, if an adolescent is arrested or charged with a delinquent act, that's a crisis.

The Children's Bureau of the United States Department of Health, Education, and Welfare estimated recently that one out of every six boys, and one out of nine children overall, will be hauled into Juvenile Court before their eighteenth birthday for some antisocial act.

Whether guilty or innocent, these teens need help. Legal aid societies and public defenders provide legal advice when private fees to pay for a lawyer are not available.

Court counseling is a special work in which adult volunteers help to raise bond for underage law violators who might otherwise be held in jail.

Each year more attorneys concern themselves with the legal rights of youths who are often neglected under the law. In the case that involved a person named Gault, the Supreme Court ruled that juvenile offenders have the same rights as adults before the law. Young persons now have:

- The right to know what charges have been brought against them.
- The right to consult a lawyer.
- The right to keep silent rather than serve as a witness against themselves.
- The right to have a lawyer cross-examine witnesses speaking against the juvenile.

Until recently young persons were denied these rights.

Other rights. Adults concerned about children's rights usually want to improve government programs so that all minors will get equal protection when brought to court. Decisions in recent cases have held that:

- Students are entitled to a hearing before being suspended or expelled from school.
- Rights of education shall be equally available for all children who are black, retarded, handicapped, or who speak another language.

Helping yourself. Some family crises go on and on, weaving threads of poverty, mental illness, family separations, and neglect into a terrible web that traps each new generation.

Still, things can change. It's important to know how to get help and where to turn for counseling if you need it. However, not everyone can afford professional help. Mental health clinics and other public agencies reduce fees so that persons who need counseling can get it at a reduced price. However, not everyone who needs help lives close enough to use such services.

CASE EXAMPLE

Toby's case illustrates how one boy found the strength to survive a difficult situation. He also grew stronger and more mature in the process. Toby discovered resources in himself to keep him going during a very bad time in his life. As you read, think what you might do in Toby's situation.

Toby lives in a home torn by one problem after another. He sounds like the hero of a horror tale. However, his story is true. In fact, many young people experience similar hurdles. As you read, note Toby's strengths.

When he was much younger Toby watched his mother sink into mental illness. She'd sit quietly for hours, staring at the wall. The deep and long silences made him feel nervous and worried.

One day a concerned teacher visited the home to suggest that Toby needed more attention and love. His mother's reaction was a sharp, "Yeah? Who's going to pay *me* some attention?" Twice during those painful years an ambulance pulled up to the house to take Toby's mother to a hospital for the mentally ill.

Toby says, "My family is a mess. Mother's better now, but she takes a lot of medicine. There are still times when she seems 'out of it.'

"My stepfather has no use for us kids. Both my older brothers swore they'd never come home to visit as long as he's around. My sister moved out when my mother got married the second time. She couldn't stand my stepfather either. He's got a mean temper. But there's no way I can leave yet. I have to finish school. I keep reminding myself that someday I'll be out of this mess.

"My sister and brothers help me, sometimes just by listening to my gripes. I got my first job when I was thirteen. I've paid all my school and

Charles Riker
Sometimes a teacher, coach, or older friend can help and advise a troubled adolescent.

personal expenses since. My boss praises me. He tells people that I'm mature and responsible. My mother and stepfather don't treat me that way. When they're not picking on me, they ignore me.

"I try to work out my problems in my head," Toby continued. "I tell myself that all families are not like ours. Because my mother is sick a lot and my stepfather curses me doesn't mean that I have to be like them. And I don't have to believe the things they call me. I try to urge myself on. It doesn't always work, but I'm doing OK. I have a bad day once in a while when I get depressed. Either I talk myself out of it or go see my sister."

Toby has developed his own method of living in an unhappy home. He has built his life around his job and studies. He avoids drugs and other trouble. He looks for approval and encouragement from his siblings and his boss. Even though he doesn't kid himself about the problems at home, he doesn't waste a lot of time complaining. Despite his difficulties, Toby remains a steady and strong young man. His future is promising. He is a good example of a young person who helped himself during a serious family crisis.

Something to think about. Toby proved to be a strong and sensible young man. Although he didn't get help from a professional counselor, he found others willing to advise and aid him, particularly his sister and his boss.

If you had a serious crisis in your life, to whom would you turn?

What about me? Toby got help from others, but he also helped himself. He set a goal to complete high school. He planned and worked hard to achieve that goal. Toby deserves a lot of credit.

Have you ever set a long-range goal? If you reached it, then you know how you have to keep working at such projects until all the details are complete.

Something to think about. Many adolescents are not yet sure about their life's work. However, it is not too early to begin thinking about your career.

Suppose that you would like to work with people in one of the helping professions. Which of the following careers appeals to you most?

Guidance counselor
Teacher of the mentally retarded
Teacher of the physically handicapped
Dentist
Dentist's assistant
Doctor
Psychiatrist
Psychologist
Mental health worker
Nurse
Nurse's aide
Police officer
Social worker

Where to get more information. For details about the helping professions, ask your school counselor, or check with the librarian in your school or at the public library.

Alcoholics Anonymous is an organization formed to help persons who cannot control their drinking. For information send a long, stamped, self-addressed envelope to:

Alcoholics Anonymous
Box 459
Grand Central Station
New York, New York 10017

Al-Anon is a branch of AA. Al-Anon is an organization for friends and relatives of alcoholics. Wives and husbands of alcoholics often need help whether the drinking person seeks aid or not. Al-Anon includes a division called *Alateen* for teenage children of alcoholics. For more information send a long, stamped, self-addressed envelope to:

Al-Anon (or Alateen)
Box 182
Madison Square Garden Station
New York, New York 10010

Parents Without Partners is an organization that serves divorced, widowed, and single parents and their children. For more information send a long, stamped, self-addressed envelope to:

Parents Without Partners
7910 Woodmont Avenue
Washington, D.C. 20014

To learn more. Select one idea or topic from this chapter that applies to you and the way you live your life.

On a separate sheet of paper describe your selection in one sentence.

In no more than three sentences explain why you chose it.
DO NOT WRITE IN THIS BOOK.

RECAP

Some crises can't be avoided. Such problems are not easily solved. However, many difficulties can be prevented if you plan carefully and make good decisions by:

- Slowing down.

- Using pauses.
- Listing pros and cons.
- Considering other choices.
- Measuring your decision against a high standard.
- Trying out decisions before making a final choice.
- Rewarding yourself for good decisions.

Some hardship during childhood and adolescence is neither good nor bad. Setbacks can test and strengthen a person. Even temporary disasters need not ruin chances for a bright future.

When faced with serious problems you can:

- Organize your life.
- Think for yourself.
- Understand and express your negative emotions.

A good friend who knows how to listen can help you through a bad time. However, if you still can't handle a crisis, outside help may be necessary. When you need help, consider seeking assistance from an understanding friend, from individual or group counseling, or from legal aid.

TERMS

Psychiatrist	Psychologist	Parents Without Partners
Diabetes	Social worker	Family counseling
Insulin	Mental health center	Legal aid societies
Counselor	Crisis center	Public Defenders
Psychotherapy	Group counseling	Court counseling
Psychotherapist/therapist	Alcoholics Anonymous	

CHAPTER 20

On the Road to Maturity

CASE EXAMPLE

Let's do a chore.
It'll be a bore.
But it'll bring money
To our door.

So went the jingle motto of a summer business founded by two fourteen-year-olds named Katina and Susan. The girls wanted to earn $75 each to buy fall clothes.

They rang doorbells to announce their services. As a team, they baby-sat, washed cars, cleaned houses, mowed lawns. Running birthday parties for busy mothers became their speciality. They even stamped envelopes for a business during a big mailing campaign.

The girls earned instant success. They provided needed services. Mothers told each other about them because the young workers seemed tireless. They always did what they promised. Often, they did three or four jobs in a day. Proud of their honesty, Katina and Susan charged only for satisfactory work.

The girls banked their money in a coffee can kept in a secret hiding place. They worked out a bookkeeping system to record every deposit. They noted withdrawals for pizza, ice cream, and movies.

McGuire Studio
Reaching out to help others is a sure sign of maturity.

A few days before school started, the girls retired. The spent an entire afternoon taping dollar bills inside the big front window of Katina's house. It was their way of shouting, "Look what we've done!" The window

Katina and Susan used their talents to work hard and earn money.

Kathy Tuite

Adolescence lasts only a few years. The picture on page 42 shows Frannie at age fourteen. Here, only two years later, she is already a young adult.

show announced their great accomplishment to the world. The final take was over $200.

Perhaps you have experienced the giddy good humor and the satisfying sense of accomplishment that go with a big job well done. Katina and Susan aren't that different from most adolescents. They just decided to put their talents and abilities to good use. Most of all, they brought *maturity* to their jobs. Maturity means a ripening and perfection of talents and abilities.

At age fourteen, Katina and Susan were strong and capable of doing adult-type work. They brought a bubbling and restless energy, a real desire for accomplishment, and great enthusiasm to their projects. They combined their friendship and their efforts to earn more than either could alone. They learned to stick with each new task and do it right the first time. A strong sense of fairness made them honest with their employers and each other. They were helped by their developing sense of good judgment. They understood what their employers expected of them.

At age fourteen, both Katina and Susan learned what maturity is all about.

STEPS TO MATURITY

To see a movie you must buy a ticket. You can't slip by the ticket taker nor sneak through a side entrance. In much the same way, to become an adult you must pass through the years of adolescence.

Sometimes the years of growing up can seem like they will never end. However, you can't grab instant maturity. You can't live any faster than day by day. You can't go back to childhood. There's only one road open to you. It runs into your future, where you will spend the rest of your life. On that road you will earn your way to maturity.

Compared to young adulthood and middle age, adolescence lasts only a short time. Think of the difference between a thirteen-year-old in junior high school and a nineteen-year-old supporting a family. Each is a teen. Still, a lot of growing and learning happens during the six years that separate them.

Adolescence is like part of a long journey. All human development goes on and on, like connecting highways across the country. One stage flows into the next. Each day builds on the day before. You can always look back to leftover business from the past. At the same time you can look down the road to make plans that will help you reach your hopes and dreams.

Each stage of life brings challenges and temporary setbacks. Adolescence

To reach adulthood you must travel through adolescence.

usually has some chuckholes and detours. However, getting a free ride into adulthood without any hard knocks at all would not be as good as it may sound. It is much more rewarding to earn maturity from day to day.

Journey. Suppose you had to travel from New York to San Francisco. You could drive at high speed on the interstate highway system, seeing little more than countryside and gas stations. On the other hand, you could go at a slower and easier pace, allowing time to enjoy beautiful scenery and to meet new people. You could stop over at historical spots like battlegrounds and early settlements, and at natural wonders like Yellowstone National Park and the Grand Canyon.

Your teen years are much the same as a cross-country tour. You must travel the adolescent route in order to reach adulthood. However, you *do* have a choice of

how you travel. You can move along looking neither to one side nor the other, or you can enjoy your journey and find satisfaction in yourself and others. You can build friendships. You can learn from mistakes, make good decisions, and begin to develop a set of personal values that will last a lifetime. The choice of how you use these teen years is up to you.

This chapter is meant to serve as a brief pause on your journey through adolescence. While reading it you can ask yourself:

"How am I doing?"

"How much have I matured so far?"

"What do I want to do with my life?"

"What must I do to reach my life goals?"

Discover yourself. If someone asked, "Who are you?" how would you answer? With your name and address? Height, weight, and age? As did one girl, might you say, "I don't know yet"?

Although much of what you are and can be is already mapped out and waiting for your discovery, your future can lead in many different directions. You will make the major decisions. You will choose the route.

Most teens do not understand themselves yet. They are not yet aware of what they can do and what they can't do. Many are not yet sure how they will spend a lifetime of energy.

This lack of awareness is normal for persons your age. Adolescence is a time to explore life. You can try on many things for size—not only sweaters and shoes, but personalities and life-styles, too.

The search for self-knowledge is an important and necessary part of maturing. Still, learning about yourself does not mean that you discover one combination of personality and character and remain the same type of person for a lifetime. In fact, a mature person is one who keeps learning and changing for a lifetime.

Persons willing to change and grow ask questions like these:

• What is the most important thing I already know about myself?

• What do I still need to learn in order to have a mature adulthood?

Then flexible persons act on their answers to the questions. The stick-in-the-muds don't.

How would you answer these questions?

Change me. Preparing for the two-hundredth anniversary of the United States (1776–1976), students at Wabash College in Indiana made exact copies of an ancient spoon found in the ruins of an old French fort near their campus. They cast a mold from the discovered spoon. When they poured hot pewter into the mold, each new spoon emerged with the same pits and nicks as the original.

It is good that neither you nor any other person is made from such a rigid mold. Even so, from the day of your birth you are gradually shaped by the things that happen to you. In turn, you help make things happen.

Of course, some things about you will always be the same. You can't alter the color of your skin, nor change the shape of your fingers. *However, you can change what you do*—how you give and take with others. Personal change is always possible but seldom easy. Perhaps that's why Oscar Wilde, an English author, once wrote that most persons die at age twenty-five but are not buried until age sixty-five. Wilde reminded us that people give up their attempts to become more mature very early in life.

Each person has the ability to improve, to develop special talents, to change for the better. Unfortunately, the spark of change is easily snuffed out. Some persons stop trying after one or two efforts. They seem to give up the idea that their lives could ever improve.

A wise man once said, "Only I can change me; only you can change you." Although you can change your own behavior, you can't force others to be different. No matter how bad their faults, friends and family members must do the hard work of changing their own way of doing things. This is true no matter how much harm they bring to themselves or those close to them. Sometimes it's possible to help others improve their lives by treating them in a different way. Of course, that requires you to do the changing first.

What about me? Have you ever tried to force others to change how they act? Did you succeed?

Kathy Tuite
Every generation has something to offer.

and understood what she said. That day students learned that it is not so much the years that get between persons who are young and old. The so-called generation gap more often results when members of one group do not notice the good qualities in others. In some ways, those boys and girls who made fun of the visiting speaker were blinder in attitude than she was physically.

When seeking friendship and company, teens most often turn to each other. Sometimes they miss opportunities to enjoy others, especially older persons. They seem to think that their parents and other adults have never been adolescents themselves.

Both older and younger persons sometimes refuse to listen and to learn from each other. That's not the way it has to be. Each person has value. Members of every generation, each age group, have something to offer. You can benefit by investing in person-to-person contacts that cut across age lines.

What about me? What is your attitude toward old persons?

Can you think of one thing that you could learn from an older person that you could not learn from a person near your own age?

Earn independence. Adolescence brings a rushing desire for independence. You want to do things on your own. You want to test and prove yourself.

The drive for independence is normal and expected. Still, independence does not require rebellion and rudeness. Independence does not mean taking the attitude, "I'm going to do what I like, take it or leave it."

Real independence must be earned. In most cases you get a chance to run your own life by proving to yourself and

Think of one way that you have changed your own behavior lately.

What is the main reason you changed?

Enjoy others. Recently, an old lady who is almost completely blind visited a high school drama class. At first she seemed out of place. Some students found her to be old-fashioned and funny looking. One whispered, "What's she doing here?" Another giggled.

Then the woman began to speak about her days as a young actress. She described the first time she ever had a lead part in a comedy. She admitted that she forgot her lines. Her vivid memories, her hearty laughter, and the jokes she told on herself wiped away the years.

The woman's perky spirit charmed the pupils. They liked her, felt close to her,

Natalie Leimkuhler

Friendships can cross lines of age and sex.

your parents that you are responsible, capable, and trustworthy. Teens earn true independence when they develop the inner controls that help them say no to themselves, and when they no longer need outside control from others.

What about me? Think of one way that you have become more independent during the past year.

Now think of one other way that you would like to become more independent during the next few months.

On a separate sheet of paper, write out the series of steps that will be necessary for you to reach your goal.

DO NOT WRITE IN THIS BOOK.

Make decisions. All persons grow older. However, not everyone becomes wiser and more mature. In fact, some adults remain like little children, selfish and uncaring of others. Simply growing older can help boys and girls to become more thoughtful. With their increased maturity they seem more able to wait for what they want.

Teens are able to make good decisions and wise choices. Through practice and experience you can learn which ideas are likely to turn out well and which should be scrapped.

Persons who make good decisions are not just lucky. They take charge of what happens to them instead of wandering without direction. They learn to think ahead in order to figure out where a certain decision will lead them. They consider more than one choice. They learn to separate thoughts and judgments from emotions. They know that

345

harmful actions can seem very attractive when considered for the first time.

Reexamine one major decision you've made in the past few days. Did your decision meet the standards present in the paragraphs just read? If yes, nice work. If no, any idea why not?

Consider one decision you must make in the near future. Write a list of pros and cons to help you see the choices open to you.

Choose values. To live a full and satisfying life everyone needs a set of personal rules to tell right from wrong. Values represent what you really believe, what you really care about.

Adolescence is the time to build guidelines for living even though you may change and choose different values as you grow older. To be able to tell right from wrong is the first step in building a personal value system.

You could live the rest of your life without stopping to think about what you believe to be important. In fact, many persons never bother to think about what issues in life they consider more important than others. The things you put first and the issues you care about will decide your future life.

What about me?
What do I prize most in my life?
What would I be willing to risk for?
What would I be willing to die for?

Set goals. Planning a long journey, the seasoned traveler sets two kinds of goals. The *long-range* goal is the final destination. Many *short-term* goals must be accomplished day by day. You can't drive across the country in one day, but you can spin off many miles.

Suppose you have a long-range goal to become a jet pilot. No matter how hard you work or how much you want to fly, you can't take over the controls to-

morrow. Years of training must come first in the form of accomplishing short-term goals.

What will happen tomorrow is much more under your control than events in the distant future. Almost anyone can set a short-term goal that will lead in the direction of a life-long plan. Completing a homework assignment in math, reading books on modern flight, and keeping in good physical condition become the building blocks that lead to a career as a jet pilot.

No matter what you want to accomplish in life, you must do it day by day, step by step. First you set a short-term goal. Then you decide *when* you will do it. Then you figure out *how* to do it. Later you check to see if you did follow through on your plans. If not, ask, "Why not?" Did you choose too big an assignment? Allow too little time to complete it? Such checks on self give you better control of your life. And you learn more about yourself in the process.

What about me? What one small step can I accomplish by tomorrow that will help me to become a more loyal friend? A more generous brother or sister? A better student? How will I accomplish my goal and check my progress?

Take risks. Part of becoming mature is knowing what risks are worth taking and then finding the courage to take them. Some plans are so dangerous or stupid that they almost guarantee failure or harm. For example, jumping from a second-story window or riding a bike down a long flight of steep stairs, or shooting a hard drug are sure ways to cause trouble for yourself.

Other types of risks involve some danger of embarrassment or ridicule, but they also offer a reward of personal growth. For example:

Do you ever wonder what you'll be doing ten years from now?

• It's risky to offer friendship when you might get turned down.

• It's risky to say what you believe when others seem to hold the opposite opinion or remain silent.

• It's risky to say, "I was wrong," or "I'm sorry."

Still, without taking such risk you'll miss a lot. After passing through the teen years many adults look back. They feel puzzled and regretful when they discover that they are not as mature as they expected to be. They ask themselves:

1. Why didn't I try more?
2. Why didn't I become more?
3. Why didn't I risk more?
4. Why didn't I give more of myself to others?

Start now. Only half-joking, a middle-aged man asked, "I wonder what I'll be when I grow up?" Of course,

he had completed his physical growth long before. However, he was still struggling to learn more about himself and to build close and rewarding friendships with others.

You need not wait until middle age to grow up. You are building your future life now. The goals and challenges mentioned in the text and in this chapter are not for the future. They are for now.

Throughout this book you've been encouraged to reach out for life, to enjoy adolescence. You've been invited to know yourself, to like yourself, to accept yourself. Liking yourself is not the same as being conceited. Liking yourself means feeling comfortable with and respecting your special abilities. It's a simple idea, but an important part of maturing.

Persons who respect themselves usually appreciate others, and are liked in return. Those with a strong self-concept work harder and earn more success. When they make a mistake they forgive themselves and try again.

Even with a bad start in life, followed by serious family problems and some bad choices, young persons can still make good. One bad break does not ruin a life. Not even the death of a parent or a permanent physical handicap means that a person can't make a satis-fying life and find joy in time spent with others.

It will always be up to you to decide which life-roads to travel and which to avoid. No one fails adolescence. By looking around at older people you will notice that most teens turn out just fine. The years you are living now are worth living well. How you live them is up to you. Be kind to yourself and to others. Have a good journey to adult maturity.

Index